Non-Production by Industry of Chemical-Warfare Agents: Technical Verification under a Chemical Weapons Convention

Non-Production by Industry of Chemical-Warfare Agents: Technical Verification under a Chemical Weapons Convention

Edited by
S. J. Lundin

Stockholm International Peace Research Institute

OXFORD UNIVERSITY PRESS
1988

Oxford University Press, Walton Street, Oxford OX2 6DP

Oxford New York Toronto
Delhi Bombay Calcutta Madras Karachi
Petaling Jaya Singapore Hong Kong Tokyo
Nairobi Sar es Salaam Cape Town
Melbourne Auckland

and associated companies in
Berlin Ibadan

Oxford is a trade mark of Oxford University Press

Published in the United States
by Oxford University Press, New York

British Library Cataloguing in Publication Data
Data available
ISBN 0 19 829129 9

Library of Congress Cataloging in Publication Data
Data available
ISBN 0 19 829129 9

Printed and bound in
Great Britain by Biddles Ltd
Guildford and King's Lynn

Abstract

Lundin, S. J., ed., *Non-Production by Industry of Chemical-Warfare Agents: Technical Verification under a Chemical Weapons Convention* (SIPRI Chemical & Biological Warfare Studies, no. 9), Oxford University Press, Oxford, 1988, 265 pp. (Stockholm International Peace Research Institute). ISBN 0-19-829129-9.

In this monograph 25 experts describe the state of the chemical weapons negotiations, practical industrial-monitoring experiments, different monitoring techniques and schemes, national reporting systems as bases for a future international reporting system, and applicable experiences from the International Atomic Energy Association. Examined are the technical possibilities of monitoring the chemical industry under a future Chemical Weapons Convention (CWC) in order to ascertain that no prohibited chemical-warfare agents are produced by the chemical industry and that certain chemicals which can be used for production of both chemical-warfare agents and for peaceful purposes are not produced in excess of agreed amounts. Suggestion are provided for possible application in the CWC negotiations. 5 annexes contain relevant parts of the negotiated CWC text, a bibliography, relevant OECD guidelines, and a schematic overview of the verification objectives of the CWC.

PREFACE

The present study was decided upon after an analysis of problem areas where SIPRI might make a contribution in providing background material of possible assistance to the negotiations on a Chemical Weapons Convention. It was decided that the problem of verification of non-production of chemical weapons in the chemical industry was one such area in which SIPRI had already made some contributions and in which much still remained to be done. This was particularly so with respect to those technical methods which might actually be available or required to meet the verification objectives. In this connection, the need to protect commercial and technical secrets is crucial for the choice and use of the verification methods.

Within the framework of its CBW Programme, SIPRI therefore invited a representative group of well-known experts in the field from a number of countries and organizations to participate in this study in their personal capacities. Their contributions thus do not necessarily reflect the views of their governments, companies or organizations. SIPRI sincerely appreciates the enthusiastic response to the invitations, which has enabled a balanced coverage of many aspects of a complex topic.

At a meeting, which SIPRI had the pleasure of convening in Geneva in January 1988, the authors were able to acquaint themselves with each others´ work and give their views on the tentative conclusions of the study. We want to express our sincere thanks to Dr Martin M. Kaplan, Secretary-General of the Pugwash Conferences on Science and World Affairs and his staff at the Geneva office for providing a meeting place and placing conference facilities at our disposal for the meeting with the authors.

The concluding remarks to this volume are those of the Editor and present his own impressions, taking into account the views presented by the authors at the Geneva meeting. They do not necessarily reflect the views of the authors, and are intended only to be indicative of where further efforts might be needed in the future. For more concrete conclusions, the reader is advised to turn to the individual chapters.

We wish to thank the OECD for their kindness in allowing SIPRI to reproduce excerpts from the March 1988 number of their *OECD Environment Monographs* in Annex 4 to this volume.

This publication could not have been finalized without the dedicated and skilled editorial work of Jetta Gilligan Borg and the sustained typing efforts of Cynthia Loo of the SIPRI staff.

Dr S. Johan Lundin
Series Editor,
Head, SIPRI CBW Programme

SIPRI
June 1988

CONTENTS

viii

IV. COLLECTION AND USE OF PRODUCTION STATISTICS, HANDLING OF SENSITIVE INFORMATION

V. EXPERIENCES FROM IAEA

VI. CONCLUSION

VII. ANNEXES

LIST OF CONTRIBUTORS

Institutional affiliations are given here for information only and do not imply participation by the people concerned in anything other than their private capacities.

von Baeckmann, Dr A.	Department of Safeguards International Atomic Energy Agency Vienna Austria
Boter, Dr Hendrik L.	Organization for Applied Scientific Research The Netherlands
Freeman, Dr Shirley E.	Department of Defence Materials Research Laboratories Ascot Vale, Victoria Australia
ter Haar, Dr Bas	Ministry of Foreign Affairs The Hague The Netherlands
Hoffmann, Professor Dr Hellmut	Bayer, AG, Leverkusen The Federal Republic of Germany
Jeschke, Dr rer. nat. Hans Joachim	General Manager VEB Synthesewerk, Schwarzheide The German Democratic Republic
Kyriakopoulos, Professor Nicholas	The George Washington University The USA
Lundin, Dr Johan	SIPRI Sweden
Mathews, Dr Robert J.	Department of Defence Materials Research Laboratories Ascot Vale, Victoria Australia
Matousek, Professor DSc Jiri	Czechoslovak Academy of Sciences Prague Czechoslovakia

Mikulak, Dr Robert	Senior Scientist Bureau of Multilateral Affairs, US Arms Control and Disarmament Agency The USA
Nishikawa, Koishi	Director, Technical Department Japan Chemical Industry Association Tokyo Japan
Perroni, Otto Vicente	Director Nordeste Quimica, Rio de Janeiro Brazil
Rautio, Dr Marjatta	Co-ordinator, The Finnish Research Project on the Verification of Chemical Disarmament University of Helsinki Finland
Rehak, Dr Walter	National Board for Atomic Safety and Radiation Protection of the GDR The German Democratic Republic
Rylov, Dr Vladimir A.	Department Head The Ministry of Chemical Industry The USSR
Schroy, Jerry	Research Fellow Monsanto The USA
Schröder, Dr Horst	Manager, Pesticide Production Bayer, AG, Leverkusen The Federal Republic of Germany
Sims, Nicholas A.	Lecturer in International Relations The London School of Economics & Political Science University of London The United Kingdom
Stock, Dr Thomas	GDR Academy of Sciences Research Department of Chemical Toxicology, Leipzig The German Democratic Republic (Presently SIPRI)

Sun Xiangyin

Ministry of Chemical Industry, People's Republic of China
China

Trapp, Dr sc. nat. Ralf

Formerly SIPRI. Since January 1988, GDR Academy of Sciences, Leipzig
The German Democratic Republic

Verweij, Dr A.

Organization for Applied Scientific Research
The Netherlands

Weinberg, Phillip

Senior Engineer
DuPont
The USA

Zeftel, Leo

Manager, Material Resources
DuPont
The USA

I. INTRODUCTION

Introductory remarks
S. J. LUNDIN, SIPRI

An overview of verification objectives under a
Chemical Weapons Convention
S. J. LUNDIN, SIPRI

Principal objectives of verification methods and results
**R. TRAPP, SIPRI/the German Democratic Republic and
W. REHAK, the German Democratic Republic**

International institutions of the Chemical Weapons Convention (CWC)
under negotiation: an introductory outline of the
emerging organization and its principal organs
N. A. SIMS, UK

INTRODUCTORY REMARKS

S. J. LUNDIN, SIPRI

I. Aim of the present study

The negotiations at the Committee on Chemical Weapons of the Conference on Disarmament (CD) made considerable progress in the work on a Chemical Weapons Convention (CWC) during 1987, and during 1988 the work has been continued. The sheer volume of this work is made evident by the latest report of the Committee, containing the so-called 'rolling text', that is, the continuously negotiated and expanded text of the future CWC. (The table of contents of that document, CD/831,[1] is reproduced in this volume in Annex 1.) The report demonstrates to what a large extent there now are common views on practically all of the politically most important issues concerning the scope and verification of a CWC.

Among the most important advances made during 1987 were those related to monitoring of compliance with the Convention, including monitoring by means of on-site verification. In the following chapter a general overview of the verification problems which pertain to the Convention as a whole will be presented, to provide a frame of reference.

The aim of the present study is to address particularly the problems associated with verifying non-production of chemical weapons by the chemical industry under the future CWC. This volume focuses on the problems most central to the discussion, the various methods of technical verification and some of the organizational aspects as seen from the perspectives of experts from different countries which are involved in, or which take particular interest in, the negotiations on chemical weapons.

The experts who have contributed to this study were invited to participate in their personal capacities, which implies that they may not necessarily express views which correspond to the official positions of their respective countries. The authors were asked not to question the agreed positions in the present rolling text, but rather to use it as a basis for their suggestions. Furthermore, any suggestions which have been made in this study concerning areas where (preliminary) agreements have not yet been reached in the CWC negotiations should be regarded only as *possible* alternatives for further technical and political consideration in the negotiating process.

One reason for limiting the study to the verification of the chemical industry is that the direct contribution to the negotiations made by the industry itself has, thus far, been rather modest. Exceptions are constituted by those instances in which workshops were arranged by particular countries to demonstrate the problems and possibilities regarding verification of the chemical industry.[2] A further important step in widening industrial participation was made during the 1987 summer session of the CD, when an informal meeting with industrial experts was held in Geneva to serve the purpose of mutual information between the experts and the negotiating delegations.[3] It has, thus, been obvious for some time that the negotiations have reached the stage where there is now an urgent need to begin the search for the technical alternatives which could be used to implement the stated verification aims. Indeed, the 1987 Pugwash Study Group meeting in East Berlin provided an important impetus to the present study.[4]

These recent developments have also underlined the need for better knowledge and understanding of what is going on in the CWC negotiations both for those who will, in the future, be affected by the provisions of the Convention and for those to whom the negotiations are of interest for a variety of reasons. Those concerned might include, among others, plant managers in the chemical industry, governmental policy-makers, national and international lawyers and journalists. Naturally the negotiators, and their technical advisors in the CD, and national decision-makers will also be affected. It is hoped that this study will reach these categories, and that it may provide useful information applicable to the formation of the future CWC.

It should be kept in mind that the provisions of the CWC will, in practice, cover only a limited portion of the activities of the chemical industry. It is *not* the goal of the negotiations to achieve a regime that would govern all production by the chemical industry.

Further, it should be remembered that were production of chemical-warfare agents or their precursors to occur in the (civilian) chemical industry this would merely be a reflection of other, more important political or military factors which had led a state to make the decision to acquire chemical weapons. The verification of non-production of chemical weapons in the chemical industry is thus one of many measures required to enable States Parties to trust that there will be compliance with the CWC.[5]

It should also be emphasized that this study deals only with the verification of non-production of chemical-warfare agents and their precursors, and not with other elements (such as shells) which are also defined as chemical weapons in Article II of the rolling text of the CWC (that is, munitions and other equipment which can make possible the use of chemical weapons). This area constitutes another verification problem which has not yet been thoroughly addressed in the negotiations.

Some of the material in this study is presently too tentative or too technical to have any immediate application in the negotiations or in the forming of the text of the Convention. However, the material in the study could possibly also serve as a useful contribution once the so-called Preparatory Committee[6] starts its work.

It has been agreed that a Preparatory Committee is to be instituted prior to the entry into force of the Convention in order to prepare for the legislation and technical verification measures, both national and international, which must then take effect immediately. This is not foreseen as happening until after the Convention has been signed by an agreed number of countries; which might not take place for some time after the Convention, as such, has been negotiated and presented for signing. It would be an interesting and politically very important step if early agreement could be achieved among the members of the CD to negotiate and sign a separate agreement on instituting the Preparatory Committee, which could then start its work parallel with the remaining negotiations. Such suggestions have already been put forward.[7]

Should it not be legally possible or politically feasible to arrange for an early Preparatory Committee, another approach might be to start a separate

Group of Experts, similar to the Group of Seismic Experts working on the verification of a Comprehensive Test Ban on nuclear-weapon tests. Such a Group could start the much-needed work on the more technical aspects of the verification of a CWC at the earliest possible opportunity. The work could also be easily followed and directed by the Committee on Chemical Weapons. The present study could also be of interest for the work in such an Expert Group.

In this context it can be observed that to the extent national efforts are being made to develop technical-verification methods, it might be useful to have them reviewed by an Expert Group (or in the Preparatory Committee) before becoming subject to the negotiation process. Accordingly, since some countries have already started national efforts[8] to work out technical-verification methods and others may do likewise in the future, it is hoped that this study may help to give an overview of the present situation and point to new technical-verification developments which might be needed.

The problems of the amount of resources and the economic costs which will be incurred for the verification activities are not dealt with in this study. However, some aspects of these matters are touched upon by different contributors. An attempt to evaluate these factors was made some years ago,[9] and a model for calculating these costs has recently been published.[10]

II. Available sources

The rolling text of the Convention reported in CD/782[11] was the last version of the rolling text available when the invitations to participate in this study were given. The portions of the rolling text of relevance to the question of verification of the chemical industry are to be found in Article VI and its Annexes 1-4--presenting, among other things, the lists (Schedules) of chemicals and the measures for verification of production or non-production--and in Article VIII; they have been used as the 'points of reference' for this study. However, since the rolling text has developed further during the course of work on this study, it was considered more useful to reproduce the later versions of Article VI and its Annexes as they were reported in CD/831 (Annex 2 to this volume).

The subject of verification of the chemical industry under a CWC is, as mentioned above, not in itself a new one. Actually it has been addressed in different contexts over approximately the last twenty years. Some of the earliest efforts were made by SIPRI in the early 1970s.[12] Continuous efforts have also been made by the Pugwash Study Group on Chemical Warfare,[13] sometimes in co-operation with SIPRI.[14] Also many other efforts have been made. These have sometimes been of a technical nature; at other times they have dealt with matters of principle. They have, however, lacked the firm basis which the present rolling text now provides in its more specific presentation of the aims of the proposed verification measures. Nevertheless, these earlier efforts represent a considerable amount of thought which should not be lost to those who will work out the final version of the Convention text. It has, therefore, been considered useful to include in this study a separate bibliography listing a number of these contributions. They are presented in Annex 3.

Other useful background material for the study of verification of the chemical industry is, of course, to be found in previously produced agreements in the area of verification. Among these can be mentioned particularly the IAEA Safeguards,[15] which are also discussed in Dr von Baeckmann's contribution to this volume, and the West European Union verification agreement of 1954.[16] Of particular interest for this study are the OECD recommendations regarding preservation of commercial secrets and technical know-how.[17] Excerpts are annexed here (Annex 4) in order to serve as background information for the papers which discuss this problem.

The most recent and probably most interesting treaty, in terms of comparison, is the recent INF Treaty between the USA and the USSR, which was concluded on 8 December 1987.[18] It contains many verification provisions which correspond to those of a future CWC, even if the objects and activities to be verified differ from those under a CWC. Another important difference lies in the fact that the INF Treaty is bilateral, not multilateral.

References

[1]Conference on Disarmament document CD/831, 20 April 1988.

[2]Conference on Disarmament documents CD/37, 12 July 1979; CD/698, 4 June 1986 (also issued as CD/CW/WP.140); CD/CW/WP.141, 10 June 1986; CD/CW/WP.142, 13 June 1986; and CD/CW/WP.143, 1 July 1986.

[3]An informal meeting with experts from the chemical industry was held in Geneva on 6-7 July 1987, with the attendance of members from the delegations to the CD.

[4]See Jeschke, H.-J. and Stock, T., 'Report on the visit to VEB Synthesewerk, Schwarzheide, GDR, during the 12th Workshop of the Pugwash Study Group on Chemical Warfare in 1987', in this volume.

[5]Lundin, J., *Considerations on a Chemical Arms Control Treaty and the Concept of Amplified Verification*, FOA Reports, vol. 7, no. 1 (Feb. 1973), pp. 1-5; and Lundin, J., 'Stockpiles of chemical weapons and their destruction', SIPRI, *World Armaments and Disarmament: SIPRI Yearbook 1979* (Taylor & Francis: London, 1979), pp. 470-90.

[6]See note 1.

[7]Conference on Disarmament document CD/769, 10 July 1987; and ADN, ['On improving the effectiveness of the Geneva Conference on Disarmament: document of the meeting of the Foreign Ministers Committee of the Warsaw Treaty Member States'], *Neues Deutschland*, 31 Oct. 1987, p. 6 (in German).

[8]*Air Monitoring as a Means for Verification of Chemical Disarmament, C.4, Further Development and Testing of Methods*, part 3, ed. M. Rautio (The Ministry for Foreign Affairs of Finland: Helsinki, 1987); Royal Norwegian Ministry of Foreign Affairs, *Contributions by Norway to the Conference on Disarmament 1982-1987* (Printing Data Center: Aurskog, Norway, 1987); and Verweij, A. and Boter, H. L., 'Verification of non-production of chemical-warfare agents in the civil chemical industry', in this volume.

[9]Conference on Disarmament documents CCD/410, 31 July 1973; CD/445, 7 Mar. 1984; CD/532, 8 Aug. 1984; CD/589, 11 Apr. 1985; and CD/823, 31 Mar. 1988.

[10]Beck, H., *Verifying the Projected Chemical Weapons Convention: A Cost Analysis*, AFES-Press Report no. 13, Mosbach, 1988.

[11]Conference on Disarmament document CD/782, 26 Aug. 1987.

[12]SIPRI, *Chemical Disarmament: Some Problems of Verification* (Almqvist & Wiksell: Stockholm, 1973); and SIPRI, *The Problem of Chemical and Biological Warfare: Vol. 6, Technical Aspects of Early Warning and Verification* (Almqvist & Wiksell: Stockholm, 1975).

[13]See, for example, *Pugwash Newsletter*, vol. 24, no. 4 (Apr. 1987), pp. 106 and 108.

[14]*Pugwash Newsletter*, vol. 17, no. 1-2 (July-Oct. 1979), pp. 40-48; and SIPRI, *The*

Chemical Industry and the Projected Chemical Weapons Convention: Proceedings of a SIPRI/Pugwash Conference, SIPRI Chemical & Biological Warfare Studies nos 4 and 5 (Oxford University Press: Oxford, 1986).

[15]Fischer, D. and Szasz, P., Goldblat, J. (ed.), SIPRI, *Safeguarding the Atom: A Critical Appraisal* (Taylor & Francis: London, 1985); and Baeckmann, A. von, 'The Chemical Weapons Convention and some IAEA experiences', in this volume.

[16]Conference on Disarmament document CD/37, 12 June 1979.

[17]See (Annex 4 to this volume) excerpt from OECD, 'Final report of the Expert Group on model forms of agreement for the exchange of confidential data on chemicals', *OECD Environment Monographs*, no. 14, Mar. 1988.

[18]Treaty between the United States of America and the Union of Soviet Socialist Republics on the elimination of their intermediate-range and shorter-range missiles, signed on 8 December 1987.

AN OVERVIEW OF VERIFICATION OBJECTIVES UNDER A CHEMICAL WEAPONS CONVENTION

S. J. LUNDIN, SIPRI

I. Introduction

The objectives of different verification measures have now, to a large extent, been delineated in the negotiations on a Chemical Weapons Convention (CWC), and the functions of a Technical Secretariat, which would be given the task of performing such verification measures, have begun to be formulated in the rolling text. To some extent, general technical methods, which might meet the expressed aims, have been mentioned. However, still lacking is a comprehensive analysis of: (a) what the proposed verification measures might actually accomplish; (b) what resources are required for particular verification methods; and (c) to what extent particular verification methods can suitably be applied. This lack of knowledge will be particularly noticeable when the time comes to deal with the problem of adequate and effective monitoring of activities which pose a risk to the Convention,[1] but which actually are performed in compliance with the CWC by the chemical industry.

The main verification areas which would need to be analysed under the CWC are: verification of the destruction of the chemical-weapon stockpiles and production facilities; verification of the non-production of chemical weapons by the chemical industry; and investigation of the alleged use of chemical weapons.

As a background to the following contributions in the present study, this chapter aims to identify technical areas which relate to working out technical-verification methods for the CWC as a whole--not just those relating to the chemical industry.

It is helpful to keep in mind that some of the undertakings under the future Convention will be *positive* undertakings and concern activities which must cease within a limited time. In these cases, verification will be concerned with methods aimed at ascertaining that previously occurring activities have ceased and cannot possibly be started again. For example, destruction of stockpiles must be performed within 10 years after the Convention has entered into force. Verification of an activity such as destruction does not need to function for more than 10 years, after which those particular verification activities would not, in general, need to be sustained.

The other types of undertaking are *negative*, that is, they imply prohibition of, for example, the production of chemical weapons, or restrictions on the production of precursors and the like for chemical weapons by the normal chemical industry. Thus, verification methods pertaining to these types of activities would have to cope with events which are expected *not* to occur among perfectly normal, peaceful activities. They will, nevertheless, have to be functional for the life of the Convention, at least in theory. Verification measures applied in this context should thus be regarded as routine measures, even when they imply some kind of on-site inspection or recurring visits, since they must not be regarded as measures of distrust of what will most probably be normal and allowed activities.

The relations between the verification objectives, proposed verification methods and the requirements they would have to fulfil, as well as identifying necessary resources for fulfilling these requirements by the methods suggested, are given in the flow charts and tables presented below and in Annex 5.

II. Schematic overview of verification aspects

The following flow charts 1 to 4, complemented by the tables in Annex 5, are not comprehensive and do not necessarily reflect the current stage of the negotiations since they build upon Working Paper CD/782 from the CD Ad Hoc Committee on Chemical Weapons. However, they serve to illustrate the relations between the different aspects involved. At some places the tables in Annex 5 include possible alternative verification methods to meet verification aims which have not yet been precisely expressed or which have been suggested in the negotiations or other contexts. It should be pointed out that the term 'on-site inspection' is not always, in these tables and charts, qualified as systematic, continuous and the like.

The flow charts and tables attempt to summarize the rolling text, rather than to quote it, in order to obtain a more easily accessible overview of the relations to be discussed. This method might lead to the risk of possible misinterpretation. Should ambiguities arise, Working Paper CD/782 and other subsequent, relevant material should be consulted.

Under the heading 'Requirements (Information)' in the tables in Annex 5 are listed attempts to identify what is required of the verification methods or the information a Party to the Convention is required to provide in order that the stated aim of verification of an object or event can be met. These requirements are sometimes indicated in CD/782. In other cases they have been conjectured by the author. 'On- site inspection' sometimes indicates the need for personnel and the performance of certain activities.

A preliminary analysis of the relations described in the flow charts and tables results in the following general observations. Any suggested verification method to be applied under the Convention would have to be considered with respect to: (a) the statistical basis for its use (that is, how often, regularly or random, and so on); (b) the actual versus the required reliability and precision; (c) its rate of false alarms; (d) the possible measures to be taken after the method has sounded an alarm; (e) the time constraints in which it will have to work; and (f) the overall importance to the Convention of the activity it is monitoring.

In addition, the necessary resources in the form of monitoring instruments, logistics and personnel will have to be evaluated as a basis for the final constituting of the Technical Secretariat and other possible bodies under the Convention. In this context, it should be remembered that the international verification measures may be complemented by national means of verification to monitor the compliance of other States Parties with the CWC. The technique most often referred to in this context is satellite monitoring. Further national verification measures might enable a State Party to demonstrate compliance with the CWC if it is challenged for on-site inspection.

One crucial aspect of verification which has so far not really been discussed emerges from the flow charts and tables. It concerns the concept of on-site inspection. The now converging views on the acceptability of on-site inspection on whatever basis--systematic, permanent, routine or by challenge-- may not have been sufficiently analysed with respect to their consequences for the construction and performance of different verification methods. So, for instance, there must be a trade-off between cost and efficiency. A permanent on-site inspection team might offer a somewhat better reliability, but the prohibitive cost may still favour a less reliable but considerably cheaper black-box method.

As examples of different verification or monitoring techniques, and auxiliary techniques relevant to their performance, which are of interest for the Convention as a whole, the following can be mentioned: optical seals (tamper-resistant), television monitoring, surveillance of stockpile site borders by sensing devices, weighing, and volume measurements. Other techniques include chemical analyses (of the contents of weapons, destruction products, chemical production on-line and in batches, waste water, and emissions in the air); communication systems for transmission of data from on-line monitoring instruments; and sampling techniques.

Obviously several of the methods mentioned above, particularly those regarding chemical analyses, can be used for the verification of more than one undertaking under the Convention.

The required resources are indicated in the following list of *organizational units* which would most probably be needed for a Technical Secretariat. Their actual size and importance can, of course, be determined only when the amount of verification activities they would have to support has finally been decided. They may also change over time as needs shift, for instance when stockpiles have been destroyed, and need no longer be monitored. The required organizational units would include: a communications department, a statistics department including library and computer resources, a chemical analytical laboratory, a transport department, a legal department (rights of inspectors, immunity, insurance), and an education and training department.

A first attempt to identify the technologies that would have to be applied would include at least the following: techniques to supervise delimited areas and buildings; remote sensing; sensor technology; systems analysis, including false-alarm rate analyses; materials accounting, production statistics and the like; chemical analysis; chemical processing; and chemical-weapon technology.

III. Conclusions and suggestions

The presentation in this chapter and that given in the tables in Annex 5 point out that the verification aims, possible verification methods, and the requirements and relevant technologies for them can be identified rather well at the present stage of the negotiations. In order to shorten the length of time until adequate verification methods become available, it might be of value to start concrete technical investigations in these areas as soon as possible as mentioned in the introductory chapter of this volume.

One particular reason for starting such investigations early would be the need to find out what might actually be realistic and achievable in the *near* future. Working out the Convention based on assumptions which are overly optimistic about the effectiveness of different future verification techniques may, in the long run, be more damaging for the Convention than initial reliance on less sophisticated techniques, which may, however, still be able to induce sufficient confidence in the Convention. It is also important that such development work takes into account what is agreed in the existing text in order to avoid future attempts to renegotiate parts of the text on technical grounds.

Experiences from existing international organizations with some form of international control machinery should be taken into account, particularly that of the International Atomic Energy Agency (IAEA) which has already encountered many of the problems which an international regime for a Chemical Weapons Convention will also meet.

One of the IAEA experiences is that national efforts to develop verification methods would provide important contributions to solving the general verification problems, even if they are directed primarily at future national needs with respect to verification. However, it would probably be useful for the negotiations on the CWC if a detailed overall review of the problems involved could be done as soon as possible on an international basis. This present publication is an attempt to promote such activities.

Reference

[1] In this context, the expression 'pose a risk to the Convention' alludes to the fact that if non-allowed production and excess production of certain chemicals were undertaken by the chemical industry, this might indicate that a chemical-production facility or the State Party was trying to produce chemical-warfare agents secretly in violation of the obligations taken under the Convention, which would thereby run the risk of collapse. Accordingly, such chemicals and their production may 'pose a risk to the Convention' if its provisions are not complied with.

Flow chart 1. Events of relevance to the verification process of a Chemical Weapons Convention

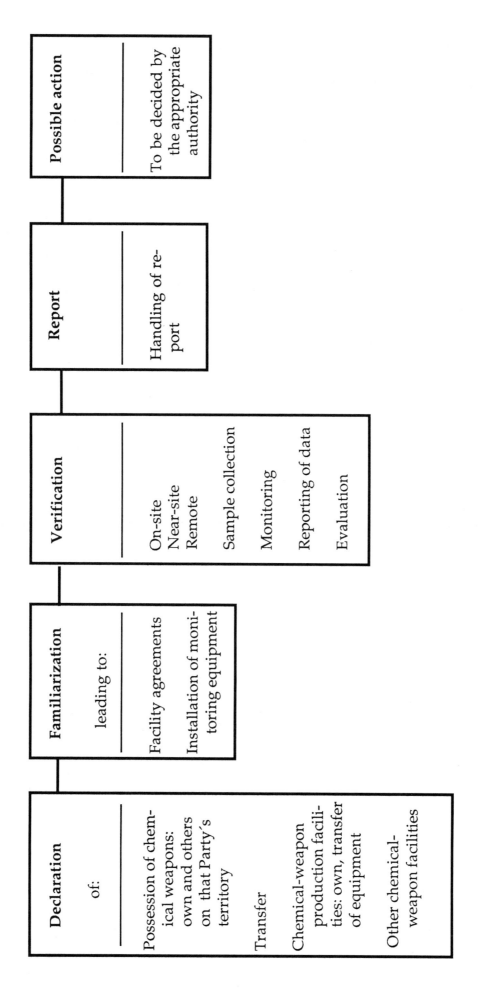

Declaration

of:

Possession of chemical weapons: own and others on that Party's territory

Transfer

Chemical-weapon production facilities: own, transfer of equipment

Other chemical-weapon facilities

Familiarization

leading to:

Facility agreements

Installation of monitoring equipment

Verification

On-site
Near-site
Remote

Sample collection

Monitoring

Reporting of data

Evaluation

Report

Handling of report

Possible action

To be decided by the appropriate authority

Flow chart 2. Verification of positive undertakings to destroy stockpiles and production facilities

Declaring of stockpiles

Destroying of declared stockpiles of chemical weapons

Declaring and destroying of production facilities for chemical weapons

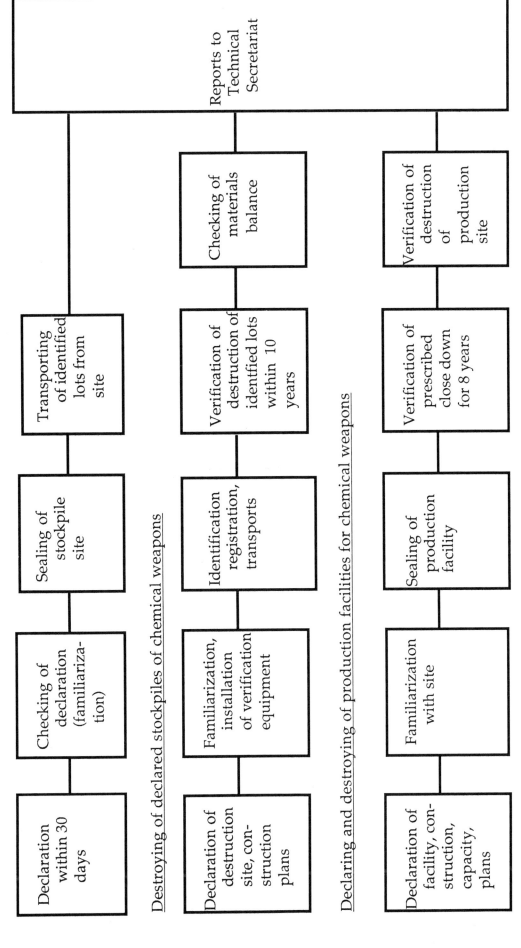

12

Flow chart 3. Verification of negative undertakings

Development of chemical weapons

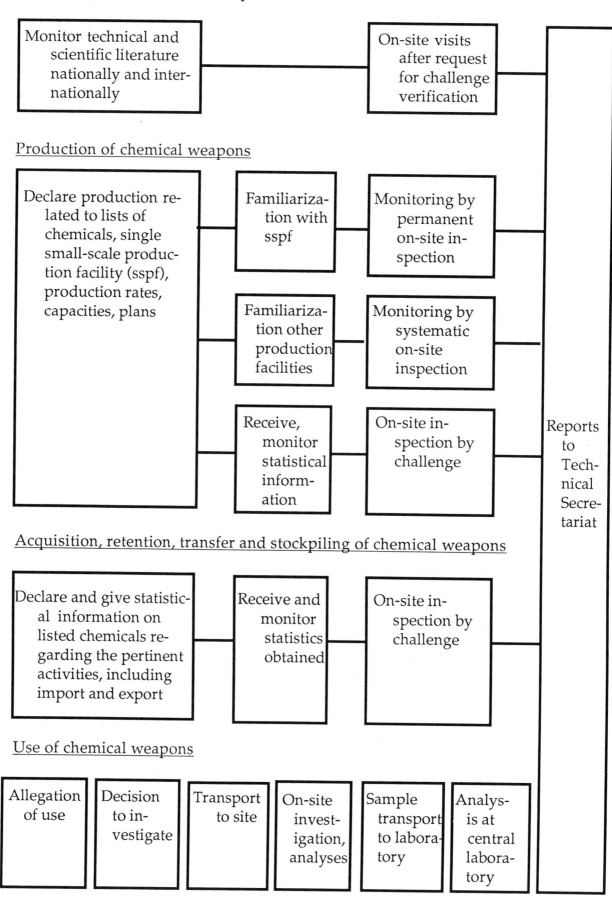

Production of chemical weapons

Acquisition, retention, transfer and stockpiling of chemical weapons

Use of chemical weapons

Flow chart 4. Description of verification parameters[a]

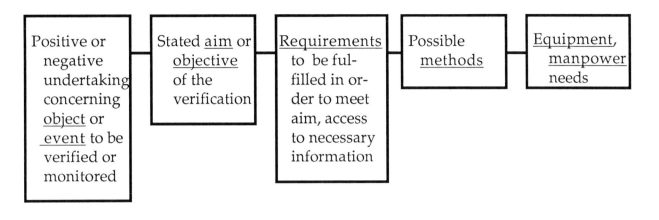

[a] See further Annex 5. The words underlined above are used as headings in tables 1 to 6 in Annex 5.

PRINCIPAL OBJECTIVES OF VERIFICATION METHODS AND RESULTS

R. TRAPP, SIPRI/the German Democratic Republic and W. REHAK, the German Democratic Republic

I. Introduction

As regards the non-production of chemical weapons, the obligations in the draft Chemical Weapons Convention (CWC) are that States Parties refrain from producing:

> (i) toxic chemicals, including super-toxic lethal chemicals, other lethal chemicals, other harmful chemicals and their precursors, including key precursors . . . except such chemicals intended for purposes not prohibited by the Convention as long as the types and quantities involved are consistent with such purposes;
> (ii) munitions and devices, specifically designed to cause death or other harm through the toxic properties of those toxic chemicals, as referred to above, which would be released as a result of the employment of such munitions and devices;
> (iii) any equipment specifically designed for use directly in connection with the employment of such munitions or devices.[1]

For verification purposes, these political obligations will have to undergo transformation into a set of technical questions to be answered during actual verification activities (see figure 1). For any verification mission to be meaningful, such technical questions will have to meet two criteria: (a) they will have to be sufficiently unambiguous (in other words, their relationship to the underlying political questions will have to be clear) to allow political judgement to be based upon the technical answers acquired during verification procedures; and (b) they will have to be solvable in technical terms (that is, designed in such a way that, from a technical point of view, there is the possibility of receiving a clear answer). In addition to this, any future verification regime would have to be:

> implemented in a manner designed in so far as possible to avoid hampering the economic or technological development of parties to the Convention and international co-operation in the field of peaceful chemical activities including the international exchange of scientific and technical information and chemicals and equipment for the production, processing or use of chemicals for peaceful purposes in accordance with the provisions of the Convention.[2]

In principle, the future verification regime will fall into two categories: (a) a routine element with the main aim of increasing and/or providing assurance of compliance; and (b) a challenge element with both deterrence and reassurance functions. The discussion here will focus on the routine element of verification.

For routine verification, the emphasis in the draft Convention, as agreed upon thus far, is on the chemical side of the definition of chemical weapons, that is, the monitoring of activities in chemical industries which might be of concern for the Convention. From the above quoted definition, used in the draft Convention, this is not at all obvious. However, chemical agents are, indeed, regarded as the key components of chemical weapons. A more comprehensive approach (which is not on record as having been discussed at any length in the Geneva negotiations on chemical weapons) might potentially lead to a degree of intrusiveness in areas outside the field of chemical warfare, for example, the domain of conventional-ammunitions production, which may be difficult for States Parties to accept.

Therefore, with the state of the agreement at the time of writing as a point of departure, the following discussion will centre on the monitoring of chemicals and facilities which produce chemicals. The chemicals of relevance to the Convention have been listed in 4 different categories (Schedules). Obligations as well as verification aims and requirements will be different for each of these categories. The Schedules as well as related provisions, as laid down in the Annex to Article VI of the Convention, are reproduced in an annex to this publication.

II. Verification aims related to the different categories of chemicals which would be monitored under the verification regime

Chemicals listed in Schedule 1 of the Convention

Chemicals listed in Schedule 1 of the draft Convention relate to actual chemical-warfare agents and their precursors. The mere existence of these chemicals under any other circumstances than those expressly permitted would be regarded as a violation of obligations assumed under the Convention. In other words, the aim of verification is to assure that these chemicals will not be produced under any other circumstances than those provided for by the Convention, and that facilities which are not entitled to produce them did indeed refrain from doing so. In the context of this discussion on the verification of non-production, we are not considering the problem of the so-called small-scale facility as defined in the proposed CWC.

Chemicals listed in Schedule 2 of the Convention

Schedule 2 of the draft Convention comprises key precursor chemicals which are regarded as high risks in terms of compliance with the Convention, because their transformation into Schedule 1 chemicals is rather simple in technical terms. These are also chemicals which, at present, are only produced in modest quantities for permitted purposes. This is, of course, a reflection of the present state of industrial development and may change in the future.

Production of these chemicals, as well as of the facilities producing, processing or consuming them, would be subject to notification, reporting and international routine verification. The aim of verification would be to assure that:

(i) facilities . . . [declared as producers of Schedule 2 chemicals] are not used to produce any chemical listed in Schedule 1.

(ii) The quantities of chemicals listed in Schedule 2 produced, processed or consumed are consistent with needs for purposes not prohibited by the Chemical Weapons Convention.

(iii) The chemicals listed in Schedule 2 are not diverted or used for purposes prohibited by the Chemical Weapons Convention.[3]

Chemicals listed in Schedule 3 of the Convention

These are chemicals which are produced industrially in large quantities. They are of concern to the Convention because they could either be converted into Schedule 2 or Schedule 1 chemicals, or have actually served as fills for chemical weapons during World War I or II but are regarded as obsolete for chemical-warfare purposes under modern military conditions. The aim of verification is (although not yet specified in the draft Convention) to assure non-conversion of these chemicals to chemical-warfare purposes. Less risk is attributed to this category by the negotiating parties as compared to those Schedule 2 chemicals. On the other hand, this category of chemicals is the one where the most significant economic and developmental concerns of future States Parties would be involved.

Chemicals listed in Schedule 4 of the draft Convention

Schedule 4 represents a list of chemicals which are relevant to the Convention, but which were not listed under the other three Schedules. In particular, these are chemicals which are commercially manufactured in quantities larger than a limit not yet agreed upon. 10, 100 and 1000 kilograms have been mentioned in the rolling text. These chemicals have acute toxicities below the threshold of super-toxic lethal chemicals (STLCs). There is no final agreement yet as to whether these chemicals will, indeed, form a separate schedule, or whether they may be incorporated into Schedule 2. However, for this discussion it is worth noting that the stated aims for verification of them are basically the same as for Schedule 2 chemicals.

III. Technical principles applicable to verification of non-production

The following set of (technical) questions would have to be answered for verification of non-production:

1. Have chemicals listed in Schedule 1 of the Convention been produced at any location other than those subjected to [systematic] [permanent] international verification?

2. Has any diversion taken place of chemicals listed in Schedules 2, 3 or 4 for purposes prohibited by the Convention?

3. Were the quantities of chemicals listed in Schedules 2, 3 and 4, and produced in a State Party, consistent with the aims allowed under the Convention?

In other words, two distinct verification aims have to be considered: verification that some specific chemicals are not being produced, and that another set of chemicals is not being diverted subsequently to their production. To these ends, technical principles have to be found which allow verification techniques to be applied in a meaningful way. The question to be asked is: What kind of information, with what statistical reliability and at which points in time, has to be gathered by verification techniques to make possible evaluations which give answers to these questions?

Material accountancy and detection of irregularities seem to be implied in the draft Convention for verifying (non-production).

Material accountancy

Verification based on material accountancy is a process whereby inputs and outputs of material are measured and verified within well-defined boundaries ('material balance area, MBA'[4]) and for a given period of time. Combined with an inventory verification of the material present at the time when the material balance is closed, such accountancy enables one to detect inventory losses ('material unaccounted for, MUF'). These may or may not be caused by intentional diversion.

A material balance equation can be formulated which calculates MUF as the difference between book ending (BE), when the balance is closed, and the inventory at that same point in time (physical inventory ending, PE): $MUF = BE - PE$.

The inventory book ending, BE, for inventory period j is calculated from the original inventory (beginning physical inventory, PB, which is at the same time the book beginning, BB), from the sum of all material entries into the MBA (X), and from the sum of all material exits out of the MBA (Y): $BE = PB + X - Y$. The book beginning in period j+1 is identical to the ending physical inventory in period j: $BB(j+1) = PB(j+1) = PE(j)$. Thus, the final material balance equation (without correction for measurement errors) is: $MUF = PB + X - Y - PE$.

Inventory verification at the beginning and at the end of a material balance period is indispensable. On the other hand, verification of material flows within a material balance period may be optional provided independent and/or remote possibilities to verify these flows can be applied. Such balances would have to be calculated separately for each category of material within each MBA.

There are four interconnected parameters which have to be discussed in connection with material accountancy procedures, and the relationship of which is crucial to the applicability of the principle: (a) the 'significant quantity' (that is, the quantity the diversion of which has to be detectable by the verification procedure); (b) detection time (that is, the time which will elapse between a diversion and its detection by the verification regime), in relation to the conversion time (that is, the time necessary to convert a quantity of diverted material into chemical weapons); (c) detection probability; and (d) false-alarm rate.

In addition, there is the problem of how to design material balance areas in a proper way.

Detection probability versus verification requirement

Verification by accountancy is, strictly speaking, only possible if the minimum amount of diverted material which has to be detected (the accountancy verification goal, 'AVG') is significantly bigger than the detection limit. In statistical evaluations a signal-to-noise ratio of 3 (in terms of standard deviations, a 3-sigma criterion) is often applied. The IAEA uses a 4-sigma criterion. In other words, a statistical fluctuation in a material balance would have to be 3 (or 4) times the statistical background fluctuation before being regarded as a signal. In IAEA practice, this is not always achieved and in such cases 'additional containment and surveillance measures (C/S) with their detection capabilities are . . . necessary to enable the detection of the diversion of a significant quantity SQ by application of a combination of methods'.[5] The problem is typical for large facilities or for large production volumes.

The uncertainty involved in verifying a material balance is due to two different possible sources of measurement errors, that of the facility itself and that of the inspector. In IAEA practice, the fundamental procedure is that the facility provides a statement about its material balance (that is, the material balance is closed and stated by the facility, not the inspector), and the inspector then verifies the correctness of the statement. This means that both possible measurement errors have to be taken into account in defining the 3- (or 4-) sigma criterion. The facility operator and the state have thereby effectively (and legally) to commit themselves to the statement and all data provided therein, which has far-reaching consequences in case significant diversions have been detected. The same reasoning may be valid for verification of non-production of chemical weapons.

Measurement errors can be both systematic and statistical. An example of a systematic error would be a miscalibrated instrument. Statistical errors will always occur when instruments are used to measure data. Whereas systematic errors would tend to produce inconsistencies in one direction or the other, statistical errors would be responsible for background fluctuations. It is essential to stress that both types of errors may occur, and may do so wtih the facility's own instruments as well as those used by the inspection team.

The next key question, then, is: What is the verification requirement (significant quantity)? In other words, what is the minimum quantity of a certain chemical the diversion of which has to be detected by the verification measure? In attempting to answer this question, one has to take into account that the material accountancy would cover a certain period of time (material balance period). The possibility of accumulating chemical weapons over a longer period of time, by diverting relatively small quantities of chemicals over several accountancy periods ('protracted diversion'), has to be taken into consideration. On the other hand, if there were a deliberate diversion it would take place within a reasonable time-scale, so the requirement for detectability of diversion per material balance period is not negligible. (For a discussion of the complexities involved, see the section 'The time factor', below.)

The present text of the draft Convention gives rather little help in arriving at any such requirement; two questions require answers:

1. What constitutes a militarily significant stockpile of chemical agents?

2. Which period of time should be considered in defining the verification goal quantity?

The different thresholds for notification mentioned in the draft Convention, albeit not finally agreed upon at the time of writing, may in the future serve to define such criteria.

The problem of accountancy boundaries

Material balancing requires definition of material balance areas, and thereby boundaries for the accountancy. These boundaries can be physical (that is, the walls of a reaction vessel or a storehouse) or functional (for example, before and after a measurement. Thus, a certain amount of material may cross the boundary between two MBAs without any physical movement at all).

In theory, there is no limitation as to how the boundaries of an MBA are set as long as all inputs and outputs can be measured and verified with sufficient reliability, and an inventory verification is possible within the boundaries. However, the proper design of the accountancy boundaries is not trivial. If borderlines are misplaced, an undesired complexity might result which could be entirely unjustified for the verification task, or the accountancy may not be able to provide the information necessary for the verification task.

It is IAEA practice to subdivide complex facilities into several (interconnected) MBAs. For example, one such sub-MBA may be for feed material, another one for material processing, and yet another for products. The specific design would depend on the characteristics of the facility, but that part of a facility where chemical reactions take place should, in any case, be separated from those areas where physical storage alone occurs, thereby forming a separate MBA. Two possibilities are illustrated in figure 2.

For verification of non-production under a CWC, a significant difference from the nuclear-safeguard approach must be considered. In the case of nuclear safeguards, access to raw materials for the production of material which would have to be verified under the safeguard system is limited, both in quantity and in terms of suppliers. Hence, material balances in the nuclear case are usually closed balances. In addition to this, chemical reactions are rare in the nuclear case, and in those cases where they occur the yields are practically 100 per cent.

In the case of chemical production of relevance to a CWC, access to raw material is ready and suppliers are numerous. Material balances are thus bound to be open at the input end (that is, verification of the material input is uncertain at best), the more so in cases where the material used to manufacture the monitored chemicals has multiple application in a given facility. In addition to this, the reactions involved are usually organic reactions with yields well below 100 per cent. It is thus essential to combine material balance verification with independent verification means to confirm those data in the accountancy which cannot be verified reliably by the material balance verification itself.

The time factor

Two different aspects must be discussed here, the problems of the closing date of a material accountancy and of the timeliness of inspections (detection time).

A material balance should be closed at a specific and well-defined point in time. Owing to the fact that there will always be material in transfer, within the inspected facility as well as between the facility and the outside world, a very specific time must be chosen. Merely agreeing on a date for balance closure would not suffice.

Another problem related to measuring and verifying inventory of the MBA is exemplified by situations where the MBA is a processing area. As long as a production facility is operating, the closing of a material balance is very difficult to achieve. Thus, verification should be scheduled in accordance with the operating schedule of the facility if undue interference with the operations of the facility is to be avoided and verifiability still guaranteed. Furthermore, any inspection regime will need to deal adequately with periods of time, not just points in time. Within this regime, a distinction should be made between inspections aimed at verification of the ending inventory of a material balance, and those aimed at verification of inventory changes in the course of a material balance period. Inventory verification is an indispensable element of the inspection regime. Inventory-change verification, on the other hand, is of a different nature and can be performed either by interim inspections or by remotely controlled instruments.

The second time factor is that of the timeliness of inspection, which in principle, depends on two time factors: detection time, the time period between diversion and detection; and diversion time, the time period between diversion and conclusion of conversion into weapons.

Based on the definition of chemical weapons in the draft Convention, diversion time is identical with the time period required to manufacture a significant quantity of a chemical agent listed in Schedule 1 (which is different from IAEA practice where diversion time would equal time needed to convert a significant quantity of a certain material into a nuclear weapon). Timeliness would be achieved in those cases where the detection time is smaller than this time period. Thus, depending on the specifics of the facility at hand, timeliness criteria can be formulated in connection with the capacity of the facility, its design features, its raw material supplies, the characteristics of the particular product which is manufactured (and verified) and other factors. It is certainly not trivial to measure the production capacity of a certain chemical plant. However, for the purposes of defining the timeliness of inspections, rather general estimations should be sufficient.

There is, however, a more general problem. Detection time comprises the time period needed for the inspection, the time required to analyse data (this may include chemical analysis and statistical analysis) and the evaluation period. Only after having prepared an inspection report can the international organization issue a statement regarding compliance. It has to be taken into account, however, that a potential violator has the option of diverting large quantities of chemicals for chemical-warfare purposes just before he intends to use them. By the time this fact became known, he might thus already have acquired a significant stockpile of chemical weapons ready for use. This would only be a short-term advantage, but that would, in any case, be all he could expect from a deliberate violation. That is to say, the routine-verification system aimed at providing assurance of compliance with the production ban should not be confused with an early-warning system.

The problem of false alarms

Verification starts from a hypothesis of innocence; it is assumed that no diversion has taken place at a verified facility. During an inspection this hypothesis is either rejected or accepted. The higher the sensitivity of the verification procedure (that is, the lower the detection limit), the higher the probability that diversion will be detected (and the verification hypothesis correctly rejected). However, the opposite situation must be taken into account as well--the hypothesis is rejected and diversion is assumed although diversion has not, in fact, been carried out.

Verification activities will produce a number of signals which may or may not result from non-compliance. In other words, there will inevitably be false alarms which in the process of technical evaluation would have to be eliminated if the ultimate statement of the international authority regarding the compliance status were to be unambiguous. To that extent, an alarm (genuine or false) is not more (but also not less) than a trigger for other compliance-assurance procedures to resolve the problem. It is no proof of a violation, but it cannot be ignored either.

If such reasoning were accepted, then the acceptable false-alarm rate could be set quite high for the sake of a high detection probability (based on technical criteria alone). This may, however, psychologically be far from easy. It would result in a considerable number of problem-resolution undertakings which may be viewed as politically counter-productive. In any case, an alarm in a verification regime is bound to elicit political concerns both for the Party verified and for other Parties.

On the other hand, demanding a low false-alarm rate inevitably means accepting a lower detection probability. It has to be re-emphasized that the fundamental parameters for material accountancy (significant quantity, detection time, detection probability and false-alarm rate) are interconnected. There is, thus, a trade-off situation which would require political agreement to arrive at mutually acceptable parameters. In IAEA safeguards, figures of 95 per cent detection probability for a significant quantity (or the accountancy verification goal) and a tolerable false-alarm rate of 5 per cent have been accepted.[6]

Detection of irregularities

The second technical-verification principle which has been suggested for verification of non-production is that of detecting irregularities (anomalies). For the purpose of this discussion, a definition of the term irregularity (anomaly) is necessary. It may be helpful to recall what definition is used by the IAEA for the same purpose. There a safeguard anomaly is defined as 'an unusual condition which might result from diversion (of material) or misuse (of a facility) or which frustrates or restricts the ability of the Agency's inspectorate to draw the conclusion that diversion or misuse had not occured'.[7] It seems that a similar definition could also be applied for verification under a CWC. If so, it becomes obvious that there are two distinct types of anomalies: quantitative and qualitative irregularities. Quantitative anomalies would be connected with the material balance or its closure, whereas qualitative anomalies would comprise other signals which indicate compliance problems.

Without attempting comprehensiveness, such irregularities could be: the detection of chemicals at places, or in points of time, at which under the obligations entered into such occurrence would not be expected; design features in a facility which give rise to doubts about compliance (for example, bypasses to circumvent measuring devices installed by the International Inspectorate); the malfunction of, or tampering with, an automatic-surveillance instrument; or the occurrence of circumstances which effectively prohibit the closure of a material balance (for example, an 'unaccounted loss' of a certain monitored chemical due to technical malfunctions or human error). The application of this principle favours 'negative-proof' methods, in other words, an inspection would not usually have to establish all that has happened at a verified facility, but rather that certain things have not occurred.

Time is again a significant factor to be taken into account, in a twofold meaning. The first consideration regards the reaction time between detecting an irregularity and an actual compliance-assurance measure. Some irregularities can be detected remotely, such as the malfunction of a surveillance instrument or inconsistencies in reports provided by States Parties. The decision when to send an inspection to the spot would then depend very much on the circumstances, such as: are there other instruments operating so that, besides a loss in data, verifiability is still provided for with some tolerable unreliability; or is the irregularity a severe one, perhaps suggestive of a violation, or would the consequences of ignoring it for a while be tolerable?

This is actually a trade-off between some losses in reliability of data versus costs of verification.

The second consideration relates to all verification missions, and to the detection of irregularities in particular. An inspection can, indeed, detect evidence of non-compliance only if present at the time of inspection, or when they are remotely recordable. First, this requires that the sequence and timing of inspection of a particular facility cannot always be predicted by the facility beforehand (that is, that there is a provision for unannounced inspections). Second, it may mean that inspections could be combined with some kind of automatic recording of data, be these chemical data (that is, autonomous automatic sampling), optical data or any other data. There would also have to be sufficient redundancy in this automatic recording to assure that a simple malfunction would not let the entire verification set-up break down.

An example of such recording is the 'SNAL approach' (sample now, analyse later) as proposed during the 1987 Helsinki workshop on automated monitoring.[8] Under the SNAL system, continuous automatic sample-taking is performed in a monitored facility to provide the possibility of later analysing production streams for those time periods when the facility was not inspected. Such analysis could, under routine circumstances, be done according to statistical principles (that is, the entire sample collection would not need to be analysed) and by applying negative-proof methods.

The requirement of unpredictability

The main reason for demanding unpredictability of routine* inspections, it is often argued, is to enhance the deterrence effect of verification. At the same time, it is meant to strengthen confidence in the verification regime. Simultaneously, unpredictability (randomization) may serve to reduce the actual inspection effort. Unpredictability may in fact mean two different things: unpredictability in time, or unpredictability of inspection activities.

Unpredictability in time calls for unannounced inspections. Such a provision is indeed already incorporated into the rolling text of the draft Convention. Its applicability depends to a certain extent upon the verification principle applied.

If the major verification principle applied in a particular facility is material balance accounting, unannounced inspections are not without problems. It would be by mere chance that such an inspection would be able to contribute to the verification of the material balance of the facility, because the facility would in all probability be operating. Material balance closure might be almost impossible at that point in time (if the facility were not shut down thus creating a major interference with facility operation). In addition to this, the books of the facility would not be ready for examination, and the facility operator could hardly be expected to be prepared to give a comprehensive and binding statement about the material distribution and movement within the facility. Thus, all an inspector could possibly do under those circumstances is look for qualitative irregularities and perform an interim-inventory verification and a book audit.

In other words, under circumstances of unannounced inspections other principles than material balance evaluation would have to be favoured. This also means that in order to perform verification based on material balance accountancy, it may be preferable to announce the inspection in good time for the facility operator to prepare the required documentation. A correlation between inspection timing and facility operation schedule also seems advisable.

But even if announced, it should be recalled that the actual inspection steps which will be taken cannot be fully predicted by the facility. It will be the inspector who decides upon which parts of the facility data will be verified, with which methods (that is, precision) and where. It will be the inspector who decides upon sample-taking and sampling points, and so on. Thus, even an announced inspection is to a great extent unpredictable for the facility operator.

---

*This discussion does not concern on-site inspections by challenge.

This does not mean that unannounced inspections would not have their merits. Non-production verification means, in fact, a combination of verification of non-diversion of one category of materials, and non-production of another. For the latter, detection of anomalies is a key principle, and unannounced inspections would undoubtedly be valuable.

Relationship between verification principles and verification methods

The implementation of verification principles requires the application of technical methods of both qualitative and quantitative nature. Detection of irregularities would favour the use of qualitative methods while material balance evaluations require quantitative methods as well. For the choice of such methods, criteria would have to be established. These depend on a set of factors, such as: the principle applied for a particular verification task; agreed verification requirements (for example, for material balance evaluations the level of the four parameters--detection probability, significant quantity, false-alarm rate, and timeliness); the specifics of the facility under verification (type of chemical produced and production volume, type of facility, technological particularities and others); and economic factors.

The kinds of criteria which would have to be established comprise, among others: required sensitivity; required selectivity; accepted intrusiveness (that is, amount of information which would be gathered by applying the method, and which would exceed the needs for verification or would, by its very nature, be regarded as sensitive by the facility which is verified); the possibility of applying 'negative-proof methods'; level of acceptable statistical error of a method; reliability of the method; possibilities as well as limitations for automatization in case a method is supposed to be remotely operated; and cost.

As can easily be seen from this list, the choice of a particular method is not trivial and requires acknowledgement of the agreed verification goal as well as the specifics of every single verification task. To that extent, the design of a specific verification scheme for a given facility is an iterative process whereby practical experience produces feedback for the improvement of the system. Simultaneously, it should be emphasized that this design process is a co-operative enterprise involving the international authority as well as the facility operator and state officials.

For the detection of anomalies, proposed verification methods range from visual observation via auditing to sampling and analysis. For material balance evaluations, auditing, sampling and analysis, and statistical evaluations would be typical methods utilized. It should, in any case, be borne in mind that no single method would be applied, but rather that an inspection would make use of a combination of several methods. The crucial 'instrument' in such a scenario would be the inspector himself and his ability to make appropriate judgements.

The problem of 'undeclared facilities'

Routine verification of non-production of chemical weapons presents a certain dilemma. If non-production verification is based on notification regarding chemical-production plans of States Parties, it may potentially leave facilities unmonitored which although not actually producing the chemicals, and hence not under international surveillance, have a capability of doing so ('undeclared facilities'). If, on the other hand, the system were based on a rigid facility-related approach (that is, designed so as to include all facilities which potentially are capable of producing one of the relevant chemicals), it would not only become very costly but also conflict with Article VI, paragraph 8 of the rolling text of the Convention.

Hence, routine verification of non-production as presently outlined in the CD presents a rather sophisticated and costly system of international monitoring with a high potential of detection for events which actually only represent one possible treaty-violation scheme. On the other hand, the system would not be capable of detecting another plausible way of violation: clandestine chemical-weapon production in an undeclared facility. This would be left to national technical means, with the mandatory international on-challenge inspection provision as the deterrent against its occurrence, and as the fall-back position in case such a suspicion actually arose.

How big would that residual risk be? Could chemical weapons be produced in facilities which are not declared for routine international verification, and could they be produced in significant quantities? For at least some of the chemicals listed in Schedule 1 the answer is probably yes. Why then are the negotiating parties seemingly willing to tolerate this risk?

There seem to be several answers to this question. First, the mere existence of a routine international on-site regime for a number of facilities belonging to States Parties would reduce the potential field where violations might be suspected. Second, the international authority would also have at least some information about some of those facilities outside the on-site regime which have the capability of producing Schedule 1 chemicals. These facilities would, in all probability, fall under the regulations pertinent to Schedule 3, and would thus be subject to national-reporting activities. Third, the alternative (that is, a comprehensive inclusion of all capable facilities into a routine on-site verification regime) does not seem acceptable to a good many negotiating parties, for both commercial reasons and reasons concerning development of the chemical industry of a State Party.

Still, national reporting would certainly not reveal clandestine production of Schedule 1 chemicals. Relying on the last resort of the on-challenge procedure may, on the other hand, be politically imprudent. If the opportunity for some low-key, on-site access below the level of on-challenge inspection could be established which was distinct from the routine on-site inspections thus far conceived (for example, on-site spot checks requested by the International Inspectorate), there would be the possibility of receiving indications of the occurrence of clandestine production of chemical-warfare agents. The verification principle to be applied would be anomaly detection.

Information processing

As explained at the outset of this discussion, verification is a loop of translating political questions into technical questions, applying technical principles and methods to gather technical information, evaluating the technical information and reaching technical conclusions which can be retranslated into political judgement. Every element of this chain of information processing is important, as are the relationships between them. If a judgement on compliance by all parties is to be furnished in a fashion which will be acceptable to all parties, the process of information gathering, evaluation and conclusion has to be designed in an appropriate and agreed way, and should be fast enough to provide an acceptable detection time. This demands standardized formats of national reporting and notification as well as standardization, to the extent possible, of verification reports.

There will be a considerable flow of data under the non-production verification regime alone. In addition to this, much additional data flow from the other verification tasks will have to be dealt with.

For the preparation of political conclusions, which is the sole purpose of the entire effort, the evaluation process is as important, if not indeed more crucial than the information gathering. Here, signals have to be interpreted for their meaning in respect to the compliance question, and technical findings become connected with political judgement. If this process is to be objective and unbiased, there is again a strong case for standardized data formats. At the same time, data reliability, safety from tampering and confidentiality of the entire information process must be guaranteed. This may in particular be true of information gathered during on-site visits. As long as the information remains within the international authority, this is basically a problem of appropriate procedures, technical safeguarding against outside access and quality of personnel.

However, the Convention also provides for circumstances where some information-carrying material might leave the international authority. For example, the service of outside laboratories can be called upon by the future Inspectorate to analyse samples taken during on-site inspections. The information content of such samples may, in many cases, be regarded as sensitive by the facility from which the sample originated. Hence, appropriate safeguarding of this information has to be provided.

In a more general sense, there has to be agreement about the rules governing the accessibility of information gathered during verification procedures, be it by States Parties or Parties outside the regime of the Convention. If the practice of the IAEA is used as a guide here, then 'statements' concerning the results and conclusions of inspections would be kept 'safeguards confidential', and thus not be accessible to anyone except the inspected party and entitled members of the international authority. An exception would be made for the annual Safeguards Implementation Report on the status of compliance which does not disclose names of States or facilities. Only in the case of serious anomalies are the names of countries and facilities listed in IAEA information to its Board of Governors.[9]

Such an approach would certainly not be advisable for most of the verification tasks under a CWC, where States Parties have a legitimate right to be reassured about, for example, the destruction of existing chemical-weapon stocks and former chemical-weapon production facilities. However, Article VI, paragraph 9 of the rolling text of the Convention does not as yet give a clear indication of how far confidentiality would be pursued in non-production verification. This leaves the option to obtain more specific statements of compliance which might be issued by the appropriate international authority.

IV. Conclusion

Although technical principles for verification of non-production verification are identified in the draft Convention, agreement is necessary on some additional conditions or requirements if these principles are to be successfully applied. In particular, such agreement would be needed for:

    1. In the case of material balance evaluations: the detection sensitivity required, in terms of diverted material per time unit (that is, the parameters-- significant quantity and detection probability); an agreed false-alarm rate which the system could tolerate; and an agreed approach to provide timeliness of inspections.

    2. In the case of irregularity detection: an agreed definition of the meaning of 'irregularity' and a list of potential such anomalies for future inspections, as a guide for verification activities.

    One persistent problem will be that of coping with facilities which, although capable of manufacturing one or more of the monitored chemicals, will remain outside the proposed system of international routine controls. To cope with this problem, additional international low-key, on-site procedures might be regarded as appropriate, and would then require CD approval.

    Further thought has to be given to the whole system of information processing and evaluation to assure that a future international authority would, indeed, be able to furnish compliance-status reports according to an appropriate time schedule, and with sufficient unambiguity. At the same time, thought must be given to the potential distribution of this information, its confidentiality and its safeguarding.

    It should be finally emphasized that designing a verification regime is an iterative process (compare figure 3, which is adapted from the IAEA safeguard glossary[10]). In other words, it seems impossible and imprudent to assume that such a system could be designed without the feedback of practical experience gathered during its actual implementation, let alone without due regard to the specifics of the facilities at hand. The Convention should thus provide sufficient flexibility to adjust the practical verification arrangements to the real world, and incorporate future experience as well as particularities of the facilities which it will scrutinize.

References

[1] Draft Chemical Weapons Convention, as published in: 'Report of the Ad Hoc Committee on Chemical Weapons to the Conference on Disarmament', Conference on Disarmament document CD/782, 26 Aug. 1987, Appendix 1, Article II, paragraphs i to iii, pp. 5-6.

[2] CD/782, Article VI, paragraph 8, p.16.

[3] CD/782, Annex to Article VI [2] , paragraph 4, p. 65.

[4] Throughout the following discussion, IAEA terminology will be applied wherever appropriate. Compare *IAEA Safeguards Glossary*, IAEA/SG/INF.1.

[5] IAEA/SG/INF.1, p. 26.

28

[6]IAEA/SG/INF.1; see also Tempus, P., GOV/OR.676, paragraph 50.

[7]IAEA/SG/INF.1.

[8]'Automatic monitoring of non-production: report of working group 3', *Automatic Monitoring in Verification of Chemical Disarmament: Proceedings of a Workshop in Helsinki, 12-14 Feb. 1987* (Finnish Project on Verification of Chemical Disarmament: Helsinki, 1987), pp. 101-104.

[9]Rehak, W., 'The institutional machinery of implementing a CW Convention seen in the light of IAEA's nuclear safeguards experience', discussion paper presented at the Implementing a Global Chemical Weapons Convention Conference, Ottawa, Canada, 7-9 Oct. 1987.

[10]Adapted and modified from IAEA/SG/INF.1, p.19.

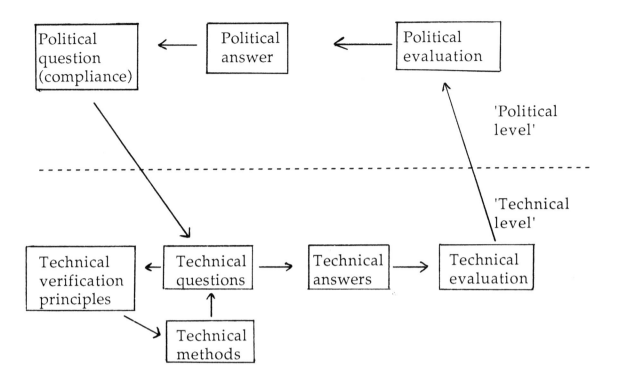

Figure 1. Information loop for verification

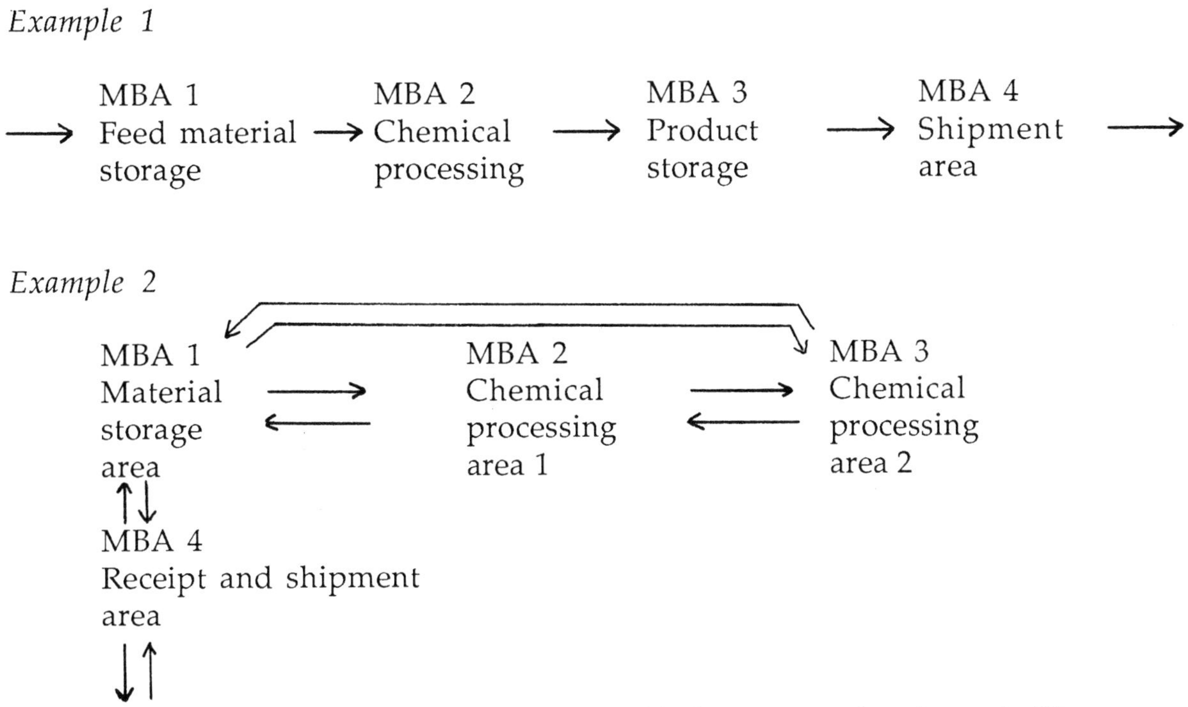

Example 1

MBA 1   MBA 2   MBA 3   MBA 4
⟶ Feed material ⟶ Chemical   ⟶ Product   ⟶ Shipment   ⟶
   storage   processing   storage   area

Example 2

MBA 1   MBA 2   MBA 3
Material   ⟶ Chemical   ⟶ Chemical
storage   ⟵ processing ⟵ processing
area   area 1   area 2

MBA 4
Receipt and shipment
area

Figure 2. Examples for the design of material balance areas in a large facility

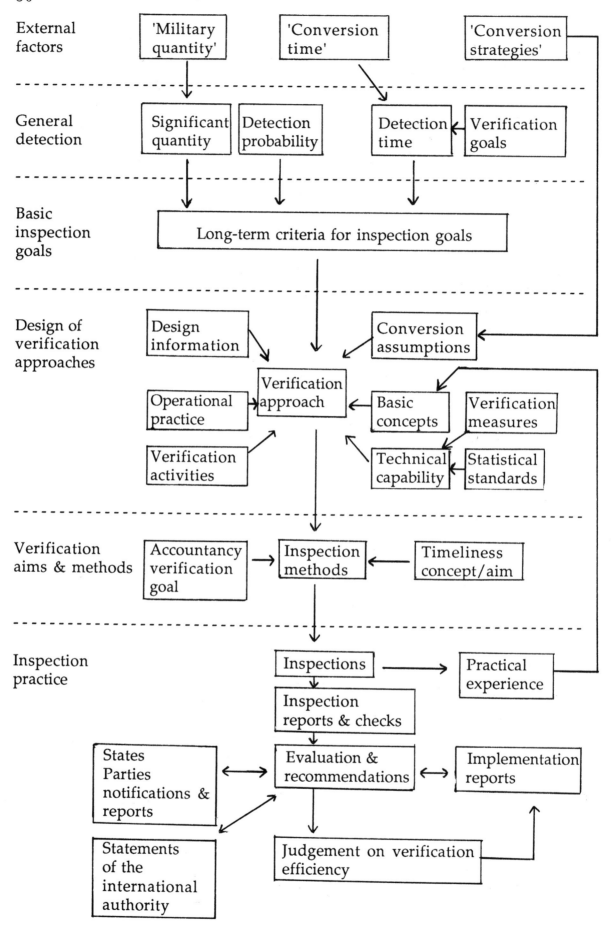

Figure 3. Development of verification principles and corresponding methods

INTERNATIONAL INSTITUTIONS OF THE CHEMICAL WEAPONS CONVENTION (CWC) UNDER NEGOTIATION: AN INTRODUCTORY OUTLINE OF THE EMERGING ORGANIZATION AND ITS PRINCIPAL ORGANS

N. A. SIMS, the United Kingdom

I. Introduction

For many years now the Conference on Disarmament (CD) in Geneva has been regularly exhorted by the General Assembly of the United Nations (UN) to pursue the successful conclusion of the far-reaching project of a Chemical Weapons Convention (CWC) as a matter of the highest priority. The sense of urgency embodied in UN resolutions has been reflected in the CD, where an Ad Hoc Committee on Chemical Weapons has been meeting in increasingly frequent sessions and intersessional consultations, with an increasingly well-articulated substructure of working groups and other discussions (some grouped in 'clusters') spanning the wide range of issues which have to be encompassed in such a comprehensive Convention.

Pursuit of a CWC is also a formal treaty obligation for the more than 100 states which are Parties to the 1972 Convention on Biological and Toxin Weapons. Under Article IX of that Convention, they have solemnly undertaken to continue CWC negotiations 'in good faith with a view to reaching early agreement on effective measures': a treaty obligation which was reaffirmed by the States Parties in the Final Declarations of their first two Review Conferences (March 1980 and September 1986) together with expressions of deep regret that the CWC had not yet been concluded.

Many issues of principle are now settled. One of these concerns the institutional structure, in broad outline, which is needed to ensure confidence in States Parties' compliance with their CWC obligations. An 'appropriate mix of national and international means of verification' has long been the agreed requirement. This formula implies two kinds of institution: one national, the other international.

In the 'rolling text'[1] of the evolving CWC, as currently (autumn 1987) drafted, Article VII (National Implementation Measures) provides for each State Party to adopt a number of measures including the obligation to designate or establish a National Authority. This would be the body primarily responsible, at the national level, for ensuring compliance with all CWC obligations assumed by the State Party. In order to fulfil this responsibility it would need to ascertain and verify patterns of compliance by all relevant entities within the jurisdiction, or under the control, of that State Party: including most obviously all government agencies, the armed forces, the chemical industry and research-and-development establishments within both public and private sectors. It would be the statutory recipient of information collected for onward transmission to other States Parties and international institutions, with which it would maintain close liaison on behalf of the State Party.

Article VIII provides for specifically international institutions. These institutions are intended to complement the National Authorities to be established under Article VII, and thereby to provide further reassurance to all States Parties that the CWC is being universally respected in every particular. They are envisaged as institutions operating impartially in the service of the States Parties as a whole. They must consequently be responsible to the same collectivity of States Parties; and this can only be achieved by very careful delineation of the functions, powers and procedures of each institution so as to ensure that the States Parties in their totality remain in control, and to exclude so far as possible the risk that control of the CWC machinery may be seized by any State Party or group of States Parties.

This chapter provides an introductory outline of the international institutions with which the CWC is likely to be endowed. Because of their special relevance for the chemical industry, particular attention is paid to the planned International Inspectorate, the guidelines under which it is to perform its designated functions and the Technical Secretariat within which it is is to be located.

Taken together, this International Inspectorate and the other institutions envisaged may well be regarded as constituting a distinct international organization, which some delegations think should be designed and recognized as such from the outset. Such an International Organization for the Prohibition of Chemical Weapons, or International Chemical Disarmament Agency (or Authority), would have as its principal organs the following:

1. a *General Conference* (or *Consultative Committee,* to give it its older but increasingly inappropriate title), composed of all States Parties and retaining ultimate authority within the provisions of the CWC;

2. an *Executive Council,* composed of a limited number of States Parties and meeting more frequently than the Conference, to which it would be responsible for the performance of most of the functions appropriate to an intergovernmental organ and for the supervision of subsidiary organs and the Technical Secretariat; and

3. a *Technical Secretariat,* headed by a Director (who might also be the Director-General of the Organization) and composed of a staff of international officials responsible to the Council for the day-to-day operation of the treaty regime established by the Convention. This Secretariat would comprehend the *International Inspectorate.*

The concept of a three-tier structure of this kind goes back to a Netherlands proposal[2] of 1973; the titles of the two intergovernmental organs (originally 'plenary Conference' and 'Board') are, however, of subsequent origin. The notion of a *Consultative Committee,* in particular, developed from 1976 to 1987, when the title General Conference was proposed by the Co-ordinator for Cluster IV in the Ad Hoc Committee on Chemical Weapons on the grounds that the body in question would be too large to warrant the name *committee* and have other functions besides *consultative* ones.[3] *Consultative Committee* persisted, however, in the 'rolling text' of 26 August 1987 (CD/782, Appendix I).

The three principal organs listed above are intended to come into being upon the entry into force of the Convention.

Until it enters into force the Convention will be endowed with temporary machinery, in the shape of a single intergovernmental organ, the *Preparatory Commission,* and a staff of international officials headed by the

Commission's Executive Secretary. The Commission will be convened within 30 days of the number of signatory states reaching a specified total (yet to be agreed), and will consist thereafter of all signatories. It will take decisions by consensus or two-thirds majority (the procedure remains to be decided), and will concentrate on making all necessary preparations for the Organization to swing into action as soon as the Convention enters into force. The conditions for the CWC's entry into force have not yet been agreed. It seems likely, however, that one requirement will be the deposit of instruments of ratification by a large number of signatories. On the precedent of the Third UN Convention on the Law of the Sea (the 1982 Montego Bay Convention, or UNCLOS-III), a requirement of 60 ratified signatures has been proposed. Even if the requirement is less stringent than that, there is certain to be a significant interval--probably of several years--between the CWC's opening for signature and its entry into force. During much of this time (or even the whole of it, if enough states sign the Convention at the very outset) the Commission and its staff will play an important part as a 'provisional technical secretariat' (see below) in setting the scene for the assumption of responsibilities by the permanent organs of the Convention. ('Growing out of the Preparatory Commission, . . . the Technical Secretariat should, for example, be able to function in an orderly manner from the first day on'.[4]) This transitional machinery accordingly deserves notice in any outline of the CWC's international institutions.

All these institutions, and even more so the Organization (or Agency, or Authority) which together they may constitute, are still under negotiation. It must therefore be emphasized that this outline relates to the CWC's international institutions as they are currently defined, some more tentatively than others, in the work of the CD at Geneva. The version of the 'rolling text' used here (CD/782, Appendix I) together with the report of the Co-ordinator for Cluster IV (in CD/782, Appendix II) represents the progress made in the CD's Ad Hoc Committee on Chemical Weapons up to the end of its 1987 summer session. It does not take account of the outcome of subsequent intersessional consultations which opened in November 1987 and continue while the CD itself is in recess. The 'rolling text' in its successive versions will, moreover, not bind any delegation until the CWC negotiations are successfully concluded. Accordingly the present description must be regarded as provisional, not definitive.

It must also be emphasized that this outline is no more than an introductory outline. In particular, it omits the negotiating history which provides the background to the institutions considered. The CWC's institutions as now envisaged have emerged out of many different proposals. These proposals, and the evolution of various concepts of relevant international organization through the first 15 years of negotiations for a CWC, are explored more fully in my book *International Organization for Chemical Disarmament*, which has been published in the series SIPRI Chemical & Biological Warfare Studies.[5]

II. The General Conference

The General Conference will be the supreme organ of the Convention. It will consist of all States Parties to the Convention, each possessing one vote. If there is an Organization, or Agency, or Authority, all States Parties will automatically be members of that entity, and the General Conference will possess overall authority within it. Although this is not yet finally agreed, decisions are most likely to require a two-thirds majority.

The General Conference will hold its first meeting not later than 30 days after the Convention enters into force. Thereafter it will meet at least once a year in regular session; at less frequent intervals (perhaps triennially or quinquennially) to perform the Article-by-Article scrutiny associated with a Review Conference; and in special session on requisition by a sufficient proportion (yet to be agreed) of the membership, or by the Executive Council, or possibly as the consequence of an unresolved compliance concern on requisition by a single dissatisfied State Party under Article IX of the Convention (not yet finalized). When convened in special session, the General Conference is intended to consider issues of primary importance for the objectives or implementation of the CWC.

Its powers and functions have been substantially agreed. The General Conference is empowered to oversee the implementation of the CWC, to consider any questions relevant to the CWC or the powers and functions of any subsidiary organs, to foster consultation and co-operation among States Parties, and to promote the verification of compliance with all treaty obligations flowing from the Convention. These four broad headings of suggested activity allow the General Conference a very wide area of institutional competence.

More specifically it will be the responsibility of the General Conference to consider and approve the annual programme and budget submitted by the Executive Council; to encourage international scientific and technological co-operation in chemistry for peaceful purposes; to review scientific and technological developments which could affect the CWC's operation, especially in relation to agreed lists. (Either the General Conference or, if the task is delegated, the Executive Council will have to be responsible for establishing, and revising as necessary, procedures for exchange of information, for declarations and for technical matters related to the CWC's implementation. It will be important to ensure that procedures for revising the agreed lists strike a balance between stability and flexibility.)

While these are the main substantive fields of activity suggested for the General Conference, it must also possess the procedural powers appropriate to the supreme organ of any international organization: to adopt its own rules of procedure and elect its own officers; to elect the members of the Executive Council; to appoint the head of the Technical Secretariat; and to establish such subsidiary organs as it finds necessary. It remains to be decided whether the General Conference or the Executive Council itself shall determine the rules of procedure for the latter. A further specified function, which appears at first sight procedural but which might in practice encompass substantive matters of compliance, is that of considering and approving the reports of the Executive Council, including reports from subsidiary organs and reports on challenge inspections and other fact-finding activities.

Another set of functions, listed in successive versions of the 'rolling text' as pertaining to the Consultative Committee, relates specifically to verification. They are defined in the 'rolling text' of Article VIII as 'activities relating to measures of verification': specifying procedures for systematic international on-site inspection, overseeing systematic on-site inspection, and carrying out fact-finding activities. These functions are, however, more appropriately listed as belonging to the Organization as a whole, rather than to any one particular organ.[6]

The most testing task of all which is likely to be entrusted to the General Conference is that of dealing with any problems which are so grave that they cannot be resolved by the Executive Council. How this function will be expressed in treaty language remains to seen; but as the supreme organ the General Conference cannot escape the responsibility of acting as the court of last resort in the event of any threat to the treaty regime of chemical disarmament which it must uphold.

III. The Executive Council

The Executive Council is defined as the executive organ of the Organization, with certain statutory functions of its own and with delegated authority when the General Conference is not in session to represent the Organization and to oversee the effective implementation of, and compliance with, the Convention.[7]

Much remains to be agreed concerning its composition, procedures and voting rules, although there appears to have been movement during 1987 towards agreement on the desirability of requiring a two-thirds majority for the adoption of decisions at least on substantive issues, in the Executive Council as well as in the General Conference. The question of composition is discussed below.

There is more agreement on the powers and functions of the Executive Council, some assigned to it directly under Article VIII and others delegated by the General Conference and therefore potentially retrievable from the Executive Council. In particular it is to supervise and co-ordinate the activities of the Technical Secretariat and any subsidiary organs, especially the implementation of the annual programme and budget; enter into agreements with the UN or other international organizations, on behalf of the Organization, subject to General Conference approval; approve agreements relating to verification activities, concluded with States Parties by the Director of the Technical Secretariat; obtain, keep and disseminate under established procedures information submitted by States Parties; consider reports on on-site inspections, submitted by the Director of the Technical Secretariat; receive requests for information and clarification regarding compliance with the Convention, including requests for fact-finding, and decide and oversee specific actions to be taken upon such requests. It is also expected to make recommendations and submit draft budgets and reports to the General Conference.

One major area of disagreement continues to complicate the negotiations over the Executive Council: its size and membership remain unresolved. Before the draft CWC can be concluded, the CD will have to decide how large the Executive Council should be; whether it should be composed solely of members elected for a limited term from their regional groups, or partly of such members and partly of permanent members; and, if the latter, by what yardstick a State Party should qualify for the privilege of permanent membership.

As regards its overall size, the Executive Council will need to be large enough to ensure adequate representation of all groups and regions: the formula 'an appropriate geographic and political balance' has been suggested. Its size must also hold out to all States Parties the possibility of being elected to membership of the Executive Council from time to time. On the other hand, if it is too large it will become unwieldy: in which event it will risk losing control of the day-to-day work of the Organization to smaller committees, or the Technical Secretariat, or both. The Executive Council must be considerably smaller than the General Conference or the differentiation of functions between the two will lose all meaning.

The question of whether some States Parties should enjoy permanent membership of the Executive Council, and the other issues outstanding as regards the composition of the Executive Council, represent the major *lacuna* still remaining in the negotiation of Article VIII. There are, however, a number of possible solutions available if states are willing to search for a workable compromise. The deadlock is not quite intractable. The whole issue is fully explored in *International Organization for Chemical Disarmament* (chapter IX).[8]

IV. The Technical Secretariat

The Technical Secretariat is outlined in a relatively well-established portion of the 'rolling text'.[9] Its general purpose is to assist the intergovernmental organs in the performances of their functions, including technical assistance to States Parties. It is to comprise a Director and inspectors and such scientific, technical and other personnel as may be required. The fully international character of the Secretariat and its staff is emphasized in paragraphs which follow very closely the language of the UN Charter (Articles 100 and 101) and thus constitute a solemn, and potentially vital, guarantee of their inviolable status. Since the integrity of the staff carrying out duties under the CWC is a matter of understandable concern to the chemical industry, these paragraphs deserve reproduction in full:

> The paramount consideration in the employment of the staff and in the determination of the conditions of service shall be the necessity of securing the highest standards of efficiency, competence and integrity. Only citizens of States Parties shall serve as international inspectors or as other members of the professional and clerical staff. Due regard shall be paid to the importance of recruiting the staff on as wide a geographical basis as possible. Recruitment shall be guided by the principle that the staff shall be kept to a minimum.
>
> In the performance of their duties, the Director of the TechnicalSecretariat, the inspectors and the other members of the staff shall not seek or receive instructions from any Government or from any

other source external to the International Authority. They shall refrain from any action which might reflect on their position as international officials responsible only to the Consultative Committee.

Each State Party shall undertake to respect the exclusively international character of the responsibilities of the Director of the Technical Secretariat, the inspectors and the other members of the staff and not to seek to influence them in the discharge of their responsibilities.[10]

Particular areas of activity for the Technical Secretariat have been specified in the draft set of provisions for the Preparatory Commission which is carried forward in parallel with the 'rolling text' of the draft Convention.[11] The Commission is to establish its staff as 'a provisional technical secretariat with units in charge of preparatory work concerning the main activities to be carried out by the Technical Secretariat created under the Convention: declarations and data; inspectorate; evaluation of accounts and reports; agreements and negotiations; personnel, qualifications and training; development of procedures and instruments; technical support; finance and administration'.

It is, of course, constitutionally open to the General Conference and Executive Council to deploy the definitive Technical Secretariat on a quite different basis once they replace the Preparatory Commission upon the CWC's entry into force. Equally it is open to the General Conference to appoint someone other than the outgoing Executive Secretary of the Preparatory Commission as the first Director of the Technical Secretariat. But there is likely to be a strong desire for continuity over these two phases--after opening for signature and after entry into force--in the evolution of the treaty regime. Negotiators in the CD have frequently stressed the need for the international institutions created under the CWC to be equipped to operate at a high pitch of effectiveness right from the start, in order to sustain the credibility of the Convention without interruption. In this context it surely makes sense to work for a close correspondence between the institutional structures preceding and following the Convention's entry into force.

V. The International Inspectorate

A passage in the 'rolling text' specifies that 'The International Inspectorate shall be part of the Technical Secretariat and carry out activities relating to the execution of international verification measures provided for in this Convention'. That is, in effect, its charter. Exactly how the International Inspectorate will fit into the Technical Secretariat, and how the Inspector-General (assuming there is one) will relate to the Director, has yet to be determined. A full discussion of these questions, together with the author's preliminary sketch of a divisional structure and senior staffing for the combined secretariat-with-inspectorate, will be found in *International Organization for Chemical Disarmament* (chapter X).[12]

The CD has, however, agreed a number of quite detailed functions for inspectors to perform, in relation for example to the verification of destruction of stocks of chemical weapons and production facilities, and verification of the non-production of chemical weapons. Draft provisions for such verification are included in the 'rolling text' of Articles IV, V and VI and more particularly in annexes to Articles IV and VI.

Recently the CD has also developed an important set of *Guidelines on the International Inspectorate*.[13] These are annexed. It should be noted that they relate to the activities carried out by inspectors conducting *routine* verification. (*Challenge* verification, special inspections and fact-finding missions will impose further responsibilities on them. Negotiations in this area are located around the 'blank page' section of Article IX provisionally entitled 'Procedure for requesting a fact-finding mission'; their outcome will have eventually to be reflected in the redrafting of Article VIII--and, it may be, in additional *Guidelines on the International Inspectorate*.)

The existing *Guidelines on the International Inspectorate* relating to routine verification activities manifest a laudable concern for the rights of plant operators, scientists and engineers in the chemical industry to have confidential information protected from unauthorized disclosure. This respect for such rights, and more generally for the industry's need to operate continuously with unimpeded efficiency, is strongly emphasized in the 'rolling text' already: as witness, for example, Article VI.9:

In conducting verification activities, the (Consultative Committee) shall:

(a) avoid undue interference in the State Party's peaceful chemical activities;

(b) take every precaution to protect confidential information coming to its knowledge in the implementation of the Convention; and

(c) require only the minimum amount of information and data necessary for the carrying out of its responsibilities under the Convention.[14]

The Guidelines may be seen as elaborating and reinforcing statements of principles such as are expressed in Article VI.9 of the 'rolling text'.

Underlying the *Guidelines* is the fundamental conviction that any intrusion in the course of inspection must be kept to the minimum required in order to be able to ascertain a pattern of universal compliance with all obligations flowing from the Convention, thereby engendering and maintaining full confidence in the integrity of the treaty regime of chemical disarmament.

References

[1]'Rolling text' is the unofficial name given to the set of draft Articles, Annexes, etc., which are forwarded periodically to the CD by its Ad Hoc Committee on Chemical Weapons and used as the basis for subsequent negotiations in that Committee and under its auspices. Successive versions of this 'rolling text' do not bind any delegation but reflect the stage reached in the negotiations at the end of each Committee session, organized in accordance with the agreed Preliminary Structure of a Chemical Weapons Convention. The version of the 'rolling text' used here, the latest available at the time of writing, is that contained in the Committee's Report of 26 Aug. 1987 (Conference on Disarmament document CD/782, Appendix I).

[2]The Netherlands, 'Working paper on an international organ for the support of a CW convention and other disarmament agreements', Conference of the Committee on Disarmament document CCD/410, paragraph II.4, 31 July 1973.

[3]CD/782, Appendix II, p. 24. (Cluster IV was established in 1987--see CD/782, page 6, grouping 'Issues pertaining to the organisation and functions of the Consultative Committee and its organs, as well as issues pertaining to consultation, co-operation and fact-finding, including challenge inspection'.)

[4]See note 3.

[5]Sims, N. A., *International Organization for Chemical Disarmament*, SIPRI Chemical & Biological Warfare Studies no. 8 (Oxford University Press: Oxford, 1987).

[6]CD/782, Appendix II, p. 26: the Co-ordinator for Cluster IV comments: 'While it is an important function of the Organization to carry out verification activities, such a function can hardly be considered a duty to be performed by one of its policy-making organs.'

[7]CD/782. This section relies more heavily on the Report of the Co-ordinator than on the 'rolling text' for its summary of the powers and functions of the Executive Council.

[8]Sims (see note 5).

[9]CD/782.

[10]CD/782, Appendix I, p. 23.

[11]CD/782, Appendix I, pp. 79-80. 'Provisions on the Commission could be contained in a resolution of the UN General Assembly commending the Convention, or in an appropriate document associated with the Convention.' Logically they cannot form part of the Conventon itself, because their *raison d'être* to serve the states signatories to the Convention while--and only while--the latter is not yet in force.

[12]Sims (see note 3).

[13]The status of the *Guidelines on the International Inspectorate* was still uncertain on 26 August 1987, so instead of including them as part of Appendix I ('rolling text') or Appendix II (Reports of Co-ordinators) the Ad Hoc Committee on Chemical Weapons attached them as a separate Addendum to its Report.

[14]CD/782, Appendix I, p. 16.

Attachment (A) to CD/CW/WP.175
Cluster IV
Guidelines on the International Inspectorate */

I. Designation

1. Verification activities in a State Party to the Convention shall only be performed by inspectors designated to this State in advance.

2. The Technical Secretariat shall communicate, in writing, to the State concerned the names, nationality and ranks of the inspectors proposed for designation. Furthermore, it shall furnish a certificate of their qualifications and enter into such consultations as the State concerned may request. The latter shall inform the Secretariat, within (30) days after receipt of such a proposal, whether or not it will accept the designation of each inspector proposed. The inspectors accepted by the State Party shall be designated to that State. The Technical Secretariat shall notify the State concerned of such a designation.

3. Should any State Party object to the designation of inspectors, be it at the time they are proposed or at any time thereafter, it shall inform the Technical Secretariat of its objection. If a State Party raises objections to an inspector already designated, this objection shall come into effect 30 days after receipt by the Technical Secretariat. The Technical Secretariat shall immediately inform the State concerned of the withdrawal of the designation of the inspector. In cases of objections to designation of inspectors the Technical Secretariat shall propose to the State Party in question one or more alternative designations. The Technical Secretariat shall refer to the Executive Council any repeated refusal by a State Party to accept the designation of inspectors if the Secretariat is of the opinion that such refusal impedes inspections to be conducted in the State concerned.

---

*/ These guidelines relate to the activities international inspectors carry out in connection with routine verification in States Parties.

II. Privileges and immunites of inspectors

1. To the extent necessary for the effective exercise of their functions, inspectors shall be accorded the following privileges and immunities, which shall also apply to the time spent travelling in connection with their missions:

> (a) immunity from personal arrest or detention and from seizure of their personal baggage;
> (b) immunity from legal process of every kind in regard to what they do, say or write in the performance of their official functions;
> (c) inviolability of all the papers, documents, equipment and samples they carry with them;
> (d) the right to use codes for their communication with the Secretariat and to receive papers or correspondence by courier or in sealed bags from the Secretariat;
> (e) multiple entry/exit and/or transit visas and the same treatment in entry and transit formalities as is given to members of comparable rank of diplomatic missions;
> (f) the same currency and exchange facilities as are accorded to representatives of foreign Governments on temporary official missions;
> (g) the same immunities and facilities in respect to their personal baggage as are accorded to members of comparable rank of diplomatic missions.

2. Privileges and immunities shall be granted to inspectors for the sake of the Convention and not for the personal benefit of the individuals themselves. The Secretariat shall have the right and the duty to waive the immunity of any inspector whenever it is of the opinion that the immunity would impede the course of justice and can be waived without prejudice to the Convention.

3. If any State Party to the Convention considers that there has been an abuse of an above-mentioned privilege or immunity, consultations shall be held between that State and the Secretariat to determine whether such an abuse has occurred and, if so, to ensure that it does not repeat itself.

III. General rules governing inspections and the conduct of inspectors

1. Inspectors shall carry out their functions under the Convention on the basis of the inspection mandate issued by the Technical Secretariat. They shall refrain from activities going beyond this mandate.

2. The activities of inspectors shall be so arranged as to ensure on the one hand the effective discharge of the inspectors' functions and, on the other, the least possible inconvenience to the State concerned and disturbance to the facility or other location inspected. Inspectors shall only request the information and data which are necessary to fulfil their mandate. States Parties shall furnish such information. Inspectors shall not communicate to any State, Organization or person outside the Technical Secretariat any information to which they have access in connection with their activities in a State Party.

They shall abide by relevant regulations established within the Technical Secretariat for the protection of confidential information. They shall remain bound by these relevant regulations after they have left their functions as international inspectors.

3. In the performance of their duties on the territory of a State Party, inspectors shall, if the State Party so requests, be accompanied by representatives of this State, provided inspectors are not thereby delayed or otherwise hindered in the exercise of their functions. If a State Party designates the inspectors' point of entry into, and departure from, the State concerned and their routes and modes of travel within the State, it shall be guided by the principle of minimizing the time of travel and any other inconvenience.

4. In exercising their functions, inspectors shall avoid unnecessarily hampering or delaying the operation of a facility or affecting its safety. In particular, inspectors shall not operate any facility or direct the staff of the facility to perform any operation. If inspectors consider that, to fulfil their mandate, particular operations should be carried out in a facility, they shall request the designated representative of the management of the facility to perform them.

5. After the inspection visit, inspectors shall submit to the Technical Secretariat a report on the activities conducted by them and on their findings. The report shall be factual in nature. It shall only contain facts relevant to compliance with the Convention, as provided for under the inspection mandate. Relevant regulations, governing the protection of confidential information, shall be observed. The report shall also provide information as to the manner in which the State Party inspected co-operated with the inspection team. Different views held by inspectors may be attached to the report.

6. The report shall be kept confidential. The National Authority of the State Party shall be informed of the findings of the report. Any written comments, which the State Party may immediately make on these findings shall be annexed to it. Immediately after receiving the report, the Technical Secretariat shall transmit a copy of it to the State Party concerned.

7. Should the report contain uncertainties, or should co-operation between the National Authority and the inspectors not measure up to the standard required, the Technical Secretariat shall approach the State Party for clarification.

8. If the uncertainties cannot be removed or the facts established are of a nature to suggest that obligations undertaken under the Convention have not been met, the Technical Secretariat shall inform the Executive Council without delay.

II. REPORTS OF ON-SITE EXPERIMENTS IN CHEMICAL PLANTS

Verification of non-production of chemical weapons and their
precursors by the civilian chemical industry
S. E. FREEMAN and R. J. MATHEWS, Australia

An experimental inspection of a multi-purpose plant
B. ter HAAR, the Netherlands

Report on the visit to VEB Synthesewerk, Schwarzheide, GDR,
during the 12th Workshop of the Pugwash Study Group on
Chemical Warfare in 1987
H.-J. Jeschke and T. STOCK, the German Democratic Republic

VERIFICATION OF NON-PRODUCTION OF CHEMICAL WEAPONS AND THEIR PRECURSORS BY THE CIVILIAN CHEMICAL INDUSTRY

S. E. FREEMAN and R. J. MATHEWS, Australia

I. Introduction

The future Chemical Weapons Convention (CWC) will ban the development, production, stockpiling, transfer and use of chemical weapons. States Parties will, however, have the right to develop, produce, otherwise acquire, retain, transfer and use toxic chemicals and their precursors for purposes not prohibited by the Convention. It is recognized that it will be necessary to monitor the civilian chemical industry to ensure that chemical weapons are not produced or their precursors diverted for purposes prohibited by the Convention.

Considerable work has already been done in examining the general principles involved in establishing a suitable regime for the monitoring process. This work is set out in a number of working papers tabled at the Conference on Disarmament (CD) and has resulted in the (as yet) incomplete provisions in the draft text of the CWC. The report on the 1987 session of the Chemical Weapons Committee[1] sets out the level of agreement that has been achieved to date. It is noteworthy that there has been a large measure of agreement as to which chemicals should be banned or monitored under the CWC. Chemicals assigned to Schedule 1 consist of super-toxic lethal chemicals (STLCs) produced for weapons and their immediate precursors. These will be banned save for a limited production for protective purposes in a single small-scale facility in each country.

Chemicals listed in Schedules 2 and 3 consist of precursors which could be diverted to the production of chemical weapons, and 'dual purpose' chemicals such as hydrogen cyanide and phosgene which could be used as chemical weapons. Schedule 2 chemicals are considered to pose a greater risk to the purpose of the Convention than Schedule 3 chemicals, because there are only a few technological steps required to convert them to chemical weapons. Monitoring of the production and use of chemicals listed in this Schedule will therefore be more stringent than for Schedule 3 chemicals.

It is envisaged that the system of monitoring will consist essentially of the collection and exchange of data covering the production, consumption and use of listed chemicals. In the case of chemicals whose diversion would pose a high risk such data will need to be verified by routine, random inspection. In some instances continuous instrumental monitoring of the production of such chemicals may be appropriate.

The processes of monitoring will, therefore, consist of data collection and exchange, on-site inspection and instrumental monitoring. A process of materials accountancy will be required for the lifetime of each listed chemical.

It is clear that it will be necessary to develop procedures for the inspection of industrial plants to verify the data which are submitted to the appropriate sub-organ of the Consultative Committee. Whether the inspection is part of a routine but random regime or whether it is part of a less systematic inspection process for Schedule 3 chemicals will not alter the criteria for the inspection. It should be effective, cost-effective and should protect commercial confidentiality.

The appropriate Australian Government agencies have for some time been in consultation with the Australian chemical industry with a view to drawing up an inspection procedure which would meet these criteria. An inspection was developed which was later tested in a 'trial inspection' of an Australian chemical facility.

The results of this 'trial inspection' are set out in CD/698.[2]

The objective of the trial inspection was not to 'prove' that a regime of on-site inspections for the civil chemical industry can be easily implemented. Rather, it was to examine whether it was possible to conduct an on-site inspection in a way that was acceptable to the operators of the facility, while still providing objective data sufficient to enable an inspection team to make a reasonable judgement whether or not the facility was being used for purposes prohibited by the Convention. It is hoped that the experience gained from this inspection will assist in devising procedures of sufficient generality to cover different circumstances in different countries.

II. The inspection format

The following outline of the stages of the inspection is suggested as a basis for further study of possible arrangements for the Convention's inspection regime:

1. Notice of inspection. The facility should be notified of the intention to inspect approximately 24 hours prior to arrival of the inspection team and advised of requirements for documentation relevant to the conduct of the inspection (see list A annexed).

2. (a) On arrival the team should make a tour of the facility either on foot or by bus (depending on the size of the facility) in order to identify its main subdivisions. (b) Documentation relevant to the conduct of the inspection should be provided by the management of the facility on the team's arrival. The team should be provided with office space in order to study this. A management representative and some clerical assistance should be available. The documentation should be used: (i) to check for consistency with data already in hand from the National Verification Authority; and (ii) to plan an inspection of those sections of the facility known or likely to be making or using listed chemicals.

3. Inspectors would check items 1-5 of list A (annexed) to establish which chemicals designated by the Convention are made or used by the company. The trend towards computerization of company records could facilitate this process. Where chemicals are traded, but not made or used by the facility, this should be evident from item 5 of list A. Products which are listed by trade or proprietary names should be identified from the facility's 'Product Handling and Safety Bulletin' or equivalent document. This document should also serve as a check on items 1-5, taking into account that it may cover products made in quantities less than the agreed threshold.

4. Inspectors would request information on production and use of listed chemicals. This information should include: (a) the quantity handled in the previous 12 months (or other reporting period as appropriate); (b) the location

in the facility where the chemicals were made or used; (c) the end-products of use and quantity of end-products; and (d) the buyers, if sold as such, and quantity sold.

5. After consultation with the works manager the inspectors should decide on the areas to be inspected on day two. This inspection plan would develop with reference to the site plan of the facility, in conjunction with relevant operating manuals. It should be remembered that a multi-purpose facility might make or use listed chemicals intermittently.

6. The physical inspection would take place on day two. All locations handling listed chemicals should be inspected. In the process plant inspectors should note: (a) the capacity of the facility for the specified annual production taking into account possible intermittent production; (b) the presence of safety equipment in excess of that expected from the declared use; and (c) the presence of items of equipment listed in list B (annexed) which might indicate use of the facility for production of a non-declared product.

7. Samples should be taken from quality-control sampling points or other 'safe' sampling points as deemed appropriate. The operating manual should provide information sufficient to cover all sampling. Three samples should be taken per sampling point and might be coded to preserve confidentiality (see below). One sample should be retained at the facility, one be retained by the inspection team, and one sent for analysis.

8. Inspectors should decide on the basis of all information available whether it would be necessary to inspect a part of the facility not indicated as involving listed chemicals. This option should be available since a clandestine production process might be hidden in another part of the facility.

9. Inspectors should examine all bulk-storage areas including any small subsidiary areas. Samples should be taken on a random basis. Particular attention should be paid to relabelled drums or drums located in areas with low accessibility.

10. Inspectors should check dispatch or shipping areas for consistency with items on list A.

11. In the case of large multi-purpose facilities, inspectors might need further time to evaluate their findings and request additional information.

12. The final report on the facility would be made following the analysis of samples by appropriate laboratories, or on-site if this is feasible.

13. The facility itself would be notified of the completion and results of the inspection.

Problems arising because of the size of very large facilities may in some cases be offset by their use of single-purpose processes which could not readily be changed to the production of listed chemicals.

The inspection carried out in Australia did not take account of information that might be available from instrumental monitoring. Valuable information could be obtained by the use of tamper-resistant flow meters to check on quantities of chemicals used or produced in a prccess. Other devices are possible and should be the subject of a separate study.

III. Protection of information confidential to the chemical facility

The guidelines should be such as to protect confidential information obtained during an inspection. It will be necessary to develop detailed procedures to ensure that facilities inspected will not be commercially disadvantaged by the inspection process. Thus all information obtained by technical inspectors should be protected. In particular, documents such as operating manuals should not be removed from the plant, or copied. Reporting to the Consultative Committee should be in general terms, and should not reveal names of plants inspected or analytical details of samples taken. The Consultative Committee would only scrutinize detailed reports on a need-to-know basis.

It is recognized that certain products or certain parts of facilities to be inspected might require a higher level of confidentiality than this. An organization might request that part of its operation be treated as a commercial secret. A special procedure could then be adopted to ensure that identification of the nature of the product with the name of the producer and the associated commercial arrangement would be available only to designated senior officers of the Technical Inspectorate. In such cases the inspectors would encode samples taken. The analyst would examine a coded sample of unknown origin. The analyst should be given details of the general class of the compound and any special handling procedures required. Complete information identifying the chemical, the facility and the country of origin would only be available to a small, senior group of technical inspectors.

In many instances samples might be analysed on-site. Quality-control procedures used at the plant could provide valuable information.

Portable analytical instruments in a mobile field laboratory might also be appropriate. However, the option to take samples out of the plant should be preserved to confirm on-the-spot analyses.

Plans and strategies to ensure commercial confidentiality and also to ensure compliance with the Convention should be developed by the National Authority and the International Authority along guidelines laid down by the appropriate sub-organ of the Consultative Committee. The guidelines should take account of differences in the organization of the chemical industry in different countries. Some suggestions follow:

1. The Technical Inspectorate must have sufficient authority to ensure that an inspection is meaningful and likely to demonstrate compliance in a convincing way.

2. The aim of the inspection should be to demonstrate compliance or otherwise. The inspectors should not investigate more fully than is necessary to achieve this aim.

3. All data obtained in the process of data exchange or during an inspection should be held securely.

4. The Technical Secretariat should report to the Consultative Committee in sufficient detail to illustrate the scope of its verification activities but not so as to breach commercial confidentiality.

IV. Role of the National Authority

It is anticipated that States Parties will enact domestic legislation to cover the local implementation of the Chemical Weapons Convention. An important role in implementation will be played by the National Authority. This authority will collect and collate all information required by the Convention and forward it at appropriate intervals to the International Authority. A representative of the National Authority should accompany the International Inspectors during visits to chemical plants and should facilitate their task in all ways.

The chemical industry in Australia is required to report regularly on its activities to government at the local and at the federal level. The National Authority should collect all such information and sort it to decide what is relevant to the Convention.

The National Authority should report: (a) production, use, transfer or export of all listed chemicals taking account of threshold values which are to be decided; (b) all facilities producing, using or transferring such chemicals; and (c) new facilities which will produce, use or transfer such chemicals. Major structural changes to existing facilities should be noted. Also changes to production lines that might be relevant, or changes to the product profile of a facility should be noted.

The role of the International Authority will be to verify data supplied by the National Authority. Detailed and consistent data will be easier to verify than incomplete data.

V. Familiarization visits

The International Authority should conduct familiarization visits to all appropriate facilities over a period of time. Data received from the National Authority will be more meaningful if it is interpreted in the framework of information gained at such visits. This concept has been discussed elsewhere.[3]

VI. Frequency of reporting

Data should be reported at intervals which are frequent enough to ensure the smooth running of the process of verification. Some suggestions might include the following.

The International Authority should report to the Consultative Committee annually unless some particular problem arises. The Executive Council might decide if the problem were serious enough to warrant an extraordinary meeting of the Consultative Committee.

States Parties might wish to make general declarations about their chemical industry on an annual basis. Such declarations would amount to confidence-building measures and would support the information provided by the Technical Secretariat.

On the other hand the National Authority should collect data on a continuous basis and transmit it to the International Authority on a quarterly basis, or upon specific request or whenever some unusual incident occurred. In the event that instrumental monitoring of some processes is decided upon it would be necessary for the National Authority to bracket this information with details of downtime in a facility or other changes which would be apparent from the remotely monitored instrumentation. Thus if a production line is closed for repairs this should be notified promptly to assist in the interpretation of the remotely acquired data.

VII. General considerations

The Chemical Weapons Convention will need to specify guidelines for the verification of non-production of chemical weapons and their precursors by the civilian chemical industry. The guidelines must be specific enough to ensure that verification is adequate. However national differences in the organization and regulation of the chemical industry may make it appropriate for the International Authority to negotiate specific agreement with each National Authority.

Such agreements might be subject to review. It is likely that both National and International Authorities will wish to modify procedures in the light of experience. There will be a learning process for all parties, including the chemical industry. It is particularly important that industry be consulted at all times. Industry sensitivities may not always be apparent to National Authorities who may seek to protect inappropriate information. Sensitivities will also change with time. There is no point in protecting last year's secrets which are common knowledge today. The process of verification will run smoothly if there is an adequate level of consultation and co-operation at the national and international levels.

References

[1] 'Report of the Ad Hoc Committee on Chemical Weapons to the Conference on Disarmament', Conference on Disarmament document CD/782, 26 Aug. 1987.

[2] Australia, 'Verification of non-production of chemical weapons and their precursors by the civilian chemical industry: trial inspection of an Australian chemical facility', Conference on Disarmament document CD/698, 4 June 1986.

[3] The Netherlands, 'Workshop on the verification of a chemical weapons ban held in the Netherlands, 4-6 June 1986, Verification of non-production of chemical weapons: scenario for an experimental inspection', Conference on Disarmament document CD/CW/WP.141, 10 June 1986.

ANNEX

List A: List of information/documents required on the first day of the inspection

Material to be provided by the chemical facility

1. List of all chemicals produced by the facility in the last 12 months in quantities greater than one tonne.*
2. List of chemicals purchased by the facility in the last 12 months in quantities greater than one tonne.
3. List of end users/buyers of chemicals in the last 12 months in quantities greater than one tonne.
4. List of chemicals not covered in 1-3 above but which are held in stocks in quantities greater than 10 tonnes.
5. List of all chemicals traded in quantities greater than one tonne, that is, bought and resold but not processed.
6. Safety manuals, including Product Handling and Safety Bulletins or equivalent documentation.
7. Operating manuals for particular processes.
8. Basic flow sheet for the facility.
9. Map showing plant layout.

*Threshold values suggested here will be subject to negotiation.

List B: Chemical equipment which might be used to produce designated chemicals

The possession of any of the following items individually is not suggestive of chemical-weapon production. However, location of several items at one facility would indicate that inspection may be necessary to verify that there are no chemical-weapon activities at the facility.

1. Chemical-process equipment (reactors, piping, distillation columns and the like) constructed of Hastelloy or another alloy with a high nickel or tantalum content.

2. Chemical-process equipment with linings suitable for use in a highly corrosive environment (that is, glass-, teflon- or plastic-lined equipment).

3. Pumps or valves designed for use with hazardous chemicals (for example, double-seal, magnetic drive or canned pumps, bellows or diaphragm valves).

4. Activated carbon filter units and scrubber units capable of handling large volumes of air from ventilation systems.

5. Equipment specially designed for fluorine, phosphorus or sulphur analyses.

6. Inert gas generating units.

7. Double-walled piping.

8. Sensitive detection and alarm systems for toxic substances.

9. Filling equipment for use with hazardous chemicals, including especially large glove boxes used to enclose filling machinery.

10. Incineration or scrubbing equipment for hazardous chemical-waste treatment, such as Venturi scrubbers or Brinks mist eliminators.

AN EXPERIMENTAL INSPECTION OF A MULTI-PURPOSE PLANT

B. ter HAAR, the Netherlands

I. Introduction

Between the autumn of 1985 and May 1986 an experimental inspection of a multi-purpose plant took place in the Netherlands. The purpose of this experiment was to gain experience on the problems involved in a routine inspection of a facility within a multi-purpose plant under a Chemical Weapon Convention (CWC).

A report on the experimental inspection and a visit to the factory concerned, were the centre-pieces of a workshop that was organized by the Netherlands Ministry of Foreign Affairs on 4 to 6 June 1986 for delegations to the Conference on Disarmament (CD).[1]

II. Purpose of the experimental inspection

The purpose of the experimental inspection was to study and test organizational and technical aspects involved in routine inspection of a chemical plant under a CWC. A large chemical company in the Netherlands agreed to co-operate in the carrying out of the experimental inspection. The multi-purpose plant formed part of a large (5 square kilometres) complex consisting of a variety of petrochemical and chemical facilities, including several multi-purpose ones. Among the purposes for which the facility was used was the production of an organophosphate (monocrotophos, a pesticide), for which trimethyl phosphite was one of the basic materials.

The prime aim of the experimental inspection was to verify that the phosphites used at the facility were not being used to produce methylphosphorus compounds.[2] In addition, it was investigated to what extent it was possible for the experimental inspection to verify that the phosphites were genuinely being processed into phosphates and not retained for the production elsewhere of nerve gases such as Sarin. Although the experimental inspection took place in a very specific situation, an attempt was made to plan it in such a way that it would be possible to generalize from it.

III. Proceedings of the experimental inspection

By referring to the exercise as an experimental inspection, we may have given the impression that we went to the plant on a particular day, had a look round, took samples, analysed them and then concluded the inspection. Indeed, that may have been how we ourselves envisaged going about the matter when we first started planning this meeting, but in practice the experimental inspection took far longer. In fact, six months elapsed between the taking of the first samples and of the last ones. Other samples were taken and analysed in the interim. This, of course, hardly made it a model inspection, as neither companies nor inspection teams will be very keen on inspections which take more than six months to complete.

However, in this case we were not concerned with carrying out an actual inspection but with investigating how a routine inspection ought to be carried out. During these six months many brainstorming sessions were held to consider this question. Four organizations were involved: the Prins Maurits Laboratory of the Central Organisation for Applied Scientific Research in Rijswijk (involved in research into methods of detecting chemical weapons), Shell Nederland Chemie in Pernis, the Central Environmental Protection Department, Rhine Estuary Region (involved in inspecting the civil chemical industry under the term of a number of Acts of Parliament on environmental matters) and the Ministry of Foreign Affairs.

IV. Scenario of a routine inspection

In the course of the brainstorming sessions the following scenario was drawn up:[3] (a) routine data reporting; (b) familiarization visits; (c) notification of inspection and reception at an industrial complex; (d) on-site inspection; (e) sampling and analysis; and (f) evaluation of the results. In the following paragraphs these six parts of the scenario are commented upon.

Routine data reporting

In order to monitor industry effectively, the International Inspectorate will need information on companies and plants which manufacture, process, use or transfer substances of relevance to chemical weapons. In the case of Schedule 2 substances, the knowledge and information required is of the two kinds discussed in the following subsections.

Data required for a survey of production relevant to chemical weapons

The International Inspectorate needs this information in order to assess *which* plants require routine inspection and *how often*. In addition, this information can possibly also be used to draw up a type of balance sheet on substances of relevance to chemical weapons.

Data required in order to carry out an inspection

This information is needed in order to determine *how* a routine inspection should be carried out. Only the team which is to carry out the inspection has a need to know this information. This information, could be used for the elaboration of a 'facility attachment' that would guide the inspectors during an inspection.

Familiarization visits

In order to obtain the additional information that is necessary for a proper inspection, inspection teams should make inquiries about all plants subject to routine inspection. If this information is available from national government bodies, it might be sufficient for an inspection team to visit the government body concerned. Among the documents which the inspection teams should be allowed to study during familiarization visits are, for example, licences and reports containing detailed flow diagrams and an indication of the capacity of the production plant. Insofar as the material supplied to an inspection team during a familiarization visit is confidential, the inspection team would only be allowed to study it on the spot and not to copy it or take it away.

If government bodies do not have sufficient information, a familiarization visit should also be made to the production plant. If government bodies *do* have sufficient information, a familarization visit to the plant itself would not, strictly speaking, be necessary, but would presumably none the less be useful for purposes of familiarization.

Notification of inspection and reception at an industrial complex

In order to make it as difficult as possible to eradicate all traces of illegal activities, it is very important that as little time as possible elapses between the notification and the carrying out of a routine inspection. The following measures could help to achieve this end:

1. Good preparation by the inspection team (for example, by means of familiarization visits).

2. Stage-by-stage notification of the routine inspection. It might first be announced that an inspection is to be carried out in a particular region (such as Belgium, the Federal Republic of Germany and the Netherlands). The receiving state or states would then be obliged immediately to take all necessary steps to facilitate inspection of any plant within its/their territory (visas, transport and the like). Only after the inspectors' arrival in the area would it be announced exactly which plant was to be inspected.

3. Instead of following the normal order of procedures, the inspectors could take a few samples immediately upon arrival at the industrial complex, that is, before holding detailed talks with management and so on.

On-site inspection

The list of items to look at during on-site inspection was based on the proposals by the United Kingdom in CD/575. In addition we felt that it would also be worthwhile to look at how waste is processed (effluent analysis might be used as a less intrusive verification method) to obtain a general indication of the safety measures taken, as these provide an indication of the possibility of producing super-toxic lethal chemicals at the plant concerned.

An on-site inspection will, of course, first of all check that nothing that is prohibited by the Convention takes place at the inspected facility. But it is at least as interesting to know whether anything forbidden has taken place or will take place.

Although it is not possible to obtain complete certainty about what has happened in the past or what will happen in the future, an inspection team could possibly obtain some indication by investigating the items detailed in table 1.

Table 1. Possible indications of non-permitted chemical-weapon production

	In the past	In the future
1. Plant records, etc.	x	x
2. Special technical facilities	x	x
3. Special safety measures	x	x
4. Medical particulars of staff (to evaluate workers' health--blood samples, illness, interviews)	x	
5. Presence of particular chemicals	x	x
6. Presence of illegal end-products	x	
7. Waste (small, detectable traces are persistent)	x	

Some of these indications can be concealed fairly rapidly and easily (for example, number 6), while others are far more difficult to hide (for example, number 7). The relevance of numbers 3 and 4 is, of course, limited to illegal production of super-toxic chemicals. They will not be of much help in deciding whether non-permitted production of key-precursors has taken place or will take place. The clearest indications are naturally to be found in plant records. Although these can be falsified it is very likely that falsifications will come to light during a routine inspection which has been announced only shortly beforehand. It is difficult to make full formal provision for checking up on all of the above seven points in every facility attachment, but it seems important that these agreements leave open the possibility that an inspection team takes these indications into consideration. (See also the chapter by von Baeckmann.)

Much will therefore depend on the knowledge, experience and diplomacy of the inspectors. The necessary experience will have to be built up, *inter alia* by paying visits to the plant concerned and to other similar ones.

If the plant is small, consisting, for example, of a single production facility together with everything pertaining to it, an inspection team can check all seven points with relative ease. But if the routine inspection has to be carried out at a very large complex where numerous facilities are operated that are not relevant to the CWC and which are therefore neither notified nor under inspection, it will be far more difficult to properly check the entire area for special compounds. In such cases, under normal circumstances, the inspection effort will probably be concentrated on the notified production facility and the storage facilities that are clearly related to the production facility.

Sampling and analysis

The sampling points could be arranged as follows, according to their degree of intrusiveness. (The numbers given refer to figure 1.)

Near-site verification could take place (1) at the point where process water enters the industrial complex and (2) at the point where effluent water leaves the industrial complex.

On-site verification (less intrusive) would encompass (3) effluent water from the production facility, (4) other waste and (5) effluent water from the industrial complex as a whole before it enters the purification plant.

On-site verification (more intrusive) could occur (6) at the place where the initial product is stored (for example, in order to analyse whether the trimethyl phosphite contains traces of $P\text{-}CH_3$), and (7) at the point where a product leaves the reactor vessel (in order to establish that the key precursor has been processed into a substance not relevant to the CWC).

An inspection would be most effective if the samples could be analysed before the end of the inspection so that supplementary samples can be taken if necessary in order to eliminate any uncertainties which arise. Where possible, analyses should be carried out in the laboratory of the facility.

Evaluation of the results of an inspection

The evaluation of the concrete data that have been assembled during an inspection is probably the most difficult part of a routine inspection. To conclude that no illegal *production* of chemical-warfare-relevant chemicals is taking place is relatively easy. It will be more difficult to conclude that no *diversion* has taken place, for example, because of the losses that occur during a normal production process. The most important causes of these losses are physical and chemical.

Losses owing to physical causes may occur, for example, during transport and storage as a result of evaporation, residues being left behind in vessels and pipes and so on. Examples of losses resulting from the chosen process of chemical production are the following:

1. If a reaction is to be carried out between two chemicals, one of which is more expensive than the other, a deliberate decision will often be made to use an excess quantity of the cheaper substance in order to ensure that all of the more expensive substance is converted into product.

2. During the reaction process, part of the initial product may be converted into undesirable by-products which are eliminated by means of waste-purification and air-purification processes.

V. The extent of losses

Although companies will naturally do their best to operate as economically as possible, with minimum losses, a discrepancy of 10 per cent between the quantity of initial products used and the theoretical quantity of end-product which should result is not unusual. If this end-product is, in turn, used as a precursor for another end-product, a further loss of 10 per cent may occur.

In a production process which consists of a number of stages of this kind, it is thus theoretically possible for significant losses to occur. It should be borne in mind in this respect that a company, for economic motives, will itself be the first to ascertain the reasons why raw materials are being lost. The

Inspectorate can expect management to provide a plausible explanation of any substantial loss. If they cannot, there are grounds for suspicion.

VI. Preliminary conclusions of the June 1986 workshop

After the workshop held on 4 to 6 June 1986 by the Netherlands Ministry of Foreign Affairs some tentative conclusions were presented to the Conference on Disarmament.[4] The essence of these conclusions was as described below.

The chemical industry is accustomed to inspections

The perspectives for co-operation with the chemical industry in finding adequate ways and means of verifying non-production appear to be favourable. At least part of this willingness seems due to the fact that the chemical industry in countries like the Netherlands is already used to a rather intrusive system of inspection.[5] However, it is recognized that a satisfactory solution must be found for the protection of sensitive information, particularly that pertaining to production data and lists of customers.

An important difference between the existing systems of national inspection and the proposed verification of non-production is that the second form of inspection is international. However, what seems to be possible at the national level--where competing chemical and pharmaceutical industries are controlled by the same inspectors--should in our view be feasible internationally, provided that adequate safeguards for the protection of sensitive information are devised.

Familiarization visits are essential

Proper preparation of a routine inspection requires a lot more specific data about the facility than is available on the basis of routine data reporting. As soon as a CWC enters into force, inspectors should start familiarizing themselves with the plants that will be subject to routine, random on-site inspection. The information that already exists in different branches of the governments of State Parties for purposes of national inspection can probably be used for the purpose of these familiarization visits.

No single scenario for all routine inspections

In order to make routine, random on-site inspections not more intrusive than is strictly necessary, but nevertheless effective, the peculiarities of a plant to be inspected (such as size, capabilities, current stocks and the like) will have to be taken into account. Proper routine inspection is, therefore, like a suit which is made to measure. In broad outline each one may be alike, but the details differ from case to case. In order to ensure a good comfortable fit the company must co-operate frankly and allow its measurements to be taken. Although there is no point in seeking to lay down a 'ready-to-wear' standard procedure which is both detailed and applicable in every case, it is possible and very useful to draw up a checklist of points that can be relevant and to develop verification techniques that can be used as the building blocks of an actual inspection.

Waste-water analysis can help but not always to the same degree

In the experimental inspection, extensive use was made of a method for the detection of small quantities of 'fingerprint' chemicals (containing P-CH3 bonds) in waste. This method proved to be a great help, but did not provide simple answers to all questions during the experimental inspection. The main problems were found to be: (a) the presence of very small amounts of P-CH3 in the starting material, (b) the production of very small amounts of P-CH3 as an unwanted by-product in the production process, and (c) the efficiency of waste-water treatment (traces that were found in the waste water before treatment were no longer detectable after treatment).

Highly qualified inspectors are needed

In order to be able to recognize which parts of a plant are relevant for chemical-weapon production, the inspectors will have to be very highly qualified, both in the field of chemistry relevant to chemical-weapon production and in the field of chemical engineering in general.

Non-production verification is possible at acceptable costs

The experience obtained by the experimental inspection described here has strengthened our view that an adequate system of verification can be elaborated at reasonable costs. Although a system of routine, random on-site inspection will not make an effective challenge inspection system superfluous, it will diminish the need to resort to such inspections.

VII. Review of the results of the workshop

Looking back at the experimental inspection, about one and a half year later at the time or writing, it seems that the conclusions we arrived at still stand, and that the results have, to a large extent, been incorporated in the rolling text of the draft Convention. The meeting of CD delegations with experts from industry on 6 and 7 July 1987, has given new proof of the willingness of civil chemical industry to take their part in the necessary dialogue on the development of an effective verification system. Our proposal of familiarization visits was, in a slightly modified form, incorporated in the rolling text as 'initial visit'. The idea of making use, as much as possible, of the less intrusive verification method of waste analysis now seems widely accepted. And nobody seems to question that the inspectors will have to be highly qualified, but a lot of work on the set-up of the Inspectorate still has to be done.

The need for separate facility attachments for industrial facilities on the basis of a general model agreement seems now to be generally accepted. In our conclusions we compared such a facility attachment (without using the word) with a suit that is made to measure. This comparison holds as far as the need for separate agreements for each individual type of facility goes, but it does not reckon with the flexibility of modern plants. A facility attachment for a multi-purpose plant will not only have to be tailor-made, but will also have to give to the inspection team a substantial amount of flexibility to respond adequately to changes in a facility.

As far as our last conclusion is concerned, the final proof will be in the eating. Still a lot of similar experiments will have to be undertaken before we can say with full confidence that the envisaged system does work effectively. But the progress we have made encourages hope.

References

[1] The preliminary conclusions of the workshop were introduced at the CD as Conference on Disarmament document CD/706, 20 June 1986. Four documents of the workshop were also made available as working documents of the Ad Hoc Committee for Chemical Weapons (CD/CW/WP 141, 10 June 1986; CD/CW/WP. 142, 13 June 1986; CD/CW/WP. 143, 1 July 1986; and CD/CW/WP. 144, 24 June 1986.

[2] It should be noted that according to the current rolling text of the Convention, trimethyl phosphite will be placed in Schedule 3. This means that its processing into off-specification chemicals would not be verified as intrusively as suggested by the experimental inspection. We believe that the facility selected for inspection was, nevertheless, suitable for the purpose of the experiment.

[3] This scenario was published as CD/CW/WP.141, 10 June 1986. In addition to this scenario that was drawn up in consultation with the company concerned, a number of ideas were put forward which the company did not necessarily have to agree with. These observations were published as CD/CW/WP.142, 13 June 1986.

[4] CD/706.

[5] An overview of regulations existing in the Netherlands was given in CD/CW/WP.143, 1 July 1986.

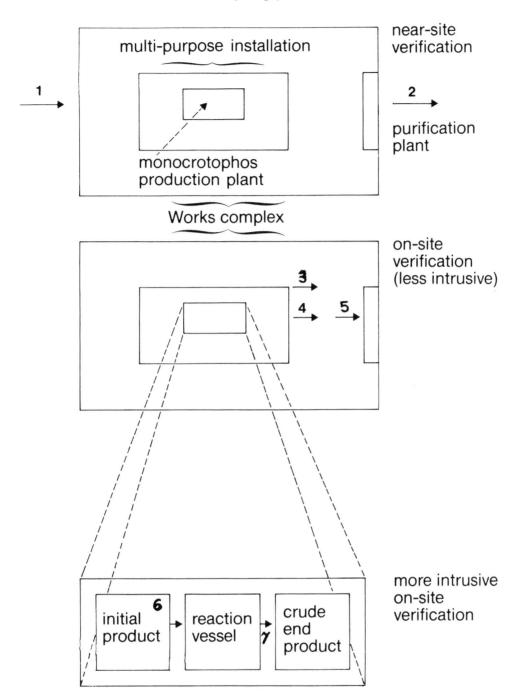

Figure 1. Possible sampling points.

Samples could be taken at the following points near site: 1. where process water enters the industrial complex; 2. where effluent water leaves the complex on-site; 3. effluent water from the production facility; 4. other waste; 5. effluent water from the industrial complex as a whole before it enters the purification plant; 6. where the initial product is stored; and 7. where a product leaves the reactor.

REPORT ON THE VISIT TO VEB SYNTHESEWERK, SCHWARZHEIDE, GDR, DURING THE 12TH WORKSHOP OF THE PUGWASH STUDY GROUP ON CHEMICAL WARFARE IN 1987

H.-J. JESCHKE and T. STOCK, the German Democratic Republic

The 12th Pugwash Workshop, which took place in March 1987 in the GDR, was devoted to verification of non-production of chemical weapons, which is one of the most important functions of the regime to be established by the future Chemical Weapons Convention (CWC). The chief topic of the Workshop was the discussion with representatives of the chemical industry about the kind of controls which the industry might have to accept in the interests of chemical disarmament.[1]   Therefore the 12th Workshop was combined with a site visit to an enterprise of a type that might become subject to certain measures: a phosgene-production unit in an integrated polyurethane complex.

Phosgene (carbonyl chloride, carbon oxychloride) has been used as a chemical-warfare agent; however, in the last 50 years it has become a major chemical intermediate. Due to its high degree of reactivity, phosgene interacts with many classes of inorganic as well as organic reactants. It is used extensively in the preparation of isocyanates leading to polyurethanes or another important group of polymers, and in the production of well-known carbamate insecticides. Besides the uses mentioned, phosgene is also present in the production of chloroformates and chlorocarbamates, which are intermediates in a variety of substances such as: flotation agents, perfumes and especially pharmaceuticals and agricultural chemicals. Phosgene is also one of the most relevant representatives of Schedule 3 chemicals (dual-purpose agents). These chemicals are defined in the present draft of the Convention as chemicals produced in large commercial quantities and which could be used for chemical-weapon purposes. For these chemicals, and the corresponding production facilities, a declaration regime is established in the Annex [3] to Article VI, in the rolling text.[2]   The declaration should contain, *inter alia*, information in relation to the location of the facility, its production capacity, the processing, consumption and transfer of the declared chemicals and the approximate yearly quantities involved.

The visit took place at VEB Synthesewerk Schwarzheide, the parent plant of the Kombinat SYS in the GDR which comprises several legally independent plants with their own cost-accounting system. In general, *Kombinate*, or combines, in the GDR are administered from the parent plant, whose management body is identical with that of the combine as a whole. A combine is headed by a General Manager who bears full political and legal responsibility for all operations. His instructions are binding on the whole work-force of the combine. General managers of combines are directly subordinated to the industrial minister responsible, in the case of Schwarzheide, the Minister for the Chemical Industry.

It was the first time that such a site visit was arranged in a chemical industry of a Warsaw Treaty Member State.

During the site visit in Schwarzheide the 38 participants from 18 countries, including outstanding experts and participants in the Geneva negotiations on a CWC, were made acquainted with the organization and operation of a major chemical plant in a socialist country.

The General Manager of the VEB Synthesewerk Schwarzheide, Dr Jeschke, briefed the study group on the production programme of the plant.

The bulk of the products are based on licences obtained from several West European countries and the United States and they are mainly produced in the polyurethane complex. This integrated polyurethane complex in Schwarzheide appears to have been the first single-site complex of this kind set up during the early 1970s in the GDR. It produces polyurethane feedstock, semi-manufactures and finished goods. A self-contained isocyanate complex in Schwarzheide is made up of nine interlinked units, which include a gasification plant for the manufacture of hydrogen; a gasification plant for the manufacture of carbon monoxide; a gas separation plant for obtaining hydrogen and carbon monoxide; as well as plants for the manufacture of TDA (toluine-diamine), aniline, pure formalin from crude formalin, phosgene and polyisocyanate; and a plant for the treatment of hydrogen chloride. Related to the polyurethane complex is a factory producing polyether alcohols and one for producing polyester alcohols. The feedstock complex is supplemented by a system prefabrication unit, which means that Schwarzheide produces not only individual components but, more importantly, user-specific polyurethane systems for direct machine processing. During the 1980s, a factory for the manufacture of elastomer semi-manufactures and finished goods was set up in Schwarzheide. While the overall production program of VEB Synthesewerk Schwarzheide is largely determined by the polyurethane complex, there are two other major production lines in the combine: the manufacture of chlorinated paraffins, used as plasticizers; and the manufacture of herbicides, that is, Omnidel (common name: Dalapon) used to protect grass, and substituted phenoxycarbonic acids based on 2,4-dichlorophenol and 4-chlorocresol, used to protect cereals.

During the site visit in Schwarzheide the participants received information from the General Manager and the Manager for Environment and Energy on waste treatment (especially waste water).[3] Extensive facilities for the treatment, storage and retention of process water have been set up to ensure that under all circumstances only properly treated waste water is discharged. The water-treatment methods at Schwarzheide comprise: high-pressure wet-air oxidation; efficient ventilation-technique biological tanks; and multi-stage, long-term biologic treatment.

The waste-water treatment line features a biological denitrification unit. Biological processes are subjected to continuous analytical monitoring. An ingenious solution has been devised: treated water is discharged two kilometres upstream from the cooling-water intake point. Thus, if water is released untreated, the facility will soon have it back with all the problems involved.

Non-reusable process waste, including toxic materials, are incinerated in cylindrical rotary kilns at temperature of 1100 ± 50 °C.

The Pugwash Study Group was also given background information on the operation of the plant. The plant meets its energy requirements from its own sources, a power station operating on raw lignite, fuel oil or natural gas, which meets its steam and electricity needs. The plant is linked by automatic, non-interruptable switching-gear to the national grid, and also has its own water-recovery and purification systems. Schwarzheide produces its own auxiliary media: nitrogen, oxygen and compressed air. Concerning transport, the plant has its own railway system, connected to the national network, and a road transportation service. A large technical department is responsible for the maintenance and replacement of facilities.

During the Schwarzheide visit, the participants were also given a brief introduction to the technology of phosgene production by the General Manager. The production technology for phosgene is technically well-known, and need not be presented here. The feedstock products in phosgene production are chlorine and carbon monoxide. The carbon monoxide gas is obtained from an external facility and is manufactured from coke oven gas. Chlorine is imported. The Schwarzheide production process of phosgene is a continuous chemical process; the final product, phosgene, is stored in 2 storage containers with a volume of 16 tonnes each. (A third storage container is held in reserve.) The production volume of phosgene is on the order of 7 tonnes per day. The entire production unit works approximately 310 days per year.

Phosgene production is an integrated part of the production process of the self-contained isocyanate complex. If there is a breakdown in the carbon monoxide or phosgene unit, the isocyanate operations must be halted.

The Pugwash Study Group visited the feedstock storage units, the production unit and the storage container for the produced phosgene. The group could observe that the size of the storage container could correspond to the requirements of the isocyanate complex. No additional phosgene stores for other purposes existed. Phosgene production is carried out on a 24-hour cycle, as is normal technical practice elsewhere.

In the course of the visit, it was demonstrated that no amount of the produced phosgene was transferred from the production facility, and that all of it was consumed in the isocyanate complex.

The Pugwash Study Group expressed interest in visiting the process-control unit of the phosgene-production facility. Here the participants could observe the control of the flow of the entire phosgene-production process by means of centralized instruments and equipment. The personnel demonstrated to the group how they monitor the actual production process, the input of feedstocks and the output of end-products as well as the quality of processing. Process parameters such as temperature and pressure are also recorded. Automatic as well as manual monitoring methods were applied.

In terms of the verification tasks concerning Schedule 3 chemicals, it was of interest for the Study Group to see that the identification of declared production data in such a central process-control unit is possible. Another important finding from the site visit was that in a fully automatic production process such as phosgene production, sample-taking from different intermediate stages is not possible without disarranging the production process unless provided for particularly. Verification of the input and output data enable comprehensive qualitative and quantitative evaluation of the production-process data.

In terms of a declaration in relation to production units for Schedule 3 compounds, the Study Group learned that it is possible to evaluate: the capacity of the phosgene-production facility in Schwarzheide; the final product or end-use of the declared chemicals; and the total amount produced, consumed, imported or exported in the previous calendar year.

As a result of the Schwarzheide site visit and of the discussions with the General Manager the following conclusions could be drawn:

1. There are differences in approaches in regard to the system of economic management and planning between socialist and Western countries. In a socialist country it is impossible to produce, import or export chemical agents without the knowledge of the central-planning institution of the government. This also concerns the export of chemicals.

2. The problem of protection of confidential information at a chemical facility is one of the most difficult ones. There exist different types of such information in relation to production, technology and commerce. From the standpoint of an enterprise, the disclosure of technical information--for example, on the volume of production, feedstocks and general information on production technology--is definitely possible. With regard to the disclosure of other kinds of information, such as on commercial relations, notably with international customers, there exist some constraints. An adequate mechanism must be found for the declaration of international customer connections that would put all enterprises on an equal footing. The competition threshold *vis-à-vis* international customers must not be allowed to hamper the declaration and verification mechanism.

3. In the field of laboratory research and development in chemistry, there exist two other problems: (a) research and development in relation to application of new chemical products, where disclosure is possible for verification without any problems for the protection of information; and (b) basic research and development in chemistry, where some problems do exist in relation to the verification scope.

4. The site visit to the Schwarzheide phosgene-production unit illustrated that an on-site inspection of intermediate phosgene stocks may permit clear identification of the size of the stocks and of the relevant processing and consumption.

5. The Pugwash Study Group learned in Schwarzheide that phosgene is not transferred outside the producing facility.

6. From the standpoint of exact verification of data on production of Schedule 3 compounds, it may be necessary to establish an internal material accountancy. The Schwarzheide site visit showed that materials accountancy in separate ledgers is possible. But for the production of intermediates, such as phosgene in Schwarzheide, a requirement for an exact material accountancy covering all steps to the final and complete end-product declaration ought to be reconsidered. (The necessity of a precise and complete end-product declaration in the event that the declared chemicals are only intermediate agents with 100 per cent processing in other chemical agents within the same facility is very doubtful).

7. Concerning verification of Schedule 3 chemicals, the main verification measures are data reporting and monitoring of the relevant data. The visit in Schwarzheide showed that data reporting and an adequate verification of relevant data is possible. The importance of the National Authority in a data-reporting system for Schedule 3 chemicals is obvious.

For a future CWC, it will be essential to find an approach that, on the one hand, takes into account the interests of the enterprises and, on the other, allows for relevant verification. For sensitive information relevant to production know-how, a non-discriminatory solution will be necessary.

References

[1]Robinson, J. P. P. and Lohs, Kh., *Pugwash Newsletter*, vol. 24, no. 4 (April 1987), pp. 108-10.

[2]Conference on Disarmament document CD/782, 26 Aug.1987.

[3]Lohs, Kh., Stock, T. and Kläss, V., *Z. Chemie*, vol. 27 (1987), p. 349.

III. APPLICABILITY OF TECHNICAL METHODS FOR MONITORING OF CHEMICAL INDUSTRY PRODUCTION

Monitoring methods in industrial production relevant to the projected Chemical Weapons Convention
J. MATOUSEK, Czechoslovakia

Verification equipment for on-site inspection teams under the proposed Chemical Weapons Convention
M. RAUTIO, Finland

Verification of non-production of chemical-warfare agents in the civil chemical industry
A. VERWEIJ and H. L. BOTER, the Netherlands

Possibilities for automatic monitoring of chemical products
O. V. PERRONI, Brazil

Some views on the control of multi-purpose plants
H. SCHRÖDER and H. HOFFMANN, the Federal Republic of Germany

Instrumented monitoring of the chemical industry under a chemical weapons ban
N. KYRIAKOPOULOS and R. MIKULAK, the USA

Reliable identification of chemical-warfare agent micro-concentrations as the basis for a system of verifying compliance with the non-production of chemical weapons
V. A. RYLOV, the USSR

Approaches to the use of instruments in monitoring the production of chemical weapons and precursor chemicals
L. ZEFTEL, P. WEINBERG and J. SCHROY, the USA

MONITORING METHODS IN INDUSTRIAL PRODUCTION RELEVANT TO THE PROJECTED CHEMICAL WEAPONS CONVENTION

J. MATOUŠEK, Czechoslovakia

I. Introduction

Verifying implementation of the provisions of any arms control and disarmament document, although not primary--compared to the provisions themselves--plays an inevitable role in the functioning of such an agreement.

Understanding and confidence among nations, states and military coalitions require necessary levels of mutual assurance. No nation can build up its security at the expense of other nations, and the global and regional system of security requires perfect routine as well as emergency verification measures.

The ideal status of international law, expressed by the phrase 'pacta sunt servanda' (treaties are to be kept) can be achieved only when the legal tools which deal with the most sensitive political and military arms control and disarmament problems contain clear definitions, non-ambiguous formulations of provisions (for example, orders, prohibitions and permitted activities) as well as a system of reliable measures for verifying both positive and negative undertakings at acceptable, feasible levels of significance as regards the military relevance of any particular provision.

The ongoing negotiations on a Chemical Weapons Convention (CWC) in the Conference on Disarmament (CD) and previous multilateral negotiating fora in Geneva (ENDC, CCD, CD) have stressed the importance of the development of a workable system of verification measures to be performed and controlled by a monitoring agency (the Consultative Committee with its subsidiary bodies) in co-operation with national verification authorities.

The reason for this approach is clear owing to a number of reasons. It is impossible to limit verification of destruction of stockpiles, for example, to only a subjective element (that is, declaration of possession) as in the Biological and Toxin Weapons Convention. Chemical weapons are very specific as a result of the breadth of their existing and potential production base which allows for extensive vertical and horizontal proliferation. The production and stockpiling of chemical weapons (as compared to biological, toxin and nuclear weapons) can occur in militarily relevant quantities with relative simplicity, low cost and at many sites. Militarily relevant quantities of chemical-warfare agents of the order of 10^2 tonnes could be produced and stockpiled, in bulk or as munitions, in many well-equipped but relatively small factories even in Third World countries. Testing of chemical weapons (as compared to nuclear devices) cannot be monitored at a distance using, for example, satellite or other remote systems. Use of chemical weapons cannot be detected using a simple physical equivalent, such as seismic verification of underground nuclear explosions or the light or electromagnetic pulse or ionic radiation present on or above ground zero in the case of nuclear explosions.

This is why negotiations on a CWC encompass a whole system of very specific provisions dealing with verification of the main objectives, composition of the organization, its personnel, and the means and methodology to be employed.

This system must assure adequate and reliable verification of a number of activities. This paper will deal only with those relating to the non-production of chemical weapons in the chemical industry.

II. Verification of non-production

Verification of non-production of chemical weapons in civilian chemical industry is based on various methods from systematic on-site inspection (according to the importance or risk which given chemicals pose for the CWC) to checking on production, import and export data as well as monitoring and analysis of statistical information.

The choice of methods will be regulated according to the four individual Schedules envisaged by the projected CWC, which establishes in Article VI certain regimes for the verification and monitoring of the production of the corresponding groups of chemicals.

The verification of production of the allowed limited quantity of super-toxic lethal chemicals (STLCs) for permitted purposes in a single small-scale facility can be regarded as a special case in the complex of verification of non-production of chemical weapons.

The production of Schedule 1 chemicals (STLCs), dangerous components/key precursors of (binary) chemical-weapon (systems) will normally be subject to the most strict verification measures. An aggregate production of no more than one tonne per year will be allowed.

These verification measures will comprise on-site inspection (systematic to permanent), use of equipment for surveillance of the site, verification of production output, analysis of produced agents, reporting of data and continuous monitoring.

Schedule 2 is principally comprised of some P-alkyl compounds and (key) precursors; Schedule 3 contains precursors and dual-purpose chemicals (like phosgene, hydrogen cyanide and cyanogen chloride) produced in large quantities for peaceful purposes purposes; Schedule 4 contains highly toxic chemicals not listed in other Schedules, but which might be relevant to the CWC.

The methods, used in verifying (monitoring) production of chemicals, corresponding to individual Schedules (2-4) must assure *inter alia* that no dangerous Schedule 1 chemicals are produced.

III. Possible methods of monitoring industrial production

It seems clear that with the exception of verifying alleged use of chemical weapons, all other monitoring tasks under the CWC would have to do with technological activities, typical of production, storage and transport of harmful industrial chemicals. Even some methods which would be regularly employed in investigations of alleged use (detection and identification of trace amounts of toxic chemicals, their metabolites and degradation products) can be successfully used in verification of technological activities, especially for on-site, near-site (downwind and downstream) and remote monitoring.

Monitoring methods will no doubt utilize the benefits of the combination of national means (proper methods, procedures and authorities)[1] and international means, represented by the system of the Consultative Committee and its subsidiary executive and technical bodies which will, of course, be determining for the execution of the verification activities.

Generally speaking, all monitoring methods consist of an intercorrelation of *facts and events* to be observed, detected, checked, determined or measured; *modes* of observation, detection, measurement and determination; *instruments* (devices and equipment) for observation, surveillance, locking, sealing, detection, determination, measuring, evaluation, storage, transformation, communication of data and so on and *inspectors*.

The choice of corresponding methods depends upon the degree of risk from the point of view of the objectives of the projected CWC. The highest aspect of risk for the CWC (it is in this context production of Schedule 1 chemicals) would require the continuous presence of inspectors. Medium-risk elements (for example, the verification of the production of Schedule 2 chemicals) would need the possible presence of inspectors and of monitoring devices; the lower-risk areas (for example, verification of the production of Schedule 3 chemicals) would need the random presence of inspectors, monitoring devices and statistical monitoring.

It is obvious that essentially all verification tasks must be performed and controlled by inspectors to at least some extent. Even in the case of the low-risk activities, inspectors would need to install, check and inspect automatic-monitoring equipment or validate statistical data.

The current possibilities and requirements for methods to implement verification can be described as in the following review of monitoring methods, which can be grouped together according to the categories listed below:

1. by main characteristics of the monitoring methods;
2. by the place of performance or the distance to the verified object;
3. by the absence or presence of personnel;
4. by the delay in obtaining results; and
5. by the particular type of verification method.

Such categorization presents a better chance to structure methods vs. tasks, to assess the current possibilities, to look for the weak points of verification schemes and to estimate the required further development of (technical) monitoring methods, as well as to outline concrete tasks for developing presently inadequate or non-existent methods. Below follows an expanded discussion of these 5 categories.

1. *Monitoring methods by main characteristics* can be divided into direct and indirect methods. Practically all of these, which are performed with technical means or by inspection of a given object, as summarized below under 2-5 are *direct. Indirect* methods are based on the evaluation of data, on drawing conclusions from statistical monitoring and the like.

2. *Monitoring methods by the place of performance or the distance to the verified object* can be divided into on-site, near-site and remote methods.

On-site methods would be the most effective and would be performed by inspectors and/or (automatic) monitoring equipment. While for various kinds of routine inspection methods there would be various specific combinations of personnel and equipment or equipment only, with respect to inspections on request (by challenge), inspectors would always be present.

Near-site methods would usually be applied to detect and identify trace amounts (concentrations) of monitored chemicals (and their by-products or breakdown products) in environmental samples downwind or downstream. They consist of point analytical devices (kits, analysers, alarms, sampling equipment) or remote analytical instruments (long-path infra-red (IR), laser techniques). The concept of 'near-site' range (of the order of 1-10 km) here coincides with the term 'remote'--ordinarily used for analytical instrumentation of the same range.

Remote methods usually involve the checking of the geographic co-ordinates of declared facilities by satellite monitoring for area-surveillance. These can also be used for identification of suspect production and storage facilities; for surveillance both of those facilities which have been declared as no longer producing chemical weapons as well as those which have been closed down--stockpiles and the like.

3. *Monitoring methods by personnel* can be divided into manual and automatic monitoring.

Many operations which would be performed on-site such as checking, testing, comparing plans with reality, locking, sealing, measuring and the like will be *manual*, including installation of automatic devices and equipment which operates automatically without personnel. At present, there is not enough automatic equipment which is sufficiently resistant against possible physical, mechanical and chemical influences to substitute for personnel in all cases for a very long period of time. On the other hand, with respect to security equipment, some relevant experience with IAEA Safeguards and applicable instrumentation has been presented recently.[2]

4. *Monitoring methods characterized by the delay in obtaining results after operation* can be divided into immediate and delayed.

Monitoring methods which give results (response to the activity to be verified) in real time can be referred to as *immediate* monitoring methods. This is typical of most methods performed by personnel. Automatic methods do so only when attached to communication channels. *Delayed* methods are those where the response is not direct. All methods where data are stored on computer media (tapes, diskettes and so on) prior to processing, as well as television and other recorded data from security and technological equipment belong to the delayed methods. Even production or environmental sampling for later analysis in laboratories, belong to this category. They are available with the present status of scientific and technological progress.

5. *Monitoring methods by aim*, relating them to their purpose, are the most important. These methods can be divided into security, checking and testing of instruments, measuring of process parameters, sampling and analysing of chemicals, data processing, communication and others.

Security methods include locking, sealing, supervision, alarming and similar methods, which are auxiliary but necessary for performing some undertakings prescribed under the proposed CWC and assuring their verification. Improved tools for these ends have been presented recently.[3] It is clear that facilities, locked or unlocked, which are dangerous for health and environment and especially for the CWC objectives, need *supervision*, both by guards and (automatic) devices, operating in real time (TV, satellites) or on delay (video recorders, photographic satellites and the like), combined with *alarm*-giving devices when necessary.

Checking and testing of instruments are also auxiliary monitoring methods. This category includes non-destructive methods for verification of reaction-vessel construction, testing of pipeline systems, all communications, inlet and outlet tubes, testing of all measuring devices and systems and all regulations, measuring declared volumes and the like prior to putting any facility into operation, as well as testing all security and communication channels.

The measuring of process parameters is one of the key monitoring methods in the whole framework of verification methods of relevance to the chemical industry. Many of the measurements for checking purposes must be performed personally by inspectors before commencement of some operations, for example, the start-up of production at the declared small-scale facility for production for permitted purposes as well as before starting declared production of Schedule 2 chemicals. It is desirable to have automatic-measuring equipment in the course of routine production of some of the chemicals posing small risks for the CWC (for example, those on Schedules 2 and 3). Process parameters include quantitative phenomena, qualitative phenomena and reaction characteristics.

Measuring of *quantitative phenomena,* such as *mass (weight), volume* and *level* is applicable not only for destruction of stockpiled agents filled in munitions and also for verification of stocks of agents either in bulk or in munitions but also when monitoring certain industrial production. To these and other procedures can be also added simple counting or accounting methods, which will be frequent in many other verification exercises.

Measuring of *qualitative phenomena* using industrial measuring devices with registration, storage and transmission of plotted parameters is quite normal in all industrial processes and may also be so with respect to verification relevant to the CWC. All these measurements enable direct, non-destructive determinations of qualitative phenomena, related to the compounds to be monitored, their purity, content of active compound and the like. To these ends, in particular cases, measuring *density, optical density, conductivity, refractive index* and other physical phenomena can be utilized. Determination of chemical composition will be discussed below.

Measuring of *reaction characteristics* is the other key group of measurements and corresponding instrumentation in all industrial processes as well as for future verification tasks, relevant to the CWC, as discussed in the preceding paragraph.

In the monitored chemical industry in connection with production of chemicals on all 4 Schedules as well as in destruction of stockpiles, common reaction parameters will be measured, such as *temperature, pressure, pH, consumption of input chemical(s), yield of output chemical(s)* (also according to their qualitative characteristics obtained by chemical analyses) and *time* (in the case of non-continuous batch processes) or *flow rates* (in the case of continuous processes).

Sampling and analysis of chemical substances, particularly chemical-warfare agents, are among the principal and most important monitoring methods of verification as outlined under the framework of the provisions of the projected CWC.

All of the industrial problems connected with the direct analysis of chemical-warfare agents (detection, identification of the types in declared stocks and in suspected industrial facilities, semi-quantitative or quantitative determination of percentage of active compound in declared stocks with agent mixtures, verification of produced compounds and their quality in small-scale facilities for permitted production and so on) can be carried out by military personnel equipped with chemical-detection kits containing detection tubes or other simple detection means, with laboratory kits, with automatic alarms or analysers for the most toxic organophosphorus STLCs. In the case of new declared chemical-warfare agents, military and other central scientific laboratories in many states are able to perform routine analytical tasks in order to solve the problems of the chemical industry where it may be necessary to analyse toxic agents relevant to the CWC, directly or indirectly. Since a certain amount of time will elapse between sampling and analysing, this procedure is often referred to as SNAL (sample now, analyse later).

Another problem arises in sampling and analysing chemicals in connection with the investigation of alleged use of chemical weapons, as well as in the case of near-site, downwind or downstream analyses. Analytical teams would meet (depending on the amount of time since the occurrence) only trace concentrations in environmental samples, degradation products in the environment, metabolites in biological samples and sometimes even interfering chemicals. The former problem can be complicated by various forms of interference or other actions by the accusing state, which would require the co-operation of many top-level scientific laboratories.

It is beyond the aim of this paper to describe suitable sampling and analytical methods relevant to the CWC and the verification exercises envisaged according to its provisions. However, these are important subjects which also must be dealt with carefully.

Data storage, processing and handling represent an important part of many monitoring methods. These are areas which are now undergoing rapid development. Also these subjects need special elaboration, since they now constitute a new industrial branch. It is evident that data monitoring refers to scientific, technical, commercial and other relevant literature, reflecting progress in chemistry; to specific data as well as to data connected with individual provisions of the projected CWC such as monitoring of non-production; and to specific data on all verified procedures (visits to storage sites, destruction of stockpiles, monitoring of single small-scale facility, statistical monitoring and the like).

For monitoring of the civilian chemical industry, the system of collection, storage, processing, evaluation and reporting must be elaborated by the Consultative Committee, which must assure responsible handling of sensitive data connected with political, commercial interests and intellectual property. These activities cannot be jeopardized in order to ensure the objectives of the CWC.

Communication and other auxiliary methods will, no doubt, be part of the necessary monitoring process. A communication network between monitored facilities and the Consultative Committee will be necessary for ensuring the proper function of inspectors and, in the future, also for direct transmission of selected data from monitoring equipment. Experiments performed by the IAEA have shown that such a network can be based on satellite communication.[4]

IV. Necessary development of monitoring methods for industrial production

It was pointed out above that monitoring methods will need to be based principally on inspectors. This will be true also in the future, although after the most stringent period of destruction of stockpiles and of chemical-weapon production facilities, the focus would be shifted onto monitoring of civilian chemical industry. Since the period of destruction will represent a heavy economic burden *per se* and this would also be the case for verification during this period, there will be pressure to diminish the number of 'inspector-days'.

The developments envisaged in monitoring methods reflect the overall scientific and technological progress in sensors, instrumentation for laboratory, technological activities, automatization, communication and data processing. The requirements for future monitoring methods will, in fact, parallel the progress mentioned.

The necessary further development of monitoring methods would encompass the development of sensitive sensors for industrial measuring devices; resistant and reliable instrumentation for locking, sealing, supervising the measuring of qualitative and quantitative parameters (in the course of reaction processes); and sampling and analysis. The methods concern detection and identification of trace amounts of toxic agents, their by-products and degradation products and metabolites; automatic monitoring equipment with output signals suitable for input into communication systems; elaboration of communication systems for controlling inspection teams from the Consultative Committee and its executive and technical subsidiary bodies and for collection of data; and elaboration of systems of collection, transmission, storage, processsing and handling of the data delivered by inspectors and supervisory teams and automatic-monitoring instruments.

The necessary development must be accompanied by an exchange of information between the States Parties on existing technical means and methods in order to achieve a certain degree of standardization and unification.

For the performance of future verification tasks, it will be necessary to educate and train personnel for verification tasks. These tasks can be entrusted to national authorities responsible for various types of control of chemical industry--medical, veterinary, hydrological and meteorological, other environmental supervision of chemical production and use of its products--in co-operation with scientific, university and military authorities.

This development should be promoted by the international scientific community, represented by international scientific organizations such as the International Union for Pure and Applied Chemistry (IUPAC) and the International Union of Biochemistry (IUB), as well as other scientific bodies including the World Federation of Scientific Workers (WFSW) and Pugwash, and by prominent international research institutes such as SIPRI, United Nation Institute for Disarmament Research (UNIDIR) and others, and of course by international organizations linked to the United Nations as, for example, the World Health Organization (WHO), the Food and Agriculture Organization (FAO) and the United Nations Environment Programme (UNEP).

The necessary development must be carefully examined in the course of the negotiations on the projected CWC in the CD in order to formulate reasonable provisions for the work of the Consultative Committee and its subsidiary bodies. This work must start as soon as possible so that the attempt to achieve an ideal monitoring agency does not itself become an obstacle to the completion of the CWC.

V. Conclusion

The present status of monitoring technology reflects the scientific and technological progress in security techniques, sensors, measuring devices and equipment; sampling and instrumental analysis of chemical weapons; communication; data processing and other technical issues relevant to the projected CWC.

Even if the monitoring technology in its complexity has not yet been systematically developed to meet the objectives of the CWC and especially if security techniques and automatic-monitoring equipment are not broadly available, it would still be possible to implement the main verification tasks connected with all the provisions of the CWC, because especially the initial verification tasks and activities need only be performed by inspectors.

The full development of monitoring technologies in the future, after the start of the destruction of stockpiles and of chemical-weapon production facilities will be influenced by scientific and technological progress and must be intentionally oriented towards reliability, automatization, communication and data processing.

The present status of monitoring technologies does not pose any obstacle to the signing of the CWC, taking into account the necessary time required to finish the elaboration and drafting of the Convention and for its entry into force after signature.

References

[1] Lohs, Kh., Stock, T. and Kläss, V., 'Internationale und nationale Methoden der Verification regionaler und globaler Vereinbarungen zum Verbot chemischer Waffen' ['International and national methods for verification of regional and global agreements to prohibit chemical weapons'], *Zeitschrift für Chemie*, vol. 27, no. 10 (1987), pp. 349-57.

[2] Mangan, D. L., 'Hardware for potential unattended surveillance and monitoring applications', 13th Pugwash Workshop on Chemical Weapons, Geneva, 1988.

[3] See note 2.

[4] Kuroi, H. and Kyriakopoulos, N., 'Experimental monitoring of safeguards sensors', 13th Pugwash Workshop on Chemical Weapons, Geneva, 1988.

VERIFICATION EQUIPMENT FOR ON-SITE INSPECTION TEAMS UNDER THE PROPOSED CHEMICAL WEAPONS CONVENTION

M. RAUTIO, Finland

I. Introduction

Verification of the non-production of chemical-warfare agents in the chemical industry will be one of the most complex tasks of the future Chemical Weapons Convention (CWC). The following presentation discusses the kind of equipment the international inspectors will require during on-site visits to operating chemical plants.

To be acceptable to industry, verification of non-production must be reliable but not at the same time lead to leakage of proprietary information (for example, leakage of production secrets such as routes of synthesis or process intermediates). The term negative proof has been used in this context, that is, proof that banned compounds are absent but without indication of other compounds produced unless listed in Schedule 2. Such 'non-intrusive' verification of non-production will require on-site monitoring of compounds listed in Schedules 1 and 2 of the rolling text:[1] namely, that compounds in Schedule 1 are not produced and that compounds in Schedule 2 are produced in quantities consistent with the needs for purposes not prohibited by the Convention. Since, for the protection of industry, inspectors should be able to identify specific compounds only, final schedules will need to list individual compounds, rather than generic entities as at present. Registration of the identification data in the data base of each instrument will then allow monitoring for known compounds alone, leaving other production unidentified. Construction of such detailed lists is also a necessity for the customs officials who will be monitoring the import and export of the compounds.

Schedules 1 and 2 must not contain too many compounds if instrumental monitoring is to be possible. A preliminary search of the literature for compounds containing P-methyl, P-ethyl, P-propyl and P-isopropyl bonds suggested there are about 2000, which vastly exceeds the number of compounds (about 200 to 300) that can be monitored by current instrumental methods.

The samples collected during inspections would be most reliably analysed with the sophisticated instrumentation of the designated laboratory of the International Inspectorate. Aided by the analytical data base of chemical-warfare agents, legally valid results would be obtained in a short space of time. The large number of samples would soon saturate the capacity of the laboratory, however, making screening of the samples on the spot absolutely essential. On-site screening is also non-intrusive, there is little time for degradation of compounds, and potential difficulties in transporting samples are avoided. Only those few samples that proved suspect in some way would need to be transferred to the designated laboratory for verification analysis.

The present paper examines different techniques for instrumental analysis on-site. Only compound-specific instruments that can be used for identification are considered, not those required to measure quantities, for the determination of material balances or for calibration. The suitability for verification purposes of analytical instruments already installed at the facility is discussed first, along with the reliability of analyses made with these instruments. Analytical instruments that can be brought on-site by the inspectors are then considered. Specific instrumentation based on gas chromatography and capable of detecting most compounds currently listed in Schedules 1 and 2 is described in some detail, and the transportability and maintenance of the instrumentation are noted.

II. Analytical instrumentation of the facility

The analytical instrumentation available to inspectors at the facilities will certainly vary from target to target, from almost nothing to full sophistication. In some cases the facility will be part of a large complex with an extensive and well-equipped research and development unit, while in others it will be located far from any research centre with no spectrometric instrumentation for reliable identification of chemicals. An inventory of the instrumentation available for verification purposes could be made during the initial inspection or familiarization visit to each facility.

For two reasons, the instrumentation of the facility could not, however, be used as the sole means for verification. The first reason is that the analysis would almost surely be intrusive (that is, not only a negative proof) if the instrumentation were used without reference data specific for the listed chemicals. Each compound would need to be identified to determine whether it is mentioned in the lists, and this would require recording and interpreting the spectra of compounds not among the compounds to be monitored.

The second reason is that the instrumentation must necessarily be in an operable state. Inspectors will not announce the exact day of the inspection much before they actually arrive at the facility, and the visit will be futile if instruments are out of order, whether by accident or design. We suggest, therefore, that the inspectors bring along their own instrumentation to each inspection, with actual use depending on the particular situation. This procedure would shift the responsibility for the operable state of the instrumentation to the inspectors and there would be no need for an out-of-order notification on the inspection protocol, with the inevitable association of suspicion.

Before the instruments of the facility can be used for verification analyses, their reliability must be verified. The inspectors will need to have calibration samples with them, to be run before the actual samples collected during inspection. For example, if a facility producing or processing phosphorus compounds is equipped with a nuclear magnetic resonance (NMR) spectrometer with a multinuclear probe allowing detection of phosphorus nuclei, the inspectors would let the instrument be tested under the standard operating conditions defined for the listed compounds, using the calibration samples of phosphorus-containing model agents and an internal chemical shift standard in a sealed NMR tube. If spectra identical with reference spectra are obtained, the instrumentation can be used, under the same conditions, for verification monitoring of compounds containing methyl-, ethyl-, propyl- or isopropyl-phosphorus bonds. (It is important that the computer-recorded running parameters be specified in the inspection protocol.) If the facility has declared production of compounds containing these bonds, their spectra must be recorded and compared with the spectra of samples taken during the inspection, to detect any inconsistency with the declaration. If other such bonds are detected, the compounds must be identified and shown not to be prohibited ones. If the inspectors have access to the computerized data base of the international organization, detailed analysis of the spectra will not be necessary for the identification.

The same procedure holds for other spectrometric techniques. Spectra of the calibration samples containing VX, for example, must be recorded under the standard conditions used to record the spectra in the data base of the international organization. If identical spectra are obtained, the same conditions must be used for running the samples from the inspections. The data obtained are compared with data in the organization's computerized data base to detect any listed compounds. Comparison is facilitated if the inspectors have on-line access to the data base, for example, through the telephone network. If infra-red spectra are used for identification, it is important that they be recorded in the same sample matrix as the reference spectra, that is to say, in gas-, liquid- or solid phase.

Use of the gas chromatographs of the facility without coupling to a compound-specific detector such as a mass spectrometer or a Fourier transform infra-red spectrometer would require careful analysis with capillary columns supplied by the international organization. Two different stationary phases and index-standard series would be needed; indexes would have to be calculated for model agents in a calibration run, and compared with indexes of the computerized data base. If acceptable indexes were obtained for model agents, the instrument could be used for verification analysis. Such a calculation of indexes and comparison with the library data is rather time-consuming, however. The same holds true for high-performance liquid chromatographs, which cannot easily be used for sensitive monitoring of phosphorus-containing compounds in samples with high background without an enzymatic or other sensitive detector.[2]

The spectrometric capacity of the inspected facility could be used to resolve a possible inconsistency in the monitoring analysis made by the inspectors' own instrumentation. If concern were to arise as to the identity of a chemical detected during monitoring by high resolution two-channel gas chromatography (see below), for example, this ambiguity might be solved on-site. However, if the problem remained unsolved, the samples would have to be coded and delivered to the designated laboratory of the international organization, for detailed analysis with sophisticated instrumentation. Coding of the samples would be necessary to prohibit leakage of proprietary information since the analysts should not know the origin of the samples.

Analytical monitoring problems can be expected in inspections of facilities producing super-toxic chemicals for purposes not prohibited by the Convention, in the pharmaceutical industry for example. Many of these chemicals are high molecular weight compounds with complicated structures which may contaminate instruments if effective sample-preparation methods are not used. If analysis of these heavier compounds is deemed necessary, it could be done with techniques and instruments used by the facility for process control. Then, however, the verification aim, identification of banned compounds, might not always be met since the techniques used for process control would not necessarily detect compounds in Schedules 1 and 2.

The facility's own instruments might also be used in inspections of facilities with completely computer-controlled processes, where the process data are stored between the inspections and their authenticity can be reliably checked during inspection. Samples could be taken from the raw materials and end-products, analysed by the instrumentation of the facility and compared with available data produced for the standard operating procedures of the facility.

III. Portable instrumentation of the inspection team

Verification analysis on the spot would considerably dispel the fear of leakage of proprietary information. Screening of samples collected during inspection by different, properly chosen techniques would reduce or even completely remove the need for detailed analysis of the samples (for example, identification of intermediates and end-products). Monitoring of listed compounds would be based on pre-recorded identification data, easily retrieved for evaluation of the results. Identification would be reliable since the inspectors would be familiar with their own instrumentation and recognize any malfunction. For their part, the instruments would have to be easily transported and quickly assembled. Several techniques are presently available for the monitoring of the listed compounds.

High-resolution gas chromatography

High-resolution gas chromatography with two-channel retention-index monitoring (RIM) and confirmation of the results with a compound-specific detector such as a retention spectrometer, a mass spectrometer or an ion-trap detector have been tested in our laboratory for various types of matrices (excluding process-control samples). Gas chromatography can be applied to the analysis of all compounds in Schedules 1 and 2 except saxitoxin (not yet agreed upon) and arsenic trichloride. A number of compounds belonging to the nerve-agent families have been successfully analysed as well. Identification of BZ is feasible but near the upper temperature limit of the method. The other BZ analogues synthesized from the precursors of Schedule 2, which are still under consideration, have not yet been tested. Analysis of some of the precursors necessitates prior derivatization, for example, methylation of the compounds.[3]

Two-channel RIM analysis is performed by injecting the sample, together with the appropriate homologous series, straight-chain alkanes, (C-standards) or phosphorus-containing compounds (M-standards), simultaneously into two columns of either similar or different polarities and leading to two similar or different detectors. A data station identifies the peaks of the standards series, calculates retention indexes (for both channels) for all other peaks, compares the indexes with the library data, converts the peak areas (or heights) to concentration units and reports the names and concentrations of the compounds found (see figure 1).

If high background interferes with the determination of retention indexes in two-channel gas chromatography, two-stage gas chromatography can be used. Two-stage RIM analysis is performed by monitoring the effluent from one column with a single detector. Any fraction suspected of containing a banned agent is led, along with the appropriate index standards, from the first column to a second column for resolution of the overlapping components. These are observed with a second detector (see figure 2).

The reliability of the identification can be further enhanced by leading the resolved components to a column unit, or retention spectrometer, consisting of some six or more short columns of different polarity. The result is the retention spectrum of the pure compound, consisting in the ideal case, of as many peaks as there are columns in the column unit (see figure 3).

Retention indexes measured with two columns, together with retention spectra, can afford reliable identification of the chemicals in Schedules 1 and 2. Selectivity can be increased by using alkali-thermionic detectors for phosphorus-containing compounds and electron-capture detectors for halogen-containing compounds. All determinations can be performed successively with the same instrument (see figure 4).

Retention spectrometry is a relatively new technique, based on gas chromatography, for the identification of known compounds. Much work still remains to be done to standardize the method and determine its reliability in long-term use. The technique would also have to gain acceptance by the States Parties before it could be applied to the verification of chemical disarmament. Confirmation of the identifications made by retention-index monitoring with two different stationary phases could, of course, be obtained by conventional techniques such as mass spectrometry or ion-trap detection, if this instrumentation were present in the facility. Otherwise the transportation and set-up would place an extra burden on the inspectors. (A conventional, single-quadrupole mass spectrometer is fairly shock-resistant and easy to set up, but the transportability of the ion-trap detector remains to be tested). If mass-spectrometric identification of listed compounds is deemed necessary, the mass spectrometer chosen should have options for both electron ionization (EI) and chemical ionization (CI). This is important for the reliability of verification, since electron impact may cause excessive decomposition of the molecules, leading to a molecular ion with very low abundance, often not visible at all. In particular, the organophosphorus compounds do not produce molecular ions under electron impact (70 eV) but show intense fragment ions only in the low mass number region. Identification is clearly more reliable if the molecular ion can be produced by chemical ionization, and these data used to supplement the fragmentation data obtained by EI.[4]

Mobile mass spectrometer

The mobile mass spectrometer MM1 manufactured by Bruker-Franzen Analytik is another analytical possibility, demonstrated for easy transportation and operation on the spot. The instrument relies on gas chromatography for pre-separation of the compounds, a 3.5-metre column length in normal cases, and a 15-metre length when increased resolution is needed. Dilute samples are concentrated by adsorption onto Tenax GC resin. Accordingly, the same requirements as for high-resolution gas chromatography apply to the physical properties of the compounds and to sample preparation. The compounds are ionized by electron ionization, detected by multiple-ion monitoring, and identified through full EI mass spectra. The mass spectrometer monitors 22 pre-selected compounds quasi-simultaneously within a few minutes. Identification is made by comparing the EI spectra-library spectra of 900 possible compounds pre-selected for inclusion in the library. The instrumentation has been suggested for analysis of samples passively collected in a silicone membrane on a continuous basis, for example, in an inspected facility. Samples collected between routine inspections could be analysed by inspectors during their stay at the facility.[5]

As already noted above for the conventional single-quadrupole mass spectrometer electron ionization causes excessive decomposition of the molecules, leading to a molecular ion with very low abundance. Identification of a particular organophosphorus compound, from among a large group of compounds, as belonging to a particular list may necessitate information on the molecular ion. Reliability of the technique could be enhanced either by the option for chemical ionization and the possibility to select the best reactant gas, or perhaps by the inclusion of index-standard compounds in the determination. In the latter case, the monitoring limitation of only 22 pre-selected compounds in one determination would require that several additional consecutive determinations be made to cover compounds in Schedules 1 and 2, since the addition of index-standard compounds further increases the number of compounds to be monitored.

Immunoassays

Immunoassay affords a non-intrusive, specific, quick, and non-instrumental means for monitoring compounds for which specific antibodies can be produced. If an antibody can be produced for each compound listed in Schedules 1 and 2, and as long as no cross-reactions occur, a highly specific method is available for their detection in a facility. The feasibility of the method depends on the possibility and cost of producing antibodies for each compound, and accordingly, on the number of antibodies required. One solution might be to use antibodies selective for classes of compounds. If a positive reaction were obtained, the particular agent could then be identified with specific monoclonal antibodies.

The present technology for producing large amounts of monoclonal antibodies at reasonable cost makes possible the use of special detection kits. The kits could include relatively high concentrations of antibodies to speed up the reaction and to make the immunoreaction observable without any instrumentation, though large amounts of an antibody would also increase the number of possible cross-reactions and necessitate careful testing of the reliability of the method. On the other hand, no chemical analyses would be needed from intermediates or end-products if the method turned out to be reliable. In the case of a positive reaction for compounds of Schedule 1, samples should be tested with the spectrometric instrumentation of the facility or delivered to the designated laboratory of the international organization for confirmation of the result by several instrumental techniques.

IV. A specific suggestion for the equipment of the inspection team

In the following we make the specific suggestion that samples collected for monitoring of listed compounds be analysed with a two-channel gas chromatograph, equipped with valves to allow two-stage operation by heart-cutting and with a retention-spectrometer column unit. The chromatograph is operated through a microcomputer-based data station containing the retention-index library. The two-stage operation and retention-spectrometric confirmation of the identifications may be needed in the analysis of air and effluent water samples collected inside the facility, that is, in cases when the sample matrix causes identification problems. Also, retention spectrometry allows the identification of all listed compounds preliminarily identified by RIM.

The initial equipment for screening analysis comprises one 25-metre SE-54 and one 25-metre OV-17 fused silica column and two FI detectors. The columns must be tested for VX which is very adsorptive. For increased selectivity and for trace analysis of phosphorus-containing compounds, the detectors may be changed to two AT detectors. To secure successful analyses on the spot, small containers for helium and nitrogen gas and a thermal desorption and a cold-trap unit with a reservoir for liquid nitrogen may be attached. Syringes, an extra pair of columns, and a service kit for the gas chromatograph, containing items like extra fuses and heaters, should be included with the equipment.

In addition to the instrumentation, the inspectors should have solutions of retention-index standards (C-series and M-series), a methylating reagent, and standard solution of some model agents both for gas chromatography-mass spectrometry and for NMR spectroscopy, the latter in sealed NMR tubes. A set of low-volume sampling tubes containing Tenax GC and XAD-4 resins, detection tubes containing reagents for the detection of acetylcholine-esterase inhibitors, and some pumps for sample collection should be included in the equipment of inspectors.

The ruggedness of the instrumentation described above (Micromat 412 gas chromatograph) has been proved in field conditions over several years and during army refresher courses in a mobile field laboratory assembled in a trailer. A recent 'containerized' version has been constructed for easy transportation (for example, by aircraft), where all instrumentation is packed in standardized containers. The assembly of the gas chromatograph is very quick as no evacuation of lines is required. No parts have broken during transportation, leading to failures in operation. The AT detector is the most sensitive part of the instrumentation but the alkali salt bead can be held in place during transportation with a special support.

V. Sample collection and preparation

Sampling points and methods for sample preparation must be planned and tested during the familiarization visit or the initial inspection of each facility, and be recorded in the facility attachment. In unexpected situations they would be decided on the spot. The routine equipment for sample preparation could be provided by the facility. Sampling and analysis could be started from the raw materials and process products, with additional samples taken from the intermediate stages of processes only if the first round of results indicated this to be necessary.

In addition to the sampling of raw materials and end-products in storage facilities, duplicate air samples could be collected in Tenax GC low-volume sampling tubes to screen for unexpected chemicals in storage facilities and production premises.[6] Other samples could be collected from effluent water before it entered the purification plant or was destroyed by incineration, especially if doubts were aroused during the inspection of production records or where the inspected facility was a large multi-purpose one.[7]

After the analysis of raw materials and end-products, air and water analyses could be done by attaching the thermal desorption and cold-trap unit to the gas chromatograph. Duplicate samples could be stored for further analysis in the designated laboratory if suspicion arose about the constituents of a sample after the on-site monitoring analysis.

If trace analysis of effluent water revealed the presence of a listed compound, it would be the task of the inspection team to discover whether this was present as an impurity in the raw material, formed as a by-product of the process or was indicative of illegal activities in the inspected facility.[8]

A prerequisite for gas-chromatographic analysis is a dilute solution in an organic solvent such as ethyl acetate or hexane, depending on the polarity of the compounds. Solid samples, from raw-material stocks, for example, would be dissolved in an organic solvent, and aqueous solutions would be extracted with it. Gaseous samples would be collected into gas bags or gas-tight syringes, or be trapped onto an organic-polymer resin, and then analysed with a gas chromatograph equipped with thermal desorption and a cold-trap unit.

VI. Reliability of the verification analysis

Because results from the verification analyses must be legally valid in all circumstances, they must be highly reliable. The quality of the results can be assured by maximizing the reliability of the method beforehand. International validation of the monitoring method and instrumentation by interlaboratory comparison tests made according to standard operating procedures would be required before their acceptance for verification analysis.

For monitoring analysis, the most reliable, transportable techniques should be chosen. We suggest that monitoring of listed compounds during inspections of civilian chemical facilities be done with the inspection team's own instruments, tested after set-up at the facility with solutions of model compounds and retention-index standards. If the monitoring analysis raises any doubt as to the presence of compounds included in Schedule 1, control samples should be taken and analysed by an independent method, either with equipment at the inspected facility (the equipment being tested by the inspectors immediately before use), or after coding and transportation of the samples at the designated laboratory. The equipment of the facility may be used only where the reliability of the results can be unequivocally guaranteed. The acceptable instruments include a tandem mass spectrometer, a high-resolution mass spectrometer, a high-field NMR spectrometer equipped with a multinuclear probe, and an infra-red spectrometer. The specifics of the analytical method, for example, the mass-spectrometric ionization technique, the MS/MS collision conditions, and the ions selected for high-resolution multiple-ion monitoring, should be selected to be especially sensitive and selective for the suspect compound.

If the analytical result obtained at the facility is clearly negative, no samples need be transferred to the designated laboratory of the International Inspectorate. If the result is positive or there is any doubt about the identity of the compound, samples should be transferred, perhaps under the official seal of the United Nations, for analysis at the designated laboratory by at least two of the four independent methods mentioned above. The analyses should be carried out by at least two individuals until identical results are obtained (see figure 5).

VII. Conclusions

The aim of the verification of non-production is to make sure that the chemical industry is not used for the production of chemicals listed in Schedule 1 and that compounds in Schedule 2 are produced only in quantities consistent with the needs for purposes not prohibited by the Convention. Accordingly, during routine inspections of facilities producing organophosphorus compounds, for example, the inspectors would need to verify the absence of any organophosphorus compound in Schedule 1, while not intruding upon the actual production of the facility. A prerequisite for carrying out this task is a specification of the chemicals to be monitored and registration of their identification data in the data base of the monitoring instruments. Individual chemicals should be listed in Schedule 1, not unwieldy families of compounds. The inspectors must know what they are looking for! Otherwise monitoring techniques cannot be used, and the routine inspections will be extremely difficult to carry out reliably, and necessarily intrusive, if the inspectors have to identify all compounds present, possibly after tedious interpretation of different types of spectra.

It would be very difficult to substantiate suspicion about the production of undeclared, unknown super-toxic chemicals in a facility during a routine inspection. The matter might be resolved through consultations between the international organization and the national organization and, where appropriate, through sampling during an *ad hoc* inspection, followed by toxicological and analytical studies by the international organization in the designated laboratory.

Analytical instrumentation and methods suitable for reliable verification of non-production during routine on-site inspections already exist. What is needed now is agreement on the chemicals to be monitored and international validation of the appropriate instrumentation and methods.

References

[1] 'Report of the Ad Hoc Committee on Chemical Weapons to the Conference on Disarmament', Conference on Disarmament document CD/782, 26 Aug. 1987.

[2]A.2, *Technical Evaluation of Selected Scientific Methods for the Verification of Chemical Disarmament,* ed. M. Rautio (The Ministry for Foreign Affairs of Finland: Helsinki, 1984).

[3]B.1, *Identification of Potential Organophosphorus Warfare Agents: An Approach for the Standardization of Techniques and Reference Data,* ed. J. Enqvist (The Ministry for Foreign Affairs of Finland: Helsinki, 1979); B.3, *Systematic Identification of Chemical Warfare Agents: Identification of Non-phosphorus Warfare Agents,* ed. J. Enqvist (The Ministry for Foreign Affairs of Finland: Helsinki, 1982); and B.4, *Systematic Identification of Chemical Warfare Agents: Identification of Precursors of Warfare Agents, Degradation Products of Non-phosphorus Agents, and Some Potential Agents,* ed. J. Enqvist (The Ministry for Foreign Affairs of Finland: Helsinki, 1983).

[4]See *Identification of Potential Organophosphorus Warfare Agents* (note 3); and Hesso, A. and Kostiainen, R., in *Air Monitoring as a Means for Verification of Chemical Disarmament; C.2, Development and Evaluation of Basic Techniques,* part 1, ed. M. Rautio (The Ministry for Foreign Affairs of Finland: Helsinki, 1985).

[5]Odernheimer, B., in *Automatic Monitoring in Verification of Chemical Disarmament,* Proceedings of a Workshop, Helsinki, Finland, 12-14 Feb. 1987, p. 44.

[6]Kostiainen, O., in *Air Monitoring as a Means for Verification of Chemical Disarmament, C.4, Further Development and Testing of Methods,* part 3, ed. M. Rautio (The Ministry for Foreign Affairs of Finland: Helsinki, 1987).

[7]The Netherlands, 'Verification of non-production of chemical weapons: Scenario for an experimental inspection', Conference on Disarmament document CD/CW/WP.141, 10 June 1986; and Boter, H. I. and Verweij, A., in *Proceedings of the Second International Sysmposium on Protection Against Chemical Warfare Agents,* Stockholm, Sweden, 15-19 June 1986, FOA Report C 40228-C2, C3 (National Defence Research Institute: Umeå, Sweden, 1986).

[8]Boter and Verweij (see note 7).

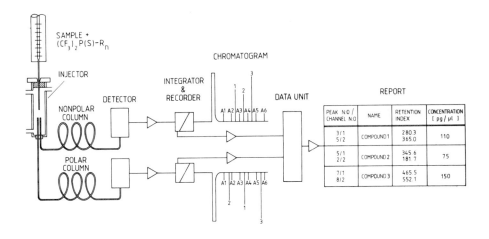

Figure 1. The principle of operation of the RIM system

Source: Enqvist, 1982.

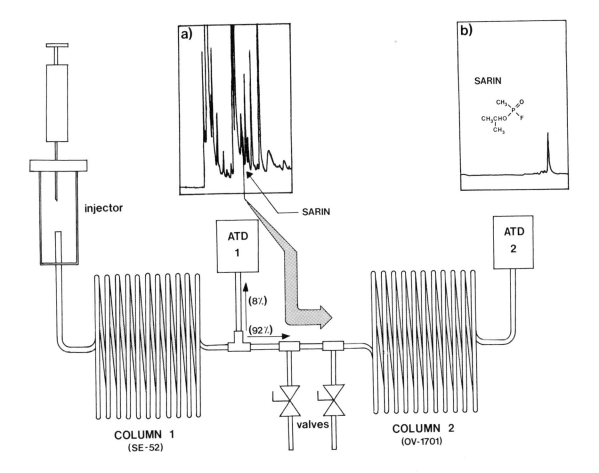

Figure 2. The principle of two-stage chromatography

Source: Rautio, 1984.

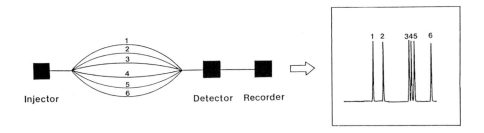

Figure 3. Operation of the retention spectrometer: (a) spectrometer-column unit, and (b) schematic-retention spectrum

Source: Enqvist, J. and Lakkisto, U-M., in *Air Monitoring as a Means for Verification of Chemical Disarmament, C.2, Development and Evaluation of Basic Techniques,* part 1, ed. M. Rautio (The Ministry for Foreign Affairs of Finland: Helsinki, 1985).

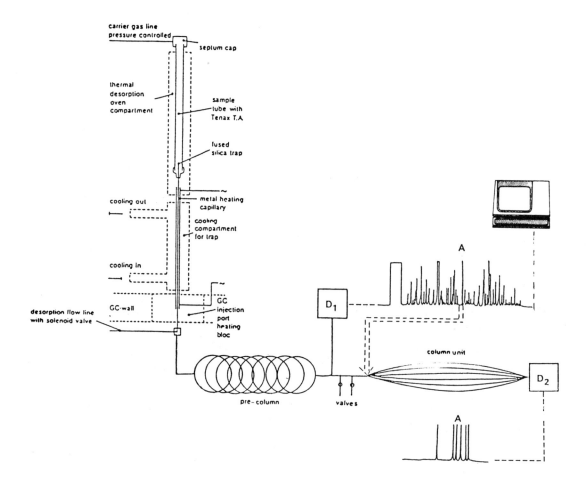

Figure 4. Schematic description of a two-stage gas chromatograph equipped with a thermal desorption and cold-trap unit and a retention spectrometer

Source: Kostiainen, 1987.

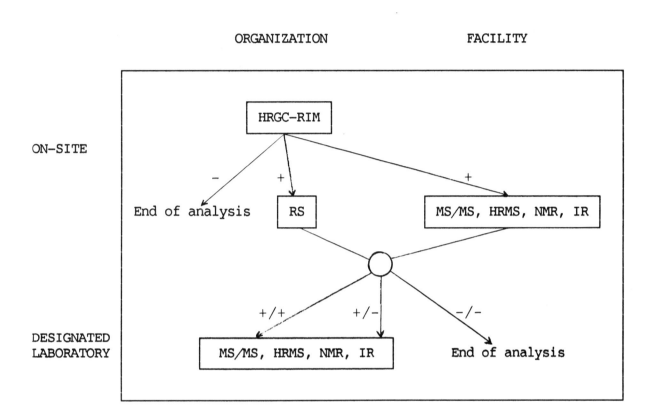

Figure 5. Analytical scheme

VERIFICATION OF NON-PRODUCTION OF CHEMICAL-WARFARE AGENTS IN THE CIVIL CHEMICAL INDUSTRY

A. VERWEIJ and H. L. BOTER, the Netherlands

I. Introduction

Since 1969 discussions concerning a treaty forbidding the development, production and stockpiling of chemical weapons and also regulating their destruction have been going on at the Conference on Disarmament (CD) in Geneva. The participating countries consider adequate verification of such a ban as a prerequisite for a treaty. The main function of an effective verification system is to deter the production of chemical-warfare agents and key precursors. To achieve adequate deterrence, procedures are necessary to ensure that there is a reasonable probability of detecting clandestine production. Clearly, the least intrusive verification methods are preferred although recently there has been a tendency to put less emphasis on this aspect.

In 1974 investigations were started which concentrated mainly on analytical methods for the near-site inspection of chemical-production plants by comparing the concentration of certain compounds in samples taken both upstream and downstream of the waste outlet. Such methods are less intrusive than a visit, which could be regarded as a possible encroachment on intellectual property. Furthermore, it was assumed that a future prohibition would most probably concern the nerve agents, because due to their superior toxic properties these compounds constitute the most serious threat among chemical-warfare agents. In view of this aspect, the P-CH$_3$ method and the intact chemical-warfare agent (CWA) procedure were developed as described in this paper.

Today the civil chemical industry shows an increased willingness to co-operate in the search for means to verify the non-production of chemical agents and key precursors, as it is generally accustomed to the phenomenon of intrusive inspection for purposes of labour safety and environmental protection. To protect industrially sensitive know-how and to cover a broader field of chemical compounds besides the above-mentioned nerve agents, it may be expected that automated universally applicable monitoring systems will be welcomed by all parties involved in a future Chemical Weapons Convention (CWC). A feasibility study was started to evaluate the possibility of applying monitors to verify the non-production of chemical agents and related chemical compounds in the civil chemical industry.

II. P-CH$_3$ procedure

Nerve agents are organophosphorus compounds that are structurally related to insecticides. Both types of compounds can be prepared in similar production plants. However, there is an important structural difference between these compounds. The majority of the nerve agents such as VX, Sarin and Soman have a phosphorus-methyl (P-CH$_3$) grouping in their molecule which is absent in the organophosphorus insecticides. The P-CH$_3$ bond appears to be directly related to high mammalian toxicity, and the production of compounds containing this group has been avoided by manufacturers of insecticides.

The P-CH$_3$ bond is very strong and resists most methods of degradation. It can be detected analytically with high specificity and sensitivity by means of gas chromatography in combination with specific phosphorus detection. Furthermore, an extensive search of the literature revealed that the P-CH$_3$ bond does not appear in nature. Thus the detection of this chemical configuration in a sample could not be due to a naturally occurring organophosphorus compound. It would appear, therefore, that a false positive identification of a nerve agent or its breakdown products would not take place. Based on these considerations, this so-called P-CH$_3$ verification procedure was evaluated in our laboratory between 1974 and 1980.

The method applied consists of hydrolysing the nerve agent or its decomposition products into methylphosphonic acid, concentrating it, converting it into a volatile compound by methylation, separating it from related compounds by means of a gas chromatographic column and detecting it in ug/litre amounts in aqueous samples using a specific phosphorus detector. Under identical conditions the insecticide will yield trimethyl phosphate which may be distinguished from dimethyl methylphosphonate by gas chromatography.[1]

In practice the detection limit could be influenced by a background concentration of P-CH$_3$-containing compounds present in the water sample under investigation. Therefore this background was measured in a number of surface-water samples obtained from several countries.[2] The mean values of the concentrations of the P-CH$_3$-containing compounds of the water samples increase in accordance with their grade of pollution. This suggests that the occurrence of P-CH$_3$ compounds is due to industrial sources. Flame retardants and experimental insecticides may be mentioned as the possible origin of the background values encountered. When using a background concentration of, for example, 0.5 ug/litre for industrially polluted water it can be established that a plant producing 12 tonnes of the nerve agent Sarin per day which discharges its waste water into a polluted river such as the Rhine will be detected by comparing a number of upstream samples with samples taken within a few hundred metres downstream of the waste outlet.[3]

The nerve agent Tabun will not be detected upon application of the P-CH$_3$ verification procedure. This compound is a derivative of phosphoric acid and will consequently yield trimethyl phosphate after hydrolysis and methylation.

Binary nerve agents are made by mixing two compounds during the delivery of the projectile to its target. For the nerve agents Sarin and Soman methylphosphonic difluoride will most probably be one of the binary compounds. This substance can be detected using the verification procedure as it hydrolyses rapidly to methylphosphonic acid. QL, the probable binary precursor of the nerve agent VX, yields methylphosphinic acid on hydrolysis. Under the conditions of the verification procedures, this compound is methylated to methyl methylphosphinate, which is detected by gas chromatography. As the signal of the phosphinate can be differentiated from that of dimethyl methylphosphonate, this provides a means of distinguishing wastes originating from classically produced VX and its binary precursor QL.[4]

One drawback of the P-CH$_3$ procedure is that its application implies considerable analysis time--amounting to about 4 to 5 days. Such a time lapse will be difficult to accept in the case of on-site inspection. Recently a promising improvement in the analysis time was achieved by the development of micro liquid chromatography in combination with a flame photometric phosphorus-specific detector which is normally used in gas chromatography.[5] This new analytical method opens the possibility of sensitive analysis of a mixture of various organophosphorus acids (among them methylphosphonic acid) omitting the laborious treatment of samples such as that required by the methylation in the P-CH$_3$ method described above. A sizeable reduction in analysis time may be possible.

III. Intact chemical-warfare agent procedure

The verification procedure mentioned above constitutes sufficient evidence to warrant an inspection of the plant under consideration to confirm or refute the indication that a nerve agent might be being produced. However, the method lacks specificity in that intact P-CH$_3$-containing chemical-warfare agents or their decomposition products are all transformed into the same compound: dimethyl methylphosphonate. Therefore a verification procedure was developed for the detection in surface water of intact chemical-warfare agents of the organophosphorus type. It can be expected that the concentration of these compounds in surface water, if at all present, will be very low because the majority of the compounds are unstable in water. As a consequence it seemed wise to aim at a procedure which could be used at a ug/litre concentration level, comparable to the detection limit of the P-CH$_3$ method.

The method consists of concentrating the agents from the water sample using a tube packed with XAD-4, removing the adhering water by centrifugation, extracting the agent from the polymer with an organic solvent and transferring the resulting solution to another tube filled with TENAX. Subsequently the compounds are injected into a gas chromatographic column and detected by a flame photometric phosphorus-specific detector. When starting with 10 millilitres of water containing ug/litre concentrations of chemical agents such as Sarin, Soman or Tabun, recoveries of 50 to 100 per cent were obtained.[6]

The procedure implies a type of negative identification in that the search is directed at, and limited to, the chemical agents and key percursors; this is of importance in the protection of industrially sensitive knowledge.

IV. Trial inspection

During a trial on-site inspection of an insecticide plant which preceded the Workshop on the Verification of a Chemical Weapons Ban held in the Netherlands in 1986, only the P-CH$_3$ procedure was applied. The purpose of this inspection was not to simulate a real inspection in every respect but to study and test organizational and technical aspects involved in routine inspection of a chemical plant under a CWC.[7] This was the first time that the P-CH$_3$ inspection method was used both in the waste-water and chemical-production flow of an insecticide plant.

The water taken from the Rhine and returned to it showed a concentration level of P-CH3-containing compounds which is normal for industrially polluted water. It was concluded that a near-site inspection would have failed in this case as it was found during the on-site inspection that a P-CH3-containing compound was involved in the production process. However, this compound appeared only as a minor by-product and was largely removed by incineration.

V. Automatic monitoring

Both the P-CH3 procedure and the intact CWA procedure have serious drawbacks with respect to on-site inspection such as (a) a considerably long analysis time (1 to 5 days); (b) an unwelcome intrusiveness while taking the samples; and (c) the need for a certified, specialized analytical laboratory located outside the production complex. Therefore, within the framework of disarmament negotiations, the application of on-site automated-monitoring systems which cannot be deceived during operation (so-called black boxes) is to be encouraged so as to enable inspection of the civil chemical industry.

The verification measures related to destruction of stored chemical weapons will differ from the methods of verifying the non-production of chemical-warfare agents or key precursors in the civil chemical industry. There would be no negative political or economic implications if a positive identification is carried out to verify the declared destruction of chemical weapons. The management of the civil chemical production plants will prefer negative verification methods and automatic-monitoring systems to visits of inspectors in view of the wish to protect the commercially sensitive know-how.

Considering the current state of the art, it seems relatively easy to verify the destruction of declared materials. The control measures can be concentrated on counting and weighing stored amounts of chemical weapons, on their movement to the destruction facility and on the reliability of an actively operating facility. The different steps in such an operation can be effectively controlled by the use of video cameras and balances to register such essential parameters as quantity, weight and movement. The actual destruction can be followed by measuring temperatures, pressures, gas or liquid flows, pH and energy consumption. In the case of incineration, the composition of the flue-gas can be traced by, for example, an SO_2-monitor. The chemical identity of the substances to be destroyed can be ascertained by taking a few, but statistically reliable, samples to be analysed by gas chromatography, mass spectrometry or infra-red spectrometry which can be carried out at the destruction site by a mobile laboratory, or off-site by a certified analytical institute.

In the case of verification measurements to control suspected illegal production of chemical agents or key precursors in the civil chemical industry, two parameters will play an essential role in the inspection--namely the chemical identity and amount of the starting materials and manufactured compounds. With the principle of negative verification in mind, these characteristics can be automatically monitored by a continuous or discontinuous registration using reliable random sampling. The measured data of the compounds in the process stream should be compared with a database system composed of chemical compounds covered by the treaty. The amount of chemicals can be traced by registering essential flows and weights in the input and output parts of a production process.

Chromatographic and, probably to a greater extent, spectrometric techniques will play an important role in the identification or characterization of the chemical compounds. It is essential to use monitoring systems that will operate reliably for long periods of time without the need of extensive maintenance, inspection and replacement or replenishment of consumable materials.

Generally, it may be expected that the industries governed by a future CWC will utilize multi-purpose plants. The respective production processes will change frequently and irregularly. As a consequence the chemical and physical parameters of the compounds in the process stream will change. Such changes may have serious consequences as regards the sampling equipment such as readjustment, replacement of analytical components or reagents, and rinsing of the sampling part of the monitor. The avoidance of valves and moving parts in the connection between the process stream and the monitor is to be preferred. If present, they will be liable to fouling, clogging or obstruction owing to corrosion or suspended matter. Chromatographic equipment including sampling devices is rather complex, difficult to adjust and liable to contamination or fouling when the production process is changed. If good instruments or sensors for in-line measurements are available, sample taking and physical or chemical pre-treatment should be avoided. Methods such as infra-red and ultraviolet spectrometry which measure the chemical process directly via optical fibre links will reduce the installation and maintenance costs. Additional advantages of these methods are simple operation and the obtaining of clear chemical-structure information. The principle of an interesting monitoring system was recently introduced by Odernheimer and designated SNAL, which stands for sample now, analyse later.[8] The samples are automatically taken at random intervals from the process stream and simultaneously deposited on a time-coded cassette tape which is stored for long periods under conditions which preserve the samples. This approach seems very flexible as the sampling and analytical aspects are decoupled.

However, the transport of the process-flow material to the sampling device still implies the disadvantage of the presence of valves or moving parts. The entire tape or a part of it can be analysed as desired by heat or liquid desorption in combination with a relevant identification technique. This can be performed by a certified laboratory outside the production facility, but it will probably be preferable to analyse the tape on-site to protect industrial know-how. In this case, a mobile mass spectrometer may play an important role. This versatile apparatus combines high mobility with reliable information about chemical identity.

In the Prins Maurits Laboratory a feasibility study has been started to study the different possibilities of the various automatic-monitoring systems to be applied in the case of verification of non-production of chemical weapons and related materials in the civil chemical industry.

VI. Conclusion

In this paper, the applicability of some analytical methods developed in the Prins Maurits Laboratory TNO concerning the verification of non-production of chemical-warfare agents and related materials in the civil chemical industry has been described. The P-CH$_3$ method and the procedure for analysis of intact agents have been shown to provide confirmation about the presence of nerve agents and related compounds, and some preliminary views concerning the use of automatic-monitoring devices have been presented.

References

[1]Verweij, A., Degenhardt, C. E. A. M. and Boter, H. L., *Chemosphere*, vol. 3, no. 115 (1979).

[2]Verweij, A., Mensingh, G. F. and Boter, H. L., *Chemosphere*, vol. 11, no. 985 (1982).

[3]Verweij, A., Boter, H. L. and Degenhardt, C. E. A. M., *Science*, vol. 204, no. 616 (1979).

[4]Verweij, A., Dekker, W. H., Beck, H. C. and Boter, H. L., *Anal. Chim. Acta*, vol. 151, no. 221 (1983).

[5]Verweij, A., Kientz, Ch. E., Berg, J. v. d., Hulst, A. and Wils, E., 'Liquid Chromatography of Organophosphorus acids', 2nd Workshop on Chemistry and Fate of Organophosphorus Compounds, Barcelona, 10-12 Nov. 1987.

[6]Verweij, A., Liempt-v. Houten, M. A. v. and Boter, H. L., *Intern. J. Environm. Anal. Chem.*, vol. 21, no. 63 (1985).

[7]For more details, see ter Haar, B., Boter, H. L. and Verweij, A., *NATO's Sixteen Nations*, Aug. 1987, p. 46.

[8]Odernheimer, B., in Finnish Project on Verification of Chemical Disarmament, *Automatic Monitoring in Verification of Chemical Disarmament*, Proceedings of a Workshop, Helsinki, Finland, 12-14 Feb. 1987.

POSSIBILITIES FOR AUTOMATIC MONITORING OF CHEMICAL PRODUCTS

O. V. PERRONI, Brazil

I. Introduction

One of the key points for the success of a Chemical Weapons Convention (CWC) is the establishment of a sound verification regime, the procedures of which ensure that the Parties to the Convention observe its provisions. These procedures include declarations, systematic on-site inspections, challenge inspections and monitoring by on-site instruments. The objective of verification is to make certain that the activity of the plant is in accordance with its declaration and that its products are not used in activities prohibited by the Convention. Systematic on-site verification by international inspectors would demand expensive, skilled labour, and would necessarily constitute a disturbance in the work atmosphere of the plant being inspected. Thus, discussion has arisen about the possibility and convenience of continuous monitoring of plants by electronic instruments operating on a real-time base.

This idea is based on the belief that in this way greater precision and reliability could be achieved, quite apart from being less intrusive in the day-to-day life of the plant. In order that the idea be practicable, however, it is necessary to have reliable instruments, suitable for qualitative and quantitative control of the production and capable of operating continuously without maintenance. It is also necessary that the system be practical and cost effective so that it can be widely used.

In order to reach a conclusion about the real possibilities and limitations of electronic monitoring of chemical plants, in view of the aim of the Convention, attempts have been made at production-control simulations of two chemical products manufactured in Brazil. The ideal situation would have been to work with a product from Schedule 2 of the Convention, that is, the group known as key precursors, but these are not produced in Brazil. The products selected instead were phosgene, made by PRONOR-Productos Orgânicos S. A., and MIPA, monoisopropylamine, made by QUÍMICA DA BAHIA S. A. Both firms are part of Camaçari Petrochemical Complex, situated in Bahia State. The reason for choosing phosgene was that it is included among the products listed in Schedule 3; with regard to MIPA, its choice was due to the fact that it is produced in a multi-purpose plant with batch operation, which could be useful in providing relevant information. The work was carried out with the aid of COMSIP Engenharia S. A., a Brazilian engineering company specialized in electronic process-control systems

The aim of the work was to design and estimate the cost of an electronic system capable of monitoring phosgene production in PRONOR and MIPA in QUÍMICA DA BAHIA, which would also be reliable and immune from possible attempts at deception on the part of the producer. This work was only possible thanks to the close co-operation of technicians from COMSIP, PRONOR and QUÍMICA DA BAHIA, to whom gratitude is due for their efforts. However, the conclusions reached do not necessarily reflect the thinking of these companies or of their technicians, and are the responsibility of the author of this paper.

II. Monitoring of the MIPA production

Brief description of the plant

The plant is a multi-purpose unit, operating in batches and in programmed working periods, in which various alkylamines are produced, MIPA being one of them.

The MIPA produced is not used by the firm, the whole output being stored in tanks ready for sale. There is no sale of MIPA via pipelines; all of it is sold in cylinders or in tanker trucks. Furthermore, there are three other ways by which MIPA may leave the plant mixed with other substances: (a) via the effluent outlet to the residue-treatment station; (b) into the residue tanks, the destination of which is in sales to third parties; or (c) via emission into the atmosphere along with other non-condensables.

Figure 1 presents a simplified diagram of the process of obtaining MIPA.

Location of control points

The control to be carried out was based on the ratio, quantity of raw material (acetone)/quantity of final product (MIPA), taking into account the yield and losses inherent in the process.

Eight control points were selected, numbered from P1 to P8, all of which were subject to quantitative control, and the first four to quality control (see figure 1). Control of these points guarantees the detection of MIPA whenever it is being produced in the plant, as well as allowing quantitative control. Besides this, it ensures that the performance and production figures declared by the firm are being adhered to. In case of discrepancy, the system will record the fact and alert the control team. The control points selected, and their purposes, were as follows:

P1. The pump outlets B9/10, before the connection with the acetic acid inlet. The aim of the control at this point was to provide analytical monitoring, both qualitative and quantitative, of one of the raw materials that is fed to the plant, namely acetone which is essential to the manufacture of MIPA.

P2. The outlet at the base of the distillation column C2. This is a key point, vital to control, and the flow that passes it was subject to qualitative control (on-line analyser) and quantitative control (flow meter). The determination of the composition of the stream at this point was important in order to check whether or not there was MIPA production in the plant at the time.

P3/P4. Outlets at the base of column C4 and at the top of column C3. The aim of the analytical control at these points was to prevent diversion of the MIPA produced between the base of column C4 and the top of C3. Moreover, this control prevented possible distortions in the quantitative control caused by the recycling of acetone.

P5. Tank outlets V18/V19. This control was only quantitive, measuring the daily production sent to the final-product tanks.

P6/P7. Consumer outlets from vessels V25A/V25B. A quantitative control served to obtain the MIPA balance and to keep track of the loading of tanker trucks and the filling of cylinders.

P8. Outlet at the top of column C4. This was only a quantitive control of production (flow) in order to close the MIPA balance.

Possible loopholes

Theoretically, the following deceptions could be attempted:

(a) Removal of MIPA from the top of column C2. The MIPA would exit mixed with ammonia, the latter being a very large quantity. To separate them would require a plant almost like the original.

(b) Fitting bypasses at points P1, P2 and P8 to remove MIPA. This manoeuvre would not be detected by the system, but, due to the high pressure (20 kg/cm^2) in line C2-C4, its implementation would require stoppage of the plant, which would be easily noticed. Apart from this, marks would be left that could always be checked by visual, on-site inspection.

(c) Feeding of acetone after the ammonia tank and simulation of the recycling. This would have to be complemented by the diversion described in (b) above, as otherwise the MIPA produced would be detected at point P2.

Configuration of the proposed system

The basic premise of the proposed system was that it should be capable of detecting quantitative diversions of production, or use of the products classified (in this case, MIPA), in relation to the quantities declared by the plant owner, taking into consideration the yield and losses of the process.

The system would have a non-automated component. It would have to rely on compulsory initial inspections that would analyse the veracity of the information received concerning the installations of the firm to be inspected. Once the information received was found to be correct, it would be passed on to the automated system. From then on, its tasks would be to register and inform about any discrepancy between the values observed in the line, or accumulated, and those declared by the firm. Whenever a discrepancy were detected, the body in charge of the control would undertake an on-site inspection of the installations so as to clarify the causes.

The system (figure 2) would be composed of three subsystems: (a) the sample-collection subsystem; (b) the analysis subsystem; and (c) the data-processing subsystem.

The sample-collection subsystem would be comprised of sample-taking devices at points P1, P2, P3 and P4 (figure 1) and an automatic collection chamber, and would execute the following sequence of steps: (a) collection of the sample at the sampling point; (b) sending of the sample collected to the analysis subsystem; (c) awaiting the conclusion of the analysis; (d) carrying out automatic cleaning of the collection chamber; and (e) carrying out the same procedure for another sampling point.

The analysis subsystem would consist of a chromatograph featuring an automatic groove injection valve, placed after the flow selector, and a column of the following type: DB1, 30 meters in height, an inside diameter of 0.32 mm and a film thickness of 1 micron (methyl-silicone column).

The computing subsystems would be constituted of a general processing (dual) unit, a memory of 512 K bytes, a 10 M byte magnetic disc unit of the Winchester type, a monitor (black and white, 24 lines), an interface for connection to the analysis subsystem, an interface for eight analogic inputs dealing with flow metering, and an interface for connection to a controlling agency.

So as to achieve the flow measurements, the plant should be equipped with suitable meters at points P1 to P8. For the purpose of cost estimates, it is considered that the flow meters would be of the micro-motion type, which are virtually maintenance free.

Cost estimate

The cost estimate for the system at the time of writing, the configuration of which has been described, is the following:

	US$
(a) Flow measurement instruments	32 000.00
(b) Collection subsystem	20 000.00
(c) Analysis subsytem	50 000.00
(d) Data-processing subsystem	120 000.00
(e) Installations and other services	28 000.00
TOTAL	**250 000.00**

In summary, the total cost of the system installed would be approximately two hundred and fifty thousand US dollars.

III. Monitoring of phosgene production

Brief description of the plant

The phosgene unit is part of an integrated plant producing TDI, the basic raw materials of which are natural gas, chlorine and toluene (figure 3).
The phosgene unit is continuous and single purpose, that is, either phosgene is produced or nothing is produced (figure 4).

The raw materials for the manufacture of phosgene are carbon monoxide and chlorine, the former produced at the plant, and the latter bought and received via a pipeline. After being produced, the phosgene is sent directly to five destinations, through pipelines: (a) three outlets for internal consumption in the plant itself, as raw materials; (b) one outlet for sale to an outside consumer; and (c) one outlet for burning in an emergency situation.

There is no other outlet from the production unit. Nor is the phosgene stored in cylinders or tanks, there being no equipment for this purpose at the plant. All the phosgene produced is consumed internally, sold or burned on line.

Location of control points

It was established as a given pre-condition that the control to be exercised over the production of phosgene would be based on the ratio raw material/finished product. A detailed study of the plant indicated that, for effective control through a material balance in the unit, it would be sufficient to control points P1, P2, P3 and P4 (see figure 4). At all the points quantitative control would be effectuated. And, at points P3 and P4, there would also be an analytical control, so as to guarantee the ratio between the phosgene produced and the phosgene piped to the caustic washer.

The combination of all the controls should ensure that, in normal operation, the values declared (yield and production) would be abided by. In the case of discrepancy, the systems should detect the fact and activate the alarm.

The control points suggested are as follows: P1--chlorine flow measurement; P2--carbon monoxide flow measurement; P3--measurements of flow and phosgene composition; and P4--measurement of flow and content of phosgene in the flow of gases sent to the caustic washer.

Potential deceptions

The following deceptions could be attempted, for example: (a) removal of phosgene at the production outlet and before P4 (Such removal could be made to seem a leak. Leaks are not uncommon. When leaks arise they are diverted to the stack as a matter of course.); or (b) modification of the units to allow feeding of chlorine and carbon monoxide after points P1 and P2, respectively, and the removal of phosgene before P3 and P4.

This procedure would not be detected by the control system and it is very easy to remove phosgene at the outlet of any reactor. The modification could be made during normal routine maintenance, as, every 40 days, removal of the bank of reactors is made to replace catalysts. Thus, the deception would be simple and easily committed, without there necessarily being any general awareness of it, provided that the raw material were available.

Proposed system

Due to the fact that, in this case, the control can be circumvented easily, the conclusion reached is that it is pointless to protect an automatic control system in the production of phosgene, as this, in practice, would not be reliable.

The possibility of monitoring the carbon monoxide production plant was also examined, or, moreover, the consumption of phosgene in the plant itself.

In both cases the control points were studied, but the examination concerning the possibility of deception led to the same conclusion, that is, the impossibility of designing a system that is deception-free.

IV. Conclusions

The first conclusion to be drawn from the study is that the automatic monitoring of classified chemical products is viable for some plants and not for others.

In the case of the two products examined, the result is somewhat surprising: the production of MIPA is made in a multi-purpose plant and keeping track of it automatically is viable; on the other hand, the production of phosgene that is made in a single-purpose plant, does not lead itself to deception-free automatic control. Thus, the matter of whether an automated monitoring system is viable or not must be studied case by case and would depend fundamentally on the degree of simplicity of the process under observation.

Another conclusion reached is that there is no entirely automated system capable, on its own, of guaranteeing the veracity of the information collected.

The system should have manual components, as it would have to rely on initial inspections by inspectors, who would analyse the veracity of the information received and pass it on to the automated system. The purpose of these mixed systems with automated control and manual inspections is to minimize the interference caused by the teams of inspectors in the controlled industries. The inspections would be reduced to random or on-challenge visits whenever a discrepancy were detected. Futhermore, this would allow a reduction of subjective factors, which are always introduced by a human presence in control work.

102

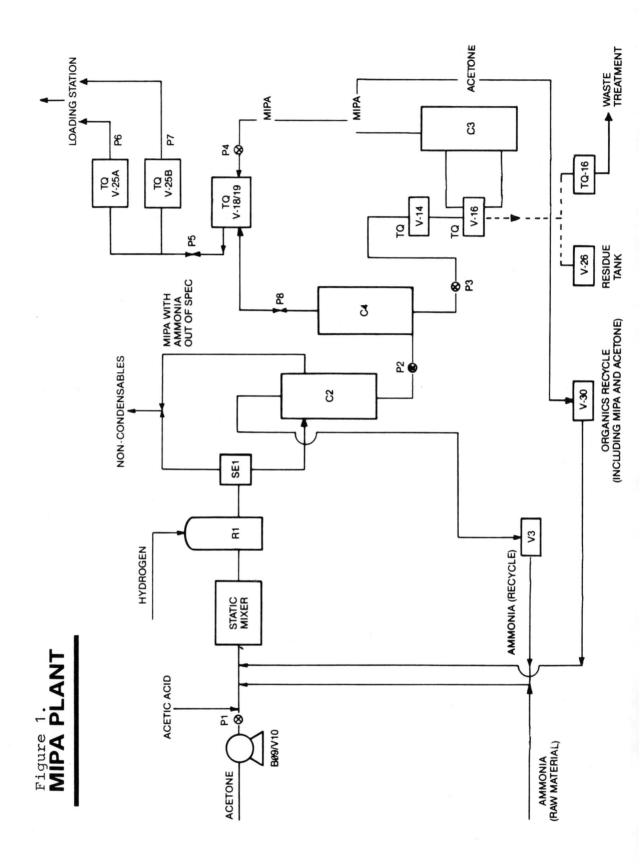

Figure 1.
MIPA PLANT

Figure 2.
PROPOSED CONTROL SYSTEM

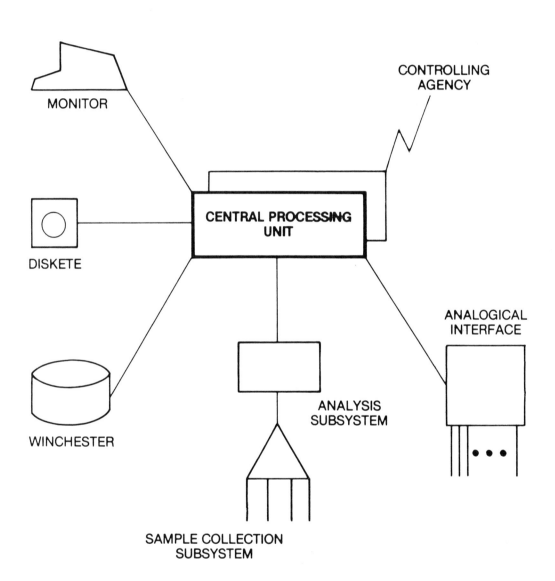

104

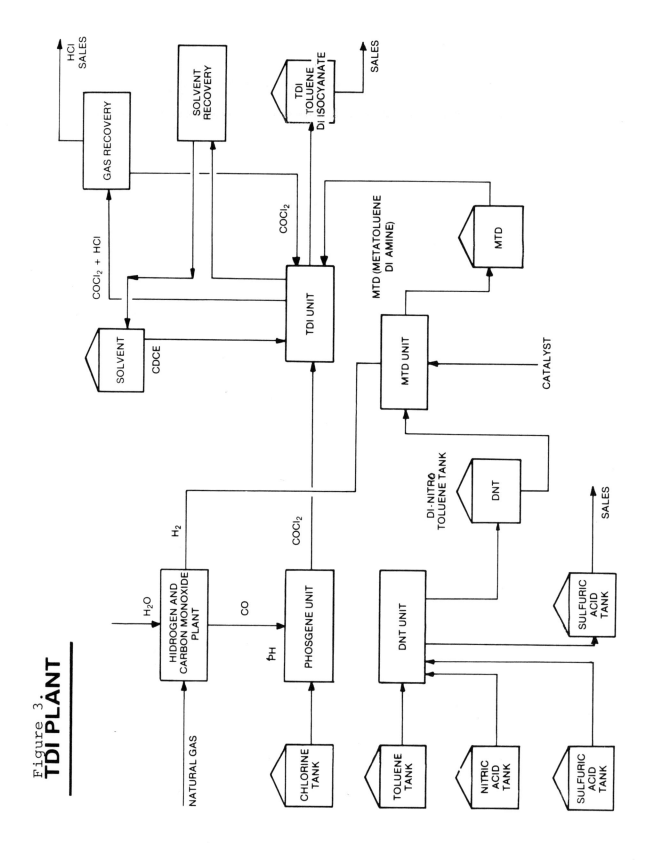

Figure 3.
TDI PLANT

Figure 4.
PHOSGENE UNIT

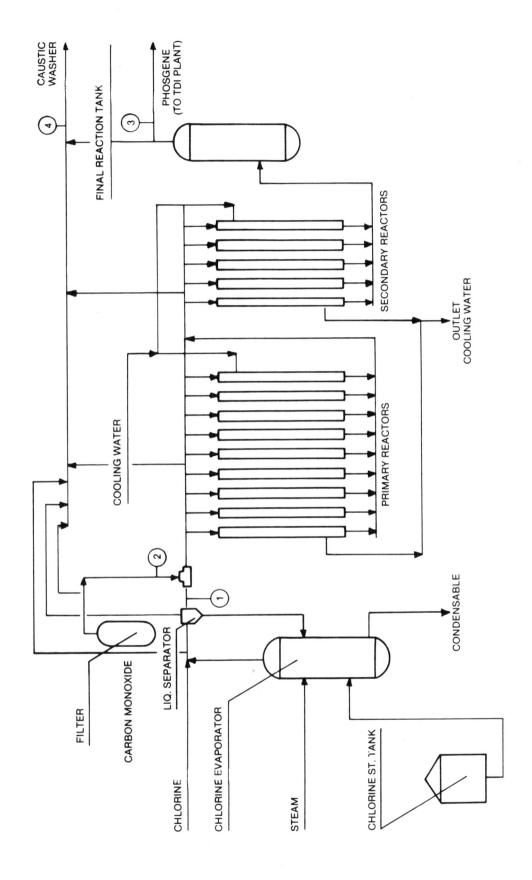

CAUSTIC WASHER

FINAL REACTION TANK

PHOSGENE (TO TDI PLANT)

SECONDARY REACTORS

OUTLET COOLING WATER

COOLING WATER

PRIMARY REACTORS

FILTER

CARBON MONOXIDE

LIQ. SEPARATOR

CHLORINE

CHLORINE EVAPORATOR

STEAM

CHLORINE ST. TANK

CONDENSABLE

SOME VIEWS ON THE CONTROL OF MULTI-PURPOSE PLANTS

H. SCHRÖDER and H. HOFFMANN, the Federal Republic of Germany

I. Introduction

The negotiations on the elimination of all chemical weapons are presently progressing at a comparatively fast pace. The verification of non-production of chemical weapons and control of permitted production are key elements of a future agreement.

During the initial discussion of the control of non-production, the question of verification by means of on-site inspection was fairly uncomplicated. At that time only the super-toxic lethal chemicals (STLCs) compounds of Schedule 1, particularly phosphorous esters, were under consideration. Production plants which manufacture these compounds require sophisticated safety installations to handle products characterized by high volatility, good skin penetration and high toxicity. This type of plant can be easily identified owing to the special provisions necessary.

The current situation is, however, a different one and can be outlined as follows:

1. The manufacture of the individual compounds of binary chemical weapons require no extraordinary safety installations.

2. Compounds of low acute toxicity and low volatility (BZ) have been added to Schedule 1.

3. The use of mustard gas in the Gulf War has shown that this World War I compound is still of importance. Considering the relatively simple technical requirements for its manufacture, it is questionable if plants used for its production are easily identifiable.

4. The addition of precursors for Schedule 1 compounds into a control regime is the change of greatest consequence. These compounds are manufactured in many countries and numerous plants. This manufacture is legal and cannot be discontinued. The aim of a control regime is therefore verification of declared production and control of peaceful use. In this final stage of negotiations, it is important to become very specific about the facilities which are to be controlled and about the means of such control. Furthermore, the discussion of gathering new STLCs in a Schedule 4 has focused attention on the versatility of chemical plants. The following discussion is an attempt to describe what can be encompassed by the term 'multi-purpose plant' and how the relevance of this term to the negotiations on chemical weapons in the Conference on Disarmament (CD) might be viewed.

II. Description of multi-purpose plants

The chemical industry has developed based on market demand and available technology. The difficulty with regard to the CD negotiations is that the industry, as such, is not structured so that definitions, requirements, organization, technology and the like fit easily into a control system under a future Chemical Weapons Convention (CWC). When an attempt is made here to develop a classification of chemical-production plants, it should be kept in mind that the reality is much more complex and that all imaginable combinations and transition states of these plants exist. The following description is valid for chemical-processing plants which are not specifically geared for chemical-weapon manufacture.

The smallest multi-purpose unit in which chemical compounds can be produced is of course the *laboratory*. It would not be necessary to consider such a small-scale production facility if the proposed low threshold value for production of Schedule 1 chemicals (1 metric tonne per year) is not included under the review system. Modern chemical laboratories are regulated by a variety of national standards of industrial hygiene and the use of closed hoods, which have minimum draught requirements, is standard. With the addition of glove boxes and the like, all types of toxic materials can be safely handled and synthesized in a laboratory, and, of course, a laboratory is normally operated by well-trained, educated personnel, able to deal with complex synthesis. Glass flasks ranging in size from 1 to 10 litres are common in a synthetic, chemical laboratory.

How would a laboratory go about producing a tonne of a particular chemical substance per year? Assuming 50 weeks of operation, this would amount to 20 kilograms per week or 4 kilograms of product per day on a five-day workweek basis. In a chemical synthesis which is not particularly developed, one can assume that approximately 10 per cent of the volume of a reactor will be obtained as a pure product, or 1 kilogram of product per batch from a 10-litre flask--not being too particular about densities, and so on when looking at such an approximation. This means that a laboratory would need a minimum of 4 x 10-litre reactor set-ups to produce the threshold value of 1 tonne per year. A laboratory with six hoods could accomplish this--a size typical of an average industrial laboratory. The number of synthesis steps has, of course, to be considered when looking at specific compounds. It is also generally assumed that a reaction can be completed within an one- or two-shift day, which is not always the case. But the point is, a dedicated laboratory has certainly to be discussed when looking at such threshold values. Cost/benefit considerations can, of course, not be applied to this tedious mode of operation.

The next size of multi-purpose facility, the *laboratory-type pilot unit*, varies in composition depending on the specific needs of the branch of chemistry one examines. In pesticide research, 1 to 10 kilograms of a product are often needed on short notice for biological, ecological, toxicological and other testing soon after the biological effect of a compound has been detected. Facilities for this task are larger than laboratories. The equipment consists mainly of glass flasks or reactors which range in size from 20 to 80 litres. Basic functions such as vent piping, vacuum generation and the like are accomplished via fixed glass piping. General connecting pipes make it easy to combine the reactor or flask sequence needed for a given task--hoses are used frequently. When supplying the first substantial amounts of different products for further testing, products may have been synthesized by a technically and economically unfeasible laboratory process. Initial studies to develop such technical processes are performed as well in this pilot unit. Owing to the use of glass equipment and the normally built-in possibility of connecting various pieces of equipment, these facilities can be called true multi-purpose units. The extent to which it is possible to handle highly toxic compounds in such a unit depends, of course, on the infrastructure of the specific installation. These facilities are designed and geared for research and development purposes and for dealing with different chemicals and processes. They carry high price tags for their construction and equipment.

As capacity increases, we find multi-purpose units which are of a more technical character. *Technical pilot plants* have test sections containing reactors ranging in size from 100 to 1000 litres and small production units with reactor sizes from 1000 to 6000 litres. The larger reactors usually serve for the work-up of reaction mixtures, where larger volumes are normally required. These pilot plants are more closely related to production units, because the reactors often are made of steel, stainless steel, enamel and the like--the same construction materials used in large-scale production plants. Wherever possible fixed piping is installed. The purpose of these plants is the development and confirmation of technical processes as a basis for the design of a commercial facility. At the same time, intermediate amounts of product are synthesized for technical development and initial market testing.

In a technical pilot plant, as much equipment as one can afford or justify is installed according to the principle of unit operations, for example, reactions, liquid-liquid separation, distillation, filtration, drying and so on. For a new product the required equipment is then combined as needed. The design is geared for flexibility, to be able to run many different types of reactions. The pilot plant is not intended for large production quantities. Since the equipment is of technical nature, changing from one process to another also involves technical changes--mainly piping changes; the length of this procedure can vary from days to weeks. Instrumentation automation is limited mostly to measuring and relating the parameters of an individual process unit. Automation of a whole process would hamper versatility. The technical pilot plant is also a true research and development tool. For extended production purpose it is too expensive, because owing to the multitude of equipment installed, some of it is bound to be idle and unused. A typical *chemical plant,* on the contrary, is designed to produce a given product by a specified process--the equipment is engineered and installed accordingly.

Much of the versatility described earlier is lost, when a *commercial multi-purpose plant,* which is built for economically acceptable production volumes, is examined. Reactor sizes are of the order of 8 to 20 cubic metres, and the reactors are constructed of different materials. The mode of operation is mainly batch process. Continuous operations are normally very specific and do not allow much variability. But as stated earlier, one seldom finds pure systems; batch operations for the reactions often have continuous process steps for work-up, such as distillation, drying and so on. Multi-purpose, in this discussion, is understood to mean that several different products can be synthesized in one given unit. A building in which several different products are manufactured, but each in a different, dedicated processing unit, is in this sense not a multi-purpose plant; one could call it multi-product.

The multi-purpose aspect of a commercial unit is narrow. It can, for instance, be the general reaction of a substituted phosphorous acid chloride with a phenol in the presence of an acid acceptor to yield a phosphor ester. Using differently substituted phenols leads to different end-products. A necessary condition for substitution is the similarity of the reactions and the chemical and physical properties of the reactants. Another example of a multi-purpose unit might be a reactor for chlorinations. The basic chlorination reaction can be applied to many compounds in such equipment and its auxiliary units. In commercial production plants the multi-purpose character, limited to the same type of process conditions and product families, is different from that of the pilot plants with their ability to handle different processes.

General discussion of converting this sort of commercial multi-purpose plant from one type of process to another is not meaningful since the necessary alteration can range from small changes to complete reconstitution. Only with knowledge of the desired process and the existing facility can an engineer judge if a process change is possible or which modifications would be required. It cannot be assumed as such that a multi-purpose plant is capable of changing *readily* from one process to another or from the production of one STLC to the next. The emphasis is on *readily*; otherwise one might as well discuss construction of a new facility.

III. Monitoring and control of multi-purpose plants

General

Before the technical aspects of monitoring and control can be discussed, one needs to define which facility is to be controlled and for what? Plants in which Schedule 1 chemicals, the active ingredients in the actual weapons, have been produced are to be dismantled. This means that, after a certain period of time, there will be no more declared facilities--besides the single, small-scale production facility--which have the proven capability to produce these listed, highly toxic chemicals. It is not possible to include, by definition, plants to be declared which fulfil some criteria for such production but which have never actually demonstrated this production. The question therefore remains where meaningful checks can be made, when stipulated by a future agreement, for the actual presence of Schedule 1 chemicals. One category which comes readily to mind is, of course, that of plants in which the precursors, the Schedule 2 chemicals, are produced or converted. Plants in which STLCs (not listed in Schedules 1 to 3) are manufactured can generally, according to present knowledge of specific compounds in this group, hardly be used for the manufacture of Schedule 1 compounds.

Pilot plants

Control of *laboratories* and *laboratory-type pilot units* should be included in the discussion of pilot plants. The monitoring of these entities does not seem justified, owing to the military insignificance of the amounts which can be produced there. Verification of the type of compounds handled could be considered. Automated control is almost impossible due to the ease with which any control mechanism can be circumvented. The frequent change of products in these facilities would also inevitably cause cross-interference in the analytical systems. The only effective control is actual sampling of the chemicals handled at a given time and analysis for the chemical properties in question. The ideal would be methods which do not reveal a whole chemical structure but only structural aspects of a sought chemical weapon--absence of phosphorus, sulphur and the like.

These facilities are, however, where the new products of a company are developed. The information available there is especially sensitive. The problem of confidentiality is of prime importance. Research activities should not be subject to a control regime. Control can only begin when the sensitive research phase is completed and production has begun. It takes 8 to 10 years from detection of a compound for pharmaceutical or plant-protection purposes till its commercial marketing. The development costs are of the order of magnitude of several 100 million Deutsch Marks.

To what extent these facilities are included in a control scheme will depend heavily on the final agreed-upon threshold value for production quantities. The non-inclusion of research facilities should be given priority when arriving at a threshold value. If this value is based upon a reasonable production quantity and relevant to the purpose of the Convention, not many of these types of research facilities will be included in a control regime. The cost of control should also be compared to the extent of verification accomplished, or undue effort might be expended to control minor elements of a regime.

Besides production threshold values, values for reactor sizes could also be introduced in a refined system as an additional criterion, to eliminate control of non-relevant facilities.

Production plants

When control of a commercial multi-purpose unit is discussed, one has to consider how a unit is integrated into a plant and how a plant is incorporated into a plant site. The following is an example of a possible multi-purpose unit with relevance to the negotiations.

Let us assume a unit exists to convert N,N-diisopropyl-aminoethan-2-ol (Schedule 2, no. 8) into its chloride (Schedule 2, no. 7).

$$iC_3H_7 \diagdown N-CH_2CH_2-OH + SOCl_2 \longrightarrow iC_3H_7 \diagdown N-CH_2CH_2-Cl + HCl + SO_2$$
$$iC_3H_7 \diagup \qquad\qquad\qquad iC_3H_7 \diagup$$

(8) (7)

Thionylchloride is used in this example. (There are other chemicals which could also be used for such a conversion.) The multi-purpose character of this unit implies that very likely different alcohols can be reacted with thionylchloride to the respective halide. The reactor would be a glass-lined reactor with auxiliary units for the absorption of HCl and SO_2. However, the work-up of the reaction mixture after the reaction with $SOCl_2$ might require different equipment, depending on the type of compound. This basic unit can be a small part within a larger production building, which again might be part of a larger complex.

In the so-called rolling text [the presently negotiated text of the future CWC] it is generally understood that the primary control applies only to a specific unit, its work-up equipment and related storage tanks. The rest of the building might have processes not related to the future Convention. Challenge spot checks might satisfy control of this unrelated part.

Quantity

The problem of quantity control during a production run in a multi-purpose unit is not different from that of a dedicated facility. A flow meter can be used if the final product is a liquid. The number of times an overflow-measuring tank fills can also be used. All this is fairly easily installed on line. Control becomes more complicated if the product is a solid, for instance, the hydrochloride salt of the compound. In this case one has to start counting bags. It is important that the model agreements to be worked out for the Convention leave enough flexibility to deal with the specific situation at a given plant.

The accuracy of material accountability or material balance from the '-ol' compound (8) to the chloride (7) depends on, among other things, the length of a production run. Usage factors/yields for a single reaction are normally well established. The accuracy varies from 1 to 5 per cent. On short production runs, however, larger deviations are possible due to clean-outs, inaccuracy of tank-level measurements and the like. This does not refer to the amount actually produced, which is always measured with the same accuracy of approximately 1 per cent or less.

The purity of a product might also deviate from the plant standard on a short run. Losses of raw materials occur through waste products or in the form of impurities in the final product. Very seldom is the usage of raw materials established for production of a single batch. Normally the yield is calculated per day or month in order to eliminate the effect of varying heels in reactors or varying amounts of in-process materials. The total amount produced does not, by itself, assure that only permitted production is occurring. It must be compared with consumption and shipments to consumers, which is not the topic of this discussion.

The problems specific to a multi-purpose unit arise when such a unit switches to the production of non-controlled chemicals. Putting existing control systems out of use or introducing additional, parallel piping can be used in order not to disrupt normal, non-controlled operation. The cost of the control system, which has to be set out of service for non-controlled production, is a factor to be kept in mind.

Identification

During a declared production run, confirmation of the declared chemical can be achieved in many ways.

Regular plant-operating records are unique to a specific reaction with regard to temperature profile, batch cycle, material flow and so on. Most of these records are normally generated in the control room. They can be complemented by shipping papers and the like. It is difficult to falsify or fabricate such documentation, which has to match in many facets. Single-batch deviations should be of no concern since, owing to necessary cleaning, production of one or two batches of a different material are highly unlikely in a production run.

Since we are dealing with non-toxic stable precursors, automatic sampling and accumulation of samples for a longer period should be feasible. One could, perhaps, utilize programmed sampling and check every second batch employing an average but random program whereby, for example, batches 1, 2, 3, 7 and 10 would be scrutinized. Verification would be performed by analysis of the samples. This type of system might be easier to run and maintain than on-line process analytical equipment. Such sampling would require a minimum degree of automatic or process control which is costly where basic installations are not already available.

Verification of non-production

Declared facility

Accepting the principle that the multi-purpose character of a large production unit is limited to the same type of reaction without major modifications, it is unlikely that the N,N-diisopropyl-aminoethan-2-ol or the resulting chloride are converted to the phosphorous compound in the described unit. A reaction type which fits into this type of unit is the reaction of thiodiglycol to sulphur mustard (Schedule 1, no. 4):

$$S(C_2H_4OH)_2 + 2SOCl_2 \longrightarrow S(C_2H_4Cl)_2 + 2HCl + 2SO_2$$

In the case described, one can probably easily recognize, by the nature of the installation alone, whether a toxic compound like mustard could be involved instead of the much less toxic amines. In addition, qualitative analysis for absence of organic sulphur would rule out any mustard production. The most meaningful sample is the one taken directly in, or close to, the reactor in question. Each reaction system has sampling points for normal process control. Analyzing waste water gives less evidence. Environmental-control agencies increasingly wish to control waste water at the discharge point from the relevant production unit and not, as presently, at the discharge point of the whole plant site. However, the parameters controlled are different from those required in the rolling text. The composition of waste water from a building, on the other hand, is of confidential nature since this can provide information on technological or trade secrets.

Undeclared facility

A future control agency under the Convention will have to rely on the declarations of the controlled party. Control measures can be bypassed by production in an undeclared facility. Following the concept 'keep it simple', the best control can probably be exercised by so-called spot checks involving the taking of a sample directly from a reactor. This system is effective, direct and of low cost. It should be considered as an exceptional measure--but could be instituted by a decision of the Inspectorate, thereby being different from a challenge inspection triggered by a third party, which is a highly political action.

This also seems to be the only means of detecting the manufacture of Schedule 1 compounds in an undeclared facility. The analysis of the sample would only be qualitative. There would be no need to discover which compounds were actually being produced; mere testing for the absence of phosphorus, sulphur and so on would suffice. In the event of a positive finding, one would need to analyse further for the next structural element. In a specific case this might lead to the actual identification of a product. This method is, nevertheless, considered to be less intrusive, because it is a very narrow control if used with care.

IV. Capacity

The US paper CD/CW/WP.171[1] provides a method for calculating the capacity of a production unit. The formal calculating scheme is able to arrive at a figure reflecting annual capacity based on actual production time or production quantity. Formally, this calculation is correct. But all the considerations discussed in this paper have to be weighed before establishing such a figure. A rigid application could lead to unrealistic figures. Capacity is one suggested factor which would determine if a facility should be controlled, and to what extent such control would be practised. The question can be raised whether capacity is a useful means of classification, especially in those instances where the actual production has been very low.

When we look at the capacity of a multi-purpose unit, we are focusing mainly upon the capacity of a batch operation. We assume, as in CD/CW/WP.171, that the production quantity produced in a given period is the basis for calculation. If this quantity is small, the matter of how extensively and at what rate auxiliary equipment has been utilized in production must be compared to the calculated production. A solvent-recovery system might create a bottle-neck. This does not become evident in a short run because the solvent can be accumulated in a storage tank, or the system can run for more hours than the main production unit. The numerical calculation could lead to higher values than are actually achievable over a longer period of time. The calculation method used illustrates technical ability. The mix of products of a plant is normally also governed by commercial-interest factors.

Many factors, besides those mentioned in CD/CW/WP.171, (such as availability of raw materials, labour, utilities and maintenance) will have to be considered. Among others, these include: plant infrastructure, repair shops, warehouses, traffic and reliability of waste-treatment facilities (biological waste-water treatment, waste-air incineration). All of these are vital for maintaining full-scale production over a longer period of time.

The same calculation cannot be used when the capacity for a similar, but different, process in the same unit has to be established. Cycle times can vary considerably. Another factor is a simple parameter like dilution. A reaction which can be run without a solvent certainly yields more tonnes per day than a process where only a 10 per cent solution of the reactants can be used. Because so many factors need to be weighed when discussing capacity, it is questionable whether capacity should be a decisive factor for a control regime. The quantity actually produced seems, to us, to be a much more readily definable and indisputable parameter.

However, when the decision has been made to control a facility, capacity should certainly be one of the many aspects considered to judge the importance of this facility, and the type and frequency of controls necessary.

V. Regulatory systems

A discussion of governmental control of the US chemical production has been presented by W. D. Carpenter in a previous SIPRI study.[2] The regulatory system in FR Germany is of comparable size, and a detailed description of its composition could fill the pages of a book. At the production level, the operating permit required by the Federal Emission Protection Law (BimSCHG)[3] acts as a comprehensive control system. This permit is a document which gives a thorough description of the plant, its equipment and processes including flow sheets. It stipulates a maximum monthly production quantity for each product or product group. All products or product groups handled, including wastes, are described. Limitation of the quantities of waste and waste-water discharges are given. These legal limitations act almost as a stronger limiting factor on the annual quantity produced than technical capacity. Although this document is approved by various departments of the permitting agency, and sometimes parts of it are even discussed publicly in the process of granting permission, this document, as a whole, is of a highly confidential nature.

There is presently no reporting system of production data which easily could be used for Convention purposes. One main system gives information to the federal statistical office. It is so structured that only product groups are reported, not individual compounds. Another problem with existing systems would also be that of their confidentiality. The future Inspectorate might have be given access to systems having more information than needed for Convention purposes; owing to this, confidentiality might be compromised.

VI. Conclusion

The present paper attempts to contribute some facts relevant to the discussion of the subject of control and verification of non-production of chemical weapons in chemical plants. The complexity and the multitude of different plants allow for no simple, universal solution. Within a framework established by the future Chemical Weapons Convention, agreements with individual plants, which are specific and tailored to the given facility, are the most effective way to achieve one of the goals of the future CWC. The chemical industry is willing to co-operate and assist with technical expertise in all aspects concerned.

References

[1]USA, 'Declaration of chemical production capacity', Conference on Disarmament document CD/CW/WP.171, 13 July 1987.

[2]Carpenter, W. D., 'Government regulation of chemical manufacturing in the USA as a basis for surveillance of compliance with the projected Chemical Weapons Convention', *The Chemical Industry and the Projected Chemical Weapons Convention: Proceedings of a SIPRI/Pugwash Conference*, SIPRI Chemical & Biological Warfare Studies no. 5 (Oxford University Press: Oxford, 1986), pp. 11-32.

[3]'Bundes Immissionsschutz Gesetz' (Bim SCHG), paragraphs 4-21.

Figure 1. Hood in a synthesis laboratory

Figure 2. Laboratory-type pilot unit

Figure 3. Reactor in a technical pilot plant

Figure 4. Reactors in a commercial production plant

INSTRUMENTED MONITORING OF THE CHEMICAL INDUSTRY UNDER A CHEMICAL WEAPONS BAN*

N. KYRIAKOPOULOS** and R. MIKULAK,*** the USA

I. Introduction

If a future chemical weapons ban is to be effective in enhancing security, states must have confidence in each others' compliance. Not only must states have confidence that existing weapons are destroyed, but they must also have confidence that chemical weapons will not be produced clandestinely in the future.

Early in the multilateral negotiations on a treaty it became clear that provisions would be needed to monitor the civil chemical industry to provide confidence that prohibited activities were not undertaken. Accordingly, considerable attention has been devoted in the negotiations to development of a monitoring regime for commercial chemical activities. The purpose of this paper is to explore the role that on-site instruments could play in this monitoring regime.

II. Verification in the chemical industry

In an approach that is under discussion in the multilateral negotiations the stringency of the provisions in a particular case is linked to the potential risk posed by the chemical or facility. The greater the risk, the more stringent the provision.

The highest risk is presented by super-toxic lethal chemicals (STLCs) such as Sarin, Soman and VX and their immediate precursors, that have been stockpiled as chemical weapons. Only small quantities of such chemicals could be synthesized and only for research, medical or protective purposes. In other words, commercial production of such chemicals would, for practical purposes, be extremely limited. Since these chemicals have no commercial significance, this limitation should not interfere with the chemical industry. The chemicals in this category would be listed in Schedule 1 of the treaty.

Commercial chemicals that pose a moderate risk would be subject to a verification regime based on data declaration and on-site verification. However, there would be no limitation placed on legitimate commercial activities. The most significant chemicals in this category are those, such as dimethyl methylphosphonate, that possess the carbon-phosphorus bond

---

*Presented at the 13th Workshop of the Pugwash Study Group on Chemical Warfare: Monitoring a Chemical Weapons Treaty, Geneva, Switzerland, 23-24 January 1988.

**Department of Electrical Engineering and Computer Science, The George Washington University, Washington, DC 20052, and US Arms Control and Disarmament Agency (ACDA), Washington, DC 20451.

***US Arms Control and Disarmament Agency, Washington, DC 20451.

characteristic of nerve gases. The chemicals in this category, considered key precursors, would be listed in Schedule 2 of the Convention.

Commercial chemicals that are produced in large quantities, but could be diverted to chemical weapons, such as phosgene and hydrogen cyanide, would be subject to a data-declaration requirement. Information would be required on the quantities produced and the location of production facilities. However, on-site verification is not envisioned. The chemicals in this category, together with other precursors, would be listed in Schedule 3 of the Convention.

The vast majority of commercial chemicals and their production facilities do not pose a significant risk and would not be subject to routine verification. However, challenge on-site inspection could be conducted to investigate any suspect activities.

III. On-site verification for moderate-risk chemicals and production facilities

As noted above chemicals and chemical-production facilities that pose a moderate risk would be subject to an on-site verification requirement. The objective of this verification regime would be twofold: (a) to provide confidence that the chemical in question is not diverted to chemical-weapon purposes, and (b) to provide confidence that the production facility in question is not used to produce Schedule 1 or non-declared Schedule 2 chemicals for chemical-weapon purposes.

The first verification task is primarily quantitative in nature. It will be necessary to verify the amount of the declared chemical produced and to verify that it is used for the purposes declared. In relatively small facilities this might be accomplished through routine, random inspections in which inspectors would examine a variety of types of records related to the production process. However, in facilities capable of producing large quantities of listed chemicals the risk is greater that militarily significant amounts of a chemical might be produced and diverted to prohibited chemical-weapon purposes. In such cases, consideration must be given to continuous monitoring of the production process. Although such monitoring might be performed by inspectors, it would be much more desirable technically and politically to use a combination of on-site monitoring instruments and inspectors if possible.

The second verification task is primarily qualitative in nature. It will be necessary to confirm that undeclared chemical-weapon-related chemicals are not produced at a facility that produces a Schedule 2 chemical for legitimate purposes. In relatively small facilities that are not suited to production of STLCs, this task might also be accomplished through routine, random on-site inspections in which inspectors examine the site, the records and take samples for chemical analysis. However, at relatively large, versatile facilities continuous monitoring of the production process, preferably through instruments and inspectors may be necessary.

The sections below explore the possible role of instruments, the types and characteristics of instruments, and approaches to data collection, transmission and processing.

IV. Role of instruments

A monitoring system consists of inspectors, instruments, data collection, data processing and data evaluation. Instrument applications fall into three categories: (a) activity monitoring, (b) product identification, and (c) production monitoring. Activity monitoring would require permanent emplacement of instruments in facilities subject to on-site verification. Product identification would require the inspection of both production equipment and storage facilities, and the analysis of products either on-site or in off-site laboratories. Production monitoring would require instruments for on-line, real-time process monitoring.

For each category, inspectors play different roles. Activity monitoring can be done by inspectors who are either continuously present in a facility or located off-site; their job is in effect to read, record and report indicators generated by the instruments. Product identification either on-site or in a laboratory demands highly trained inspectors, while the experience and training of inspectors for production monitoring depends on the characteristics and sophistication of the process-monitoring system. For this latter category cost-benefit analysis of the trade-offs between inspectors and instruments would be the most beneficial.

The specific uses of instruments in a facility depend on the verification requirements for that facility. Although verification scenarios for commercial facilities have not yet been formulated, some general observations can be made. Consider a facility declared as producing only key precursors. The monitoring system must have various levels of operation. At the first level, instruments must determine whether or not the facility is active; this could be accomplished by monitoring only a few key points such as the utilities and the temperature in the reactors. The sensors required are few, simple, and the data generated are minimal.

If part of the entire plant is activated, a second level of instruments can be envisioned. There might be circumstances such as testing or maintenance, requiring activation of certain components of the plant. The corresponding instruments should be able to discriminate between these circumstances and the actual production state; this task is relatively easy. The characteristics of the production processes for the known key precursors will be known from required declarations. These characteristics include quantities of reactants, physical state (that is, liquid, gaseous or solid), temperature and pressure ranges and flow rates. On the basis of these characteristics, models of the processes can be constructed and key monitoring points identified. Thus, the second level of instrumented monitoring would consist of sensors monitoring one or more variables which are critical to the production of key precursors. If one or more critical indicators are not present, it can be concluded that chemicals of interest are not produced, although parts of the plant are activated.

During production, the monitoring system must collect sufficient information to ascertain: (a) that undeclared chemical-weapon-related chemicals are not produced, and (b) that militarily significant quantities of allowed chemicals are not produced and diverted to prohibited chemical-weapon purposes. To meet these requirements, a process-monitoring system must be designed; it must generate both quantitative and qualitative information. It is not yet clear whether such a system can be generic or must be plant-specific; probably some components are applicable to more than one production process, but their integration into a complete system is plant-specific.

At this time, it has become evident that there is a need for developing production-process models for chemicals which are subject to the provisions of a chemical weapons treaty. On the basis of these models, the corresponding systems can be designed. In the meantime, some features of the monitoring systems can be identified on the basis of experiences from the nuclear Non-Proliferation Treaty (NPT) and from industrial process control.

Types and characteristics of instruments

Special design features are needed in instruments that will be used for international treaty monitoring. These features are dictated not only by the verification function of the instruments but also the relationships among the facility operator, the state and the international authority. These three entities have interests that are sometimes contradictory. The international authority wishes to collect sufficient information to verify treaty compliance; the operator wishes to minimize that information to protect proprietary data; the state wishes the data to be reliable to avoid false suspicions of treaty violations.

General design considerations

The design of the monitoring system for a given facility determines the type and location of instruments for that facility. Among the key design considerations are redundancy of information, the operating mode of each instrument, data reliability and data security. These considerations are discussed individually below. A good design dictates that no instrument, or type of instrument or location, be critical to the operation of the monitoring system. Redundancy in the required information can compensate for data uncertainty and data losses. Under this approach, an abnormal indication by any one instrument can be evaluated in the context of the indications of the remaining instruments, instead of treating it as an alert requiring immediate and drastic action. For example, an abnormal temperature indication in a reactor vessel would have different significance if it is accompanied by indications of flow in and out of the reactor than it would without them.

Verification requirements would also determine whether instruments operate continuously or intermittently. Usually instruments need not generate data continuously; a sampling operation is sufficient. For example, the sensing element of a temperature probe generates an analogue signal proportional to the temperature. If the function of the probe is to determine whether or not the reactor is being operated, there is no need for the data to be available on a continuous basis. It would be sufficient if the sensor would generate a signal only when the temperature exceeds a certain threshold. Such a requirement could be accommodated with a sensor having two states: 'on' and 'off'. If the analogue signal of the probe exceeds a given threshold, the state would be 'on', otherwise it would be 'off'. Such a design does not take into account the security requirements for the sensors.

Instrumented monitoring implies unattended operation of the instruments. For effective verification, there must be confidence in the indications of the instruments; confidence is eroded either by faulty operation or intentional tampering. The effects of both can be minimized through proper design. It is therefore necessary to specify a mean-time-between-failures (MTBF) for every instrument used in the monitoring system. Instruments should operate unattended and reliably for a period of at least one year. The actual number of MTBF could be determined through trade-off analysis between manufacturing costs, the costs of scheduled preventive maintenance and also the costs of reacting to faulty instrument indications.

At the instrument level, tampering can take two forms: the environment being monitored by the sensing element is altered, or the signal generated by the sensing element is altered. Protection against tampering implies that actual or attempted tampering should be detected within a predetermined time interval. To protect against altering the environment, the sensing element must be an integral part of the sensed environment. Seals and continuity sensors can ensure that removal of the probe from its environment would be detected. The signal of the sensing element can be altered by breaking into the instrument or subjecting it to some form of radiation, such as electromagnetic, thermal or nuclear radiation. Protection against intrusion can be obtained by placing each instrument in an enclosure made of continuously cast aluminium or other similar material, providing only one access port, and by shielding against external radiation. Intrusion into the instrument casing can be detected by sensors located in the instrument and at the ports. Some prototype instruments incorporating these design features have already been built and tested.[1]

Protection against tampering can also be obtained by appropriate processing of the sensor signal. If the analogue signal of the sensing element is sampled very rapidly, for example, more than 10 times per second, it would be very difficult for an intruder to substitute a fake signal for the one generated by the sensing element. Thus, the rapid sampling of the input signal prevents the substitution of a fake signal although these samples are neither needed by the monitoring system and are not processed beyond the instrument.

In view of the requirement for data reliability and security, it can be argued that the instruments used for verification be distinct from those used by the facility operator and that only the international authority should have access to them. Access to these instruments by state or facility personnel would compromise the security of the system. Use of separate instruments for verification, in addition to the complexity of the system, raises two other serious issues: (a) protection of the facility operator against disclosure of proprietary information, and (b) conflicts arising from discrepancies between the instruments of the operator and those of the monitoring authorities. These issues cannot be addressed here in detail; however, the first one can be resolved by designing the instruments so that they are sensitive to and report the minimum data needed by the verification authority to the exclusion of all other information. This can be accomplished by negotiations between the international authority and the facility operator on a facility-by-facility basis. For the resolution of conflicts between two sets of instruments, standard procedures must be agreed between the operator and the international authority.

Instruments have already been classified according to their roles as activity monitors or product identifiers. Examples of some instruments and their role in a monitoring system are discussed in the next section.

Security sensors

Security sensors have primary roles in places where little, if any, routine human activity is anticipated. Storage facilities are prime candidates for such sensors. Also, security sensors can be used to protect and to activate other sensors.

Seals are the simplest type of security sensor. If the monitoring system does not require detection of any violation of the integrity of the seal in a timely manner, seals can be checked when an inspection is performed. On the other hand, if a violation of the seal must be detected promptly, a remotely monitored seal is necessary. The most versatile seals use fibre optic cables. A bundle of light-transmitting fibres is wrapped around the part to be sealed, and the two ends of the cable are mechanically clamped together. Continuity of the seal is checked by introducing light in one end of the cable and detecting it at the other. For *in situ* verification, light is introduced by the inspector using a portable module, and the output light pattern is noted. For a multifibre cable mechanical clamping severs some of the fibres causing randomness in the light pattern emerging from the cable; this pattern constitutes the unique signature of the seal. The pattern formed when the seal is installed will be repeated every time light is shone through the fibres; if the seal has been compromised, the new pattern will differ from the original one, and the violation will be detected.[2]

For remote monitoring, light is passed through the fibres continuously.[3] The detected light is sampled very rapidly. If the seal is broken, even momentarily, the light transmission is interrupted and the violation is detected by the absence of the light signal. A remotely monitored seal can satisfy the timeliness requirement by specifying the time intervals between successive transmissions of the status of the seal to the central monitoring authority. For example, if it is required that a violation of the integrity of the seal becomes known to the central authority within 24 hours, continuity of the seal, although continuously monitored, is transmitted only once per 24 hours; the amount of data specifying the status is minimal.

To detect opening and closing of doors, continuity sensors are easy to design. Similarly, light sensors can be used to detect changes in ambient light. Within a confined area microwave or infra-red intrusion sensors can detect activity. On surfaces such as floors, walls or partitions, strain gauges can detect vibrations associated with movements or cutting.

Optical surveillance can be used not only to detect activity but also to discriminate among various activities. One of the first applications of optical surveillance in an international environment has been the use of film cameras by the International Atomic Energy Agency (IAEA) in nuclear safeguards. A pair of film cameras is enclosed in a special tamper-resistant enclosure. The cameras are under the control of a timer. At programmed intervals a snapshot is taken. In typical operating conditions with an average timer interval of 20 minutes, the film is used up in about three months. At that time the film is retrieved by an inspector for processing and examination. A camera failure or indications on the film of abnormal conditions become known to the central authorities only at the time the film cassette is retrieved or the film is processed; thus, the uncertainty about the time of occurrence of an event can extend to more than three months.

The trend in optical surveillance is to use video cameras. Local security systems utilize analogue monitors which display continuously the output of the cameras. These signals can also be recorded on video tapes or transmitted to a remote location. Continuous display, recording or transmission of the video signal would be impractical and very expensive. Instead, the efforts are directed toward surveillance systems which take, display, record or transmit frames; these systems are generally known as freeze-frame systems. The analogue outputs of the light-sensing elements are scanned at a given rate; scene frames are then formed for further processing. Under this arrangement, a picture frame can be formed either at predetermined intervals or on command from external trigger signals.

Closed-circuit television surveillance systems with picture-recording capabilities have been built in the United States under the program of support for the IAEA.[4] Similar systems are also under development in Japan. In the commercial market there exist systems with the ability to transmit picture frames over telephone channels. To conserve bandwidth and consequently to decrease the costs of transmission, various image-data-compression techniques are used; these are well established. Depending on the system design and the quality of the particular telephone line, a picture frame can be transmitted in less than 30 seconds; adaptive algorithms may be used to adjust the coding procedures and the transmission rate to the quality of the telephone channel thus preserving the quality of the images. Therefore, with respect to optical surveillance, the timeliness requirements, once specified, can be satisfied with existing technology.

Process monitoring

Sensors for monitoring elementary physical variables such as temperature, pressure, flow and weight are in widespread use; they could be adapted to treaty monitoring by rendering them tamper-resistant and by ensuring security of the data. Some prototype designs addressing these concerns have already been implemented.[5]

Considerably more complex is the problem of analysing a product through the various stages of processing. The types of sensors used depend on the method of conducting the analysis. These methods are classified as off-line, at-line, on-line and in-line.[6] Off-line analysis involves physical removal of a sample and transport to a laboratory; obviously, it requires human presence, existence of a laboratory and the logistics of transport. At-line analysis involves the use of instrumentation by the inspectors near the process line. Both approaches imply the continuous presence of inspectors near the monitored process.

On-line and in-line analysis aim to increase automation and decrease human presence. On-line analysis requires the construction of a sampling mechanism to remove the sample from the process line and introduce it to the analytical instrument; this is normally done automatically. On-line analysis can satisfy the requirement of timeliness by designing an appropriate sampling schedule; it can also reduce the need for the presence of the human element from the immediate vicinity of the process line to an area isolated from the actual process. The cost associated with such a design would involve the construction of elaborate sampling lines and the maintenance costs of the sampling apparatus.

In-line analysis involves the insertion of a probe into the process stream. This probe could either be a chemical probe designed to detect specific characteristics of the processed material, or a light probe removing information from the process stream through a light beam; the light beam, carrying information about the material, is analysed by instruments in the vicinity of the process line. The most promising analytical approach for in-line analysis is spectroscopy in conjunction with fibre optics.[7] At present, most of the research activity is centred in the infra-red and near infra-red part of the spectrum.

The advantage of spectroscopy is that sensors can be designed which are tuned to detect specific substances and exclude all others. Although the light beam is rich in chemical data, sophisticated signal-processing techniques at the front end of the analyser can be used to exclude all but the information necessary for monitoring the treaty. Therefore, spectroscopy in combination with in-line probes has the potential of providing sensors which can provide high levels of discrimination and can operate unattended.

Security and process-monitoring sensors can be used to construct a monitoring system for a process line or part of the process line. Consider, for example, the monitoring of a reactor. Temperature and pressure sensors along with load cells under the reactor can indicate the state of the reactor; flow meters in the pipes entering and leaving the reactor can indicate input and output conditions. In-line process monitors can identify the chemical substance of interest. Load cells and level indicators in the input and output holding tanks can be used to determine quantities. The integrity of the process-monitoring instrumentation is assured through a security system which ensures that the instruments are indeed in place; video surveillance may provide additional assurance that the process-monitoring instrumentation is not being bypassed. Listing of the instruments for this example does not imply that they should all be used; instead it indicates some of the options available for constructing a monitoring system for a reactor.

Integrating instruments into a system

The data generated by the sensors at a facility may be needed at the facility, the central monitoring authority or both. They may be required on a real-time or near real-time basis, or on a data-retrieval mode. Therefore, the design of the data-collection system depends on the functions of the monitoring system for each facility. The requirements for instrumentation and data processing can be generated once a verification system for each type of facility has been specified. Although such specifications have not yet been developed, some general principles affecting the design of the verification system can be made and their impact on the systems for the collection, transmission, processing and evaluation of the data examined.

Data collection

Assuming that the locations and operating modes of the sensors have been established, a local data-collection network is required to monitor sets of sensors. Since the tamper-resistant design of the sensors assures the integrity of the signals at their sources, the information must be protected during communications between each sensor and the local data-collection node. Protection may be accomplished either through encryption or through authentication. To an unauthorized observer encrypted data appear as noise; therefore, the information is neither available to nor easily alterable by unauthorized observers. On the other hand, authentication implies that information is transmitted in the clear, but it cannot be altered by unauthorized persons. Security of the data, therefore, implies that the data-collection modules must also be tamper-resistant; the principles of protection of the sensors against tampering apply similarly to the data-collection nodes.

The choice between authentication and encryption depends on the relationship between the operator and the monitoring authority, and on the principles of the design of the verification system. If the operating status is one of the parameters ensuring the integrity of the verification process, then no unauthorized persons must have knowledge of the system status; therefore, encryption is required. On the other hand, if the operating status of any one component of the monitoring system is not one of the design parameters, then, authentication would suffice, because the operator could be aware of the failure and still not be able to defeat the system. To illustrate the point, assume that one or more sensors have failed either permanently or intermittently. A verification system designed on the premise that knowledge of these failures would be sufficient to defeat it, would require data encryption. Conversely, a design relying on increased redundancy could reduce the need for hiding the failures of the monitoring instruments from the operator while still protecting the data against tampering, through authentication.

Reliable networks have no single critical node. Thus, the local data-collection network should not only provide duplication of the coverage by redundant sensors, but it should provide for redundant coverage of the sensors by duplicate data-collection nodes. The increased system reliability entails a corresponding increase in capital costs for the system. At the design phase a trade-off analysis becomes essential.

Sensor data are needed at the facility and at the central monitoring authority. When inspectors are at a facility, they must have access to the sensor data. In the interim, instruments provide the required monitoring of the facility by the central authorities. Also, there is a need for accumulating a record of sensor data regardless of the use of such data on a real-time basis. A log of past sensor data is essential for the resolution of disputes between the operator and the central monitoring organization; furthermore, sound engineering practices dictate the accumulation of operational data for the entire system.

The world-wide distribution of the facilities coupled with the centrally located monitoring authority make the system unique among techniques used to collect data. Transfer of data files on an infrequent basis, that is, of the order of months, presents no problem. If data are required on a near real-time basis, a global data-collection network must be established. At present, the location of all facilities which could possibly be subject to monitoring is not known; it may be assumed that some are located in remote sites which are not easily accessible to dedicated data networks. Therefore, the remaining alternatives are the international telephone network and satellite system.

For practical purposes the telephone network provides effective global coverage; it is difficult to envision a facility without a telephone line. The usability of the telephone network may be limited depending on the amount of data to be transmitted via this channel. Although some telephone links with appropriate modems can support data rates of 9600 bits per second (bps), more realistic data rates would be 300 and 1200 bps. Satellite telephone channels can support data rates up to 64 000 bps. The choice of the data-collection network depends on the amount of data collected at each facility by the central monitoring authority, the total number of facilities to be monitored and their geographical distribution. These parameters establish the total amount of data generated by and transferred through the system per unit of time. As the number of facilities increases, as the data generated by each facility increase and as the timeliness requirement for each facility decreases, the operating costs of using the telephone network at the central monitoring authority increase; consequently the use of satellite channels operating on a demand-assigned mode becomes cost effective. However, use of satellite channels requires the installation of earth terminals at each facility thus increasing the capital costs of the system. The choice, therefore, between the telephone network and a satellite system depends on the comparison between initial capital costs and long-term operating costs, given the geographical distribution of the facilities and the data requirements at the central monitoring authority.

Some of the ideas set forth in this paper have been used in the design of the experimental monitoring systems RECOVER (Remote Continual Verification),[8] JAEMS (JAERI Atomic Energy Monitoring System)[9] and TRANSEAVER (Transportation by Sea, Verification).[10] RECOVER was designed primarily as a demonstration of a remote security system for international nuclear safeguards; funding was provided by the US Arms Control and Disarmament Agency. The system was demonstrated successfully in 1980 using test sites in Australia, Bulgaria, Canada, the Federal Republic of Germany, Japan, the United Kingdom and the United States; the central monitoring unit was in Vienna, Austria. Following the field test, Japan Atomic Energy Research Institute (JAERI) constructed JAEMS, an upgraded version of RECOVER, which is operating at the JAERI Laboratories at Tokai-mura, Japan.

RECOVER and JAEMS are designed to monitor fixed sites. For moving platforms it is also necessary to monitor location. TRANSEAVER has been designed to monitor the security status and the location of cargo containers during sea transport. Although the cargo may be plutonium or highly enriched uranium, TRANSEAVER is usable for monitoring any standardized cargo container at sea. In addition to the basic RECOVER components, TRANSEAVER has a navigational unit and a communication-satellite earth terminal. The TRANSIT and OMEGA systems provide navigational data, and INMARSAT provides dial-up telephone communications at sea. TRANSEAVER has been constructed under a co-operative agreement between ACDA and JAERI.

The latest in the series of prototype global monitoring systems is Artemis; it also stands for Aircraft, Real Time, Encrypted, Monitoring and Information System.[11] Artemis is an extension of the RECOVER and TRANSEAVER concepts for tracking cargo aircraft; in addition, it has the capability of transmitting coded messages from escorts, and it can identify the location of the cargo containers in the event of a crash. The development of Artemis is undertaken on a co-operative basis between ACDA and JAERI; there are plans under consideration for building and testing Artemis.

The systems discussed in this paper share some common characteristics. They are designed to operate in the international environment for the purpose of monitoring international agreements; there is presumed to be an adversarial relationship between the central monitoring authority and the authorities of the sites where the sensors are located; there is global coverage and operating costs are low; the components in the remote locations are designed to operate unattended; information to the central authority is provided in a secure and timely manner; data losses due to failures in the local power supply or in the communications links are minimized; the design is modular so that the systems are easily adaptable for use in small or large facilities.

Based on experiences with these systems it can be argued that there are no technical impediments to the design and operation of global monitoring systems for multilateral verification, assuming all required sensors have been identified.

Data processing

Data collected at a facility have multiple uses. For real-time monitoring they are needed by the central authority; during the inspectors' presence at a facility, data are also needed by the inspectors. Depending on the inspection procedures, inspectors at the facility may need current data only, or past and current data. Furthermore, data available to the inspectors might be from the monitoring instruments only, or from these instruments and from the data bases of the facility operator. Therefore, the configuration of the data-processing system depends on parameters which have not yet been specified. Nevertheless, some observations may be made under some postulated parameters.

When sensors operate as threshold detectors, the amount of generated data is insubstantial. However, when a process is monitored continuously, or when there is optical surveillance even on an intermittent basis, substantial quantities of data are generated in short periods of time. Although data processing refers to handling of the data regardless of quantity, the issues raised in this section pertain to large quantities of data generated at a facility by the monitoring system.

There are two general options, data generated at a facility are processed and stored at that facility, or they are transmitted to the central authority for processing and storage. To implement the first option, substantial computing capacity is required at each facility.[12] Maintaining that capacity requires the continuous presence of support personnel; it would be unrealistic to expect a complicated data-processing system to operate unattended for extended periods of time. Under this configuration, inspectors would have easy access to the facility data base, and the operators of the facility would have high confidence that facility-related raw data remain within the facility. An additional advantage is that in case of disagreements between inspectors and the operator, there is a higher level of confidence by the operators in the integrity of the data. The major disadvantage is the high cost of maintaining a data-processing centre at each facility.

The second option involves the transmission of primary or raw data from the facility to the central authority with minimal processing requirements at each site. The necessary data-collection modules and communciations channels can operate unattended for extended periods of time; also, there are no storage requirements at each site; therefore, data-processing personnel is not needed on a continuous basis. From the point of view of personnel presence and implementation cost, the second option has substantial advantages over the first. There are also some disadvantages. Once raw data have left the facility, they are beyond the control of the operator and accessible to a wider audience. In spite of confidentiality agreements between the central authority and the operator, the feeling may persist that proprietary information has been compromised; in addition, there might be accusations that either side might have altered the data, inadvertently or otherwise. There is also the question of availability of the data to the inspectors during on-site inspections. If the inspection procedures call for the inspectors to collect only current information, then the second option presents no problems; if, however, during the inspection the inspectors need access to past data, then the system must provide for access to the data base at the central authority. Such access can be provided by a portable data terminal.

The aforementioned concerns notwithstanding, the second option is preferable because it minimizes the cost per facility of implementing a verification system. The questions of alteration of data and loss of proprietary information can be addressed through proper system design. To avoid conflicts based on analysis of different data bases, and to assure the operator that only agreed-upon information leaves the facility, the data-collection systems can be designed so that data can be made available to the operator simultaneously with the transmission to the central authority. Alternatively, the operator can be provided with a first look at the data before transmission. It would be realistic to assume that, once data leave a facility, they are no longer proprietary. It is therefore the task of the system designer to devise a system which can obtain the information for verifying compliance of a facility without relying on proprietary data. The process will have to be iterative with the focal point being which data are indeed necessary for verification and which are indeed proprietary.

V. Conclusions

This paper has addressed some of the issues related to the instrumented monitoring of a chemical weapons treaty. Individual instruments for measuring specific parameters are available or technically feasible. Security sensors are already available; physical-parameter monitors are also available; general purpose in-line product analysers are feasible, although special features may need to be designed for specific application to chemical weapons treaty verification. Data-collection modules with capabilities for unattended operation are within the state of the art.

Substantial work remains to be done in the development of verification systems. There is the question of what minimum information is necessary for each facility or class of facilities, to ensure that they are in compliance with the provisions of the treaty. Also, how can a monitoring system be constructed to collect that information, that is, what would be a cost-effective combination of instruments? Attempts to address these questions would contribute substantially to negotiating on a Chemical Weapons Convention.

References

[1] Johnson, C. S. and Martinez, R. L., 'Development of tamper-protected sensors', Report No. SAND 87-2730, Sandia National Laboratories, Albuquerque, NM, Dec. 1987.

[2] Mangan, D. L., 'Hardware for potential surveillance and monitoring applications', presented at the *13th Workshop of the Pugwash Study Group on Chemical Warfare: Monitoring a Chemical Weapons Treaty*, Geneva, 23-24 Jan. 1988.

[3] Kyriakopoulos, N. 'Global data collection via the international telephone network', *Proceedings of the International Telemetering Conference*, vol. 18, San Diego, CA, 1982, pp. 39-47.

[4] Mangan (see note 2).

[5] Johnson and Martinez (see note 1).

[6] Callis, J. B., Illman, D. L., and Kowalski, B. R., 'Process analytical chemistry', *Analytical Chemistry*, vol. 59 (1987), p. 624A.

[7] Callis (see note 6); Sander, R. K. and Buchwald, M. I., 'Some laser techniques for chemical detection', *Proceedings of Symposium on Substance Decontamination*, eds G. C. Outterson and F. M. Prociv, Battelle, Columbus, Ohio, April 1980, pp. 8-15; and 'Optical fiber spectrocopy', *Energy and Technology Review*, Lawrence Livermore Laboratories, Livermore, CA, July 1987.

[8] Kyriakopoulos (see note 3.)

[9] Kyriakopoulos, N., Kuroi, H. and Sheaks, O. J., 'TRANSEAVER: a security system for international sea transport', *Proceedings International Conference on Communications*, Toronto, 1986, pp. 949-54.

[10] Kuroi, H. and Kyriakopoulos, N., 'Experimental monitoring of safeguards sensors', presented at the *13th Workshop of the Pugwash Study Group on Chemical Warfare: Monitoring a Chemical Weapons Treaty*, Geneva, 23-24 Jan. 1988.

[11] Kyriakopoulos, N., 'Artemis: a security system for international sea transport', *Proceedings: Workshop on Automatic Monitoring in Verification of Chemical Disarmament*, Helsinki, 12-14 Feb. 1987, pp. 66-78.

[12] Koskinen, L. and Hirvonen, H., 'Technical solutions for automatic monitoring of chemical warfare agents', *Proceedings: Workshop on Automatic Monitoring in Verification of Chemical Disarmament*, Helsinki, 12-14 Feb. 1987, pp. 9-36.

RELIABLE IDENTIFICATION OF CHEMICAL-WARFARE AGENT MICRO-CONCENTRATIONS AS THE BASIS FOR A SYSTEM OF VERIFYING COMPLIANCE WITH THE NON-PRODUCTION OF CHEMICAL WEAPONS

V. A. RYLOV, the USSR

A claim that one of the parties to an agreement banning chemical weapons has violated the agreement is an extremely ponderous step and should be based on absolutely reliable data.

In this context, the key issue in verification is not just detection, but rather a reliable identification of minute quantities (10^{-10} to 10^{-12} grams and less) and concentrations (10^{-7} to 10^{-10} weight per cent and less) of substances representing certain classes, the precursors of the aforementioned substances or the products of their decomposition (hereafter referred to as 'key substances'). What is more, such detection must be carried out in the presence of numerous known and unknown substances whose concentrations exceed many times over the concentration of the compound being sought.

In view of the above, a monitoring system based on automatic sensors placed at control points cannot be effective. This is because not one of these devices assures fulfilment of the main requirement for a verification system: selective, highly sensitive and reliable identification of key substances and their chemical relatives.

Reliable, high sensitivity identification of key substances in air, water and other solvents is, in practice, possible by a comprehensive analysis of the samples under investigation using various physico-chemical methodologies. Only methods such as mass-spectrometry applying a broad range of pressures at the ion source including laser mass-spectrometry, optico-acoustical infra-red spectrometry with Fourier transformations, and multi-element plasma spectroscopy combined with multi-dimensional gas and liquid chromatography using various highly sensitive selective detectors such as those utilizing enzymatic and immunological methods give information on the structure of the micro-quantities of the substance being analysed. Reliable identification at the levels necessary for the verification of compliance with an agreement banning chemical weapons can only be achieved by a comprehensive application of these methods in combination with selective sample preparation and purification.

Extensive use of such equipment is, obviously, impossible--both from the technical and economical point of view.

Hence, from every point of view, the most appropriate method lies not in the on-site installation of verification equipment, but in the installation of automatic air-sampling devices (for the analysis of aerosols and gases), water-sampling devices and, if necessary, of those for the sampling of soil in combination with periodic transferral of sealed sample [containers] to the appropriate national and international verification centre(s) equipped with the corresponding complex of modern equipment necessary for sample preparation, concentration, highly sensitive and selective identification.

Given proper automation of sampling, sample preparation, concentration, introduction into the apparatus and data-processing work organized along the suggested lines would allow fulfilment of the verification tasks with high levels of confidence. Also fewer experts would be required and the costs associated with the organization, content and functioning of the verification system would be much lower in comparison with a system of automatic sensors even if such a system were capable of reliable identification.

Verification of compliance with an agreement on non-production of chemical-warfare agents in production facilities could be achieved by the installation of sampling devices in the immediate vicinity of entities which previously produced chemical weaponry and associated precursors. In the case of a factory (which would be declared in the framework of a future agreement) subjected to monitoring, verification of the agreement could be assured for the entire plant by the installation of such devices in the immediate vicinity (or even within) the factory grounds. In such a case, all that would be required is that a sufficient volume of sample mixture pass through the collector and then be concentrated. The subsequent selective sample preparation based on the use of multi-level liquid and gas capillary chromatography will ensure the determination of key substances at the required levels (10^{-7} to 10^{-10} weight per cent and less). If necessary, detection levels can be lowered to even 10^{-12} to 10^{-14} weight per cent (when using the appropriate equipment and system of sample preparation). Such detection levels make verification of compliance with the agreement of non-production of chemical-warfare agents with high levels of confidence possible and also point to two problems of verification which, in our opinion, have not received adequate attention so far.

The first lies in the fact that at the detection levels described above, key substances may be detected at the site of an entity which previously produced chemical weaponry for a long time after the halting of production, even if the most careful steps are taken in cleaning equipment and tubing. For that reason, it is a prerequisite to dismantle completely all the equipment in these entities and to replace it with new equipment. Another possibility is to halt production and agree upon a certain permitted detection level (higher than the detection level of the standard equipment in use today) for example 10^{-7} to 10^{-8} weight per cent below which the equipment is considered as not being used for agent production.

The second problem lies in excluding the potential for discovering the compostion of the product of a factory during verification of a chemical-warfare agent production ban at a particular site when this compostion is an industrial secret. The task of identifying sub-micro quantities of unknown components of mixtures on which no previous information is at hand is an unusually difficult task in comparison with the detection of known (key) substances--even using the entire complex of equipment outlined above. Almost the only possible solution to that problem, from the standpoint of excluding the possibility of identifying the composition of the products not subject to verification, consists in using a strictly regulated, controlled automatic methodology of sample preparation and analysis--based on introducing certain fractions of the sample (which correspond to the key substances and are produced with the help of liquid and gas chromatography) to the analysing device. The entire analytical sample (resulting from sample preparation and concentration) must be either consumed in the process of analysis or destroyed. The entire analysis would be carried out using robot technology and accordingly be accompanied by minimal human involvement.

In particular, the verification of compliance with an agreement using the system suggested here, which is based on an automatic sampling and automatic sample analysis in international and national centres (the sequence of operations when using the corresponding methods of analysis can be strictly regulated and controlled), helps to resolve not only the problem of verification but also the problem of preventing technological espionage. This is an additional advantage of the system. One must also note that limiting the detection levels for key substances would further facilitate the solution of this problem.

It is clear that a verification system based on periodic on-site inspections has many disadvantages in comparison with the centralized one we have proposed. In particular, the periodic system requires the use of highly qualified technical experts, but we are not sure they can reach a final decision without substantiating their doubts at verification centres. Under such a system the potential for industrial espionage is maximized--besides which, interference in the production activity of national enterprises would take place.

We consider that the equipment applied for the purpose of the maintenance of industrial safety measures cannot be used for verification of fulfilment of the agreement. These devices could only be used in complementary roles. For this purpose, the special equipment or the analysis methodology possessing higher selectivity and higher sensitivity for identification of key substances is needed.

As far as verification (inspection) of the production of declared quantities of any of the substances listed in Schedule 2 is concerned, it is more appropriate to use commercial chromatographs or to use continuous or quasi-continuous selective-analysis machinery in order to check on commercial productions, effluent gases or waste water. Automatic monitoring of the non-production of the contemplated substances can be assured by a multi-faceted verification system such as this at the desired levels and in a timely manner. Obviously, the appropriate analysis methodology using the same type of equipment would have to be agreed upon by all negotiating parties.

The system suggested here--based on automatic sampling, subsequent selective-sample preparation, based on multi-dimensional liquid and gas chromatography and multi-faceted physico-chemical analysis of key substance fractions--is the system, among the various verification systems compared, which fulfils the requirements of a verification system most fully. These requirements are: reliable detection of sub-micro quantities and concentrations of key substances in mixtures containing known and unknown substances, the exclusion of industrial espionage during the process of verifying non-production, and economic viability. Sample preparation and analysis must be conducted at the appropriate verification centres equipped with the necessary machinery. It should also be noted, that this system allows verification not only of factories, but also of chemical-warfare testing ranges. The equipment needed for sampling, sample preparation and identification that has been chosen by experts for the verification system and centres must be subjected to prior scrutiny by experts of the interested negotiating parties.

APPROACHES TO THE USE OF INSTRUMENTS IN MONITORING THE PRODUCTION OF CHEMICAL WEAPONS AND PRECURSOR CHEMICALS

L. ZEFTEL, P. WEINBERG and J. SCHROY, the USA

I. Introduction

The purpose of this paper is to present a review of current production-monitoring practices of the civil chemical industry to determine how these practices may interrelate with the requirements for monitoring for chemical weapons and their precursors. Since this kind of monitoring is a new concept for the civil chemical industry, the subject matter will be divided into three areas: (a) the purpose of monitoring in the civil chemical industry and industry concerns over chemical-weapon monitoring; (b) a historical overview of process-monitoring technology; and (c) general process-monitoring procedures.

II. Purpose of current monitoring practices and industry concerns

It is necessary to discuss the purpose of current monitoring practices in order to understand the impact that monitoring for chemical weapons will have on the chemical industry.

Current monitoring practices in the civil chemical industry evolved from the needs to: (a) ensure the most economic utilization of raw materials and equipment; (b) ensure the production of specification grade and quality end-products; and (c) track the emissions of solid, liquid or gaseous by-products to the environment. Basically, monitoring is done to obtain a material balance using instruments to replace or supplement people. Monitoring practices and their accuracy vary with the state of the art, the environmental regulatory requirements of the *state* where production occurs, the economics of monitoring vs. the economic benefits obtained by better utilization of raw materials and equipment, and any desired improvement in the quality of the end-product. Where environmental concerns are dominant, economics are usually of lesser concern and where there are no environmental problems, economics dictate the use and requirements of monitoring systems.

Monitoring to meet environmental concerns is perhaps more closely related to monitoring for chemical-weapons systems than monitoring for economic and quality concerns. However, as regards economics and quality concerns, all data obtained from monitoring systems are considered proprietary and confidential and are not normally disseminated outside the facility or company. Any data submitted to a *state* are usually in the form of an annual aggregate number of finished-product weight submitted on a company basis.

Occasionally a similar aggregate number may also be released to a trade association or trade journal. All numbers are usually in ranges and the narrower the range, the more confidentiality is requested to protect the commercial viability of the company submitting the data. Loss of confidential information is of concern because of intense economic competition among companies and countries. In some cases, national security may also be involved.

Where monitoring is done primarily for environmental reasons, a different relationship exists. Monitoring systems are designed to alert, record, and maintain a history for inspection by plant and/or company management, as well as by local, state or national environmental agencies. Monitoring is usually done to determine whether selected, but not necessarily toxic chemicals are released into the environment, and, if so, in what quantities. Also, monitoring is done to discover whether any unusual situations have occurred such as a spill or vapour emission which may cause a change in the environment--a spill of a non-monitored chemical, for example, an acid, which may affect the pH of a waterway or be a threat to aquatic life.

In all of the aforementioned areas, data obtained from the monitoring systems are also treated as confidential by environmental agencies unless there is concern that excessive release of a chemical to the environment will be harmful. If the data are made public, the information deals *only with the release into--and the effect on--the environment. No data that could be considered intellectual property are disclosed to the public and certainly not made available for review by competitors.*

This is a very important factor and bears repeating. *When data of environmental concern are made public, either due to new knowledge about a chemical in commercial use or due to an accidental release of a known or suspected harmful chemical into the environment, no specific data on the amount of production of the chemical product, the use of precursor raw materials or the process technology used are disclosed other than what is currently available in the public scientific and trade literature. Business confidentiality is maintained.*

It is highly probable that monitoring systems currently used in the civil chemical industry can also be used as monitoring systems for chemical-weapon control, either as is or with reasonably achievable modifications. However, since the *end requirements* of monitoring for chemical-weapon control differ significantly from current industrial controls, the data obtained and the dissemination of that data are of concern to the chemical industry in that protection of confidentiality becomes of critical importance to the chemical industry.

Confidential information will be subject to potential compromise whenever a monitoring system is required. The compromise will occur when analysing the process to determine what variables need to be monitored, through data collection, and when servicing the monitoring equipment. Some of the compromised information will be related to the processes to be monitored. However, much data on other non-treaty-designated products made in the same equipment, as well as information on products made in other equipment on the plant, may be compromised. This information will include process technology, process capability and capacity data. Also, technology related to monitoring equipment and instruments will be lost. The extent of information lost when designing a system, through the collection of data and the handling of monitoring equipment can be estimated knowing the system to be monitored, but assigning an exact economic penalty may be difficult. The amount of the information lost due to servicing the equipment will depend on how frequently service personnel visit a site, the background of the service personnel, the extent that their movement is controlled while on the plant, and the degree to which descriptive information (raw material containers, labelling of storage facilities, personnel communications and the like) is controlled.

Another issue is how much will monitoring interfere with plant operation? *Monitoring systems cannot be allowed to affect the safety of a plant.* A significant economic penalty could result if the process equipment cannot be used when the monitoring system is not working. Also, if a non-regulated product required a high level of confidentiality, it would have to be made when monitoring is not being done or the operation would have to be moved to a facility which is not monitored, at considerable economic expense.

Recognizing the aforementioned concerns of the chemical industry, let us now review the state of the art of current production-monitoring systems and practices of the civil chemical industry.

III. Historical overview of process-monitoring technology

Introduction and definitions

The objective of this section is to review the capabilities of present technology in the area of 'remote process monitoring' and describe how these technologies can be applied to chemical-production units when and where it is considered appropriate. To prevent confusion due to language differences and differences in technical perspective, a number of definitions are given below. The definitions are based on the perspective of an engineer in the United States and assume the technology discussed will be available to all the parties of the Convention.

• Remote monitoring is the process of transmitting equipment operating parameters from instruments located on or near the equipment to a location separated from the production facility by a large distance.

• Remote sensing is the process of determining a production-operating parameter through instruments not physically connected to the production equipment. The instruments may be located near the equipment or they may be at a location considered remote from the production unit.

• Remote communication is the process for transmitting data over long distances via direct or indirect communication links, such as phone lines, satellite stations or infra-red transmission systems. Long distances in these cases mean many hundreds of miles.

General description

The monitoring of chemical processes has varied greatly over the life of the chemical industry due to changes in attitudes on issues of personnel safety and dramatic changes in technologies. Most chemical processes started as batch-reactor systems with operators hand-feeding ingredients and stirring the reactors with wooden paddles. Process monitoring, in many cases, was left to the operator who used reactor temperatures, product colour or consistency, odour and so on to establish batch completion.

Since those early beginnings, many changes have occurred related to understanding process parameters and the methods for controlling reactions.

These changes have led to large continuous processes, as well as small-batch processes that produce reproducible high-quality products. This has been true in the developed countries of the world for over 50 years, but not true of the world as a whole. Naturally the degree of sophistication used in making chemicals varies from one end of the technical spectrum to the other, depending on the economics of the country producing the chemical. In most countries, economics will translate to the availability, cost and sophistication of the work-force in that country. Large and small hand-stirred reactors may still be found in some locations because of readily available low-cost labour, even though we have the technology available to run fully automated batch and/or continuous processes.

Today's technology allows fully automated processes, using distributed-control systems, to be monitored and supervised by a central computer system located halfway around the world. The supervisory computer system could also be equipped with a full process-simulation capability, which could verify the validity and security of all reported field-instrument readings. Such systems are being used as training tools for new processes and new operators to insure proper operation of the large complex systems prior to loading of chemicals. The simulation systems grew out of simulation systems used initially in the 1970s to design new processes without the need for several scale-up experiments prior to construction of a commercial-scale facility.

The advent of the small high-powered computer systems have allowed control systems to become small self-contained control devices distributed throughout the process. This distributive-control system has reduced control costs and led to improved control performance. The central control room has simply become a monitoring and supervisory control station with further reduction in manpower needs for operating the plants.

However, the systems described above are sophisticated controls dependent on sophisticated computer technology that is not available throughout the world. *In some cases, the process simulation technology may be a matter of industrial confidentiality, which makes the company competitive and profitable.*

The issues discussed above are critical in that remote monitoring can be rather simple for some facilities, while impossible in others, such as those which utilize low-cost labour in place of instruments. For those facilities where remote monitoring is not practicable, remote sensing may be possible, although more difficult and less precise. In those cases, monitoring process emissions, and relating emissions to production, would provide an indirect understanding of the production rate.

Equipment discussion

The following discussion provides a brief summary of each technology that may be found in chemical-production units. The discussion deals with the advantages and disadvantages of the monitors and highlights issues of calibration, maintenance, reliability and security of the signals. None of these issues can be covered in detail in this paper, but highlights will be presented. Systems utilizing hand-stirred reactors, which use operators as process-variable observers and controllers, will not be discussed.

Analogue monitors

The technology of using analogue devices for monitoring and controlling a chemical process dates to the 1950s. Analogue control devices are reliable, easily calibrated and offer the simplest instrument-control options available. A disadvantage of using an analogue signal for both monitoring and controlling the process involves the high cost of transmittal of low-voltage or pneumatic signals over even short distances. The fact that the controller utilizes the signal produced by the instrument directly means that calibration is only necessary to provide a read-out that the operator can understand. This constitutes a second point where the signal could be manipulated, the first point being the initial calibration. The instrument does not have to be calibrated to perform its function. It should be noted that most monitors used on process equipment produce an analogue signal, and to interface with a digital computer, an analogue-to-digital (A to D) signal converter is necessary. The use of an A to D converter allows a third point at which the signal can be changed or modified to give a fictitious value to the instrument-output parameter. This is a disadvantage of most of the monitoring equipment used in the chemical industry today. To ensure that the conversion factors are proper, validation efforts may require direct observation of one or more of the key production variables, such as product output or raw-material utilization, or use of previously mentioned process-simulation technology. To use process-simulation technology, it will be necessary to have a logging and supervisory control computer in the central control room. This technology is discussed below.

Digital monitors

The technology to utilize digital signals for control of process variables came into use in the mid-1970s and is based on the adaptation of computers to process-control functions. The hybrid technology of using analogue controllers hooked to digital computers is still in wide use, but will disappear as digital computers get smaller and have greater capacity. As new processes are installed in the late 1980s, most will employ digital-based technology which will dominate in the 1990s. For some process variables, analogue to digital converters may be necessary due to the difficulty of producing a digital signal from many process instruments. The problems encountered when using A to D converters are discussed above. The disadvantage for remote-monitoring systems of having many small digital computers located throughout the process is one of the validation of many separate systems. The person inspecting the remote-monitoring equipment will have to be thoroughly knowledgeable of the process technology being used to produce the monitored chemical. Unlike the analogue systems discussed above, the digital-control systems require that the signal produced by the instruments, either directly or via an analogue-to-digital converter, must be correct. This means the instrument must be maintained on a continuous basis. While maintenance technology for analogue instruments is easily taught, the technology involved in digital instruments and microcomputer technology is not. The availability of parts and trained labour may be a major obstacle in many parts of the world.

Distributive controls

The advent of small high-powered computers has led to the development of direct installation of the computer in a field-control loop and is known as a distributive-control system. These systems utilizing central computers as logging and supervisory control stations, are the new state of the art technology and will be the technology of the 1990s. Remote monitoring by the central control computer is quite consistent with the desire to monitor processes from great distances. With the advent of inexpensive data-transmission technology, systems using distributive controls can be monitored from great distances. The above discussion of digital monitors also applies to distributive-control systems. The one advantage that a centralized monitoring and supervisory control system offers is the ability to simulate the process to determine if the process instruments are functioning properly.

Process simulation

The development of process-simulation technology is not new. However, the advent of the small computer and the change in the role of the central control computer has allowed the application of simulation technology as part of the process-operating system to allow training and process evaluations on-line in real time. The direct application to process-control systems has provided a new level of expertise to the system and required an increased level of training of the operating staff. These systems cannot be operated by semi-skilled personnel and, for many locations, this is a significant disadvantage. The level of training for the instrument-maintenance personnel has also increased greatly.

The availability of a process simulator in an operating unit does create one additional level of complexity in the security and reliability of the data. *The remote monitoring of the process will require some method of ensuring that the signals being transmitted are from the process instruments and not from the process simulator.*

Remote transmission technology

The development of satellite-communication systems has led to the elimination of the word 'remote' from the communications language base. There is no place on earth which has electricity that can be considered remote. Any communication needs can be met using simple, easily operated equipment for the transmission of voice and data. Some potential disadvantages of utilizing this type of technology may still be the level of training required of the personnel operating and maintaining the equipment and the availability of spare parts.

IV. A general process-monitoring system

Computerized process-monitoring systems have been in existence for over 10 years, allowing the chemical industry to obtain and store process-data information in a chronological and organized fashion. This has allowed process operators and engineers to have both access to data for purposes of obtaining a better understanding of their operations and the ability to suggest and improve operational enhancements. During this time, many improvements have been made in the hardware and software used in process-monitoring systems. The hardware improvements have resulted in equipment which is more reliable, occupies less space, performs many more functions and is less costly. The software has added many more functions which allow more types of data displays, including process flow-sheet graphics, data trending, data analysis and data storage.

There are a number of systems currently available on the US market for monitoring process data. There are also systems developed by companies and used 'in-house' only. They all involve the use of sophisticated electronic equipment, including process-measuring instruments, controllers, local-data transmitters, data collectors, data communicators, and computers and video displays.

The information described below is a typical process-monitoring system with the capability of transmitting the information to locations off-site of the actual process area. Many other systems can be suggested and are capable of performing the same functions. The differences will be in terms of functional performance, cost and manageability. Figure 1 presents a typical layout of a system which can monitor several operations on one site, in addition to processes at other sites.

The layout shows equipment which is typically used in a data-monitoring and display system. Major parts include the process-measuring instruments (not shown), data-acquisition (collection) hardware, computers, data-line multiplexors, data-communication modems (not shown), display stations, printers and computers. The function and, in some cases, the reliability and relative cost of each of these will be discussed below.

Process-measuring instruments

Before selecting the measuring instruments, the first function which must be performed is a study of the process to determine the specific information which must be monitored. The stated purpose of the system will be to detect the production of disallowed chemicals or production of excessive volume of restricted chemicals. Typical process information to be monitored may include raw material and product storage-tank levels and pipeline-flow rates, including temperatures and pressures. This information may be employed in material-balance calculations to reconcile consumption of raw materials with production of product. In order to determine if the process is actually operating, selected information may be monitored which could include process-vessel pressure and temperature, as well as the on/off status of pump and agitator motors and switches. In-line composition detectors are also necessary for detecting the actual chemicals which are being handled.

Instruments vary significantly in their function, reliability and cost. Each of them must have the capability of transmitting a standard electronic (preferred) or pneumatic signal to a regionally or centrally located data collector in the process area or control room. This is usually done through a process-signal transmitter.

The measuring instrument is the part of the monitoring system where the most attention to quality equipment should be placed. A good quality instrument, well-designed for the particular application, properly located and installed, and properly maintained, will give consistent, reliable data. Failure to follow these guide-lines will result in the collection of information which may be of questionable value.

Costs may range from less than one hundred dollars for a temperature-measuring thermocouple, to several hundred dollars for a simple flow meter, and several thousand dollars for an in-line composition-measuring instrument. It should be noted that significant attention must be given to instrument maintenance. Since all data collected is considered important, procedures must be set up to service the instruments routinely, checking calibration and functionality. In-line composition-type instruments will likely require significantly more maintenance than the traditional flow, temperature and pressure types.

Data-collection systems

These instruments, or systems, function mainly as collectors of process signals and convert them to a form which may be transmitted to a computer for further processing. They can, however, perform many other functions, including data display and reporting, and--when connected to certain personal computers running special software--may serve as 'stand-alone' local monitoring and data-display systems with no other hardware requirements. However, as stand-alone monitoring and display systems, off-site data access is limited. In addition, these systems have limited data storage and data-analysis capability. As a result, it is preferred that data collected by this equipment be transmitted to a large host computer for data processing, analysis, storage and display. The collected data is transmitted via a communication cable or line using standard communication protocols acceptable to most computers.

Data-collection systems are available to handle pneumatic, as well as electronic information. The cost of such systems may vary from about US $2000 for a small system with little functionality to upwards of US $20 000 for a system which can collect large quantities of data and perform a wide variety of other functions. This hardware is quite reliable and easy to maintain. A supply of spare parts, a manual and some knowledge of the electronic equipment is required.

Data communications

This equipment consists of modems and multiplexors which help carry the process data long distances over telephone-data lines, from the data collectors to the host computer. In easily understood terms, a multiplexor is a device which combines data from several data lines onto one line for transmission to another location. At the receiving end resides a de-multiplexor which recognizes the data and redistributes it onto separate lines. The modem prepares the data for transmission by converting the signal from analogue to digital form. The modem at the receiving end converts it back to analogue form. Transmission of data in digital form is subject to less error because there is little or no signal decay.

In addition to transmitting data over telephone lines, transmission via satellite is possible. Hardware is currently available to condition the data signals to perform this operation. This technique is useful when transmitting over large distance, particularly across areas which have poor-quality telephone service (or no service).

Multiplexors may cost about US $3000 to US $4000 for a set which will combine 8 channels of data. Sets are available to handle 32 channels and possess diagnostic routines for communication problem solving. These may cost up to US $10 000 or more. They are usually very reliable and occasional failures are easy to diagnose and repair.

Modems are fairly inexpensive devices which may cost from several hundred to about a thousand dollars, depending upon transmission speed and diagnostics built into them. They, too, are reliable. If one fails, it is not normally repaired, but replaced.

Computer systems

Computer systems to handle data acquired from a chemical-process data-acquisition system vary widely in type. Available personal-computer systems are not likely to be suitable for data which must be filed for long-term use and be readily accessible for use upon short notice. They may also limit the number of users who have access to the information and provide limited-area data-analysis software capability. The minicomputer is the best selection for multiple, off-site process-data handling. It can handle significant numbers of simultaneous users, process large quantities of data within small time intervals, possess large-scale, long-term disk storage capabilities, and have the capability to provide multiple data-analysis software packages.

One scenario for designing a system is to use minicomputers (costing in the area of US $20 000 to US $30 000) at locations which are centrally located near several processes. These computers can process the collected data and distribute the information to its users. Another larger minicomputer and associated magnetic data-storage equipment (at a total cost of several hundred thousand dollars) may be used to receive data from the smaller computers for purposes of long-term data storage and data analysis, as well as data display. This design may have advantages over one which employs one large computer collecting data from all monitored sites. The multi-computer plan allows more flexibility in managing the system. For example, a single computer failure would not affect the entire monitoring system. Instead, it would affect only a part of the system. Experience with these types of computers indicates that with good management, they can have 'uptimes' of 99 per cent or greater. (This includes downtime for software and hardware upgrades and an occasional hardware failure.) The key is to manage the facility to optimize availability and to have a good maintenance support system. Computer system management is important. Depending upon the complexity of the systems, one or more people will be required to keep the equipment and software running trouble-free.

Software systems which will perform process-monitoring and display functions are widely available for personal computers. They are also available for a wide variety of commercially available Distributive-Control Systems (DCS). Unfortunately, the availability of this type of software for larger computer systems not tied to a DCS is not well known, but probably exists. Several chemical companies possess software packages developed (and used) 'in-house'. However, these may not be available for outside use. In general, systems which have been in use for several years may be considered to be relatively error-free.

Other software packages should be available on the centrally located computers. They should be capable of statistical analysis, data organization, data tabulation and graphic display.

Another function which will be very useful is chemical-process mathematical-simulation software. There are several commercially available products which are widely used and easy to learn. These can be employed to calculate material balances for purposes of discovering unusual imbalances between raw materials consumed and product produced.

Data storage

Whatever system is chosen for the process-monitoring function, it is strongly suggested that sufficient planning and design be performed to allow long-term data-storage capability. This includes the hardware to store the data, usually magnetic storage disks and tape or cassette drives, and the software to create and organize the long-term data files. The software should allow easy file maintenance and simplicity of file organization. This will minimize the need for human intervention in the maintenance of the long-term historical data. *In addition, it should be designed to allow easy, but secured and controlled access to users, should the need arise.* The system should allow sufficient data to be stored 'on-line' so that no delay or human intervention is required for authorized requests for data. Finally, the system should allow easy and organized data-file 'back-up' capability. These 'back-ups' should be stored in separate, protected facilities in case of 'on-line' storage-media destruction.

Confidentiality of data

All data should be encrypted, so that all data transmission, storage, and access will be limited to authorized personnel only. This authorized group should be as few in number as possible.

Data access

If the concept of a centrally (or several centrally) located computers is employed, they must be accessible by authorized users located on- and off-site. This is not difficult. Users on-site can be connected through commercially available local-area networks which are compatible with the computers and video-display terminals in use. Many reliable systems are available. Off-site users may be connected via wide-area networks and the technology for this is commercially available, too. In addition, the option for dial-up capability may be supplied. *In any case, care must be taken to secure the networks and computers from unwanted intruders.*

Potential problems

Despite the high reliability of a process-monitoring system containing quality hardware and software, there are many potential problems to be addressed to assure that the collected data are accurate, honest and timely. *Intentional and unintentional tampering with the systems is not something which can be overlooked and may be very difficult to police.* Several issues addressing these concerns will be discussed.

It was suggested earlier that the quality of the data collected is very dependent upon the raw data collected by the measuring instruments. These instruments must be properly maintained and frequently calibrated to ensure accuracy. This is usually a labour-intensive procedure which is dependent upon the knowledge and abilities of the person servicing the instrument. Sometimes, this operation may necessarily interfere with the production process. For example, pipe joints may leak in the measuring-element area, creating process hazards. Or, the instruments may have deleterious effects on flow through the pipes or equipment. Sometimes, flow streams must be stopped or diverted in order to repair an instrument problem. This must be taken into consideration when determining the monitoring requirements for the process.

Unfortunately, today's instruments are usually quite easily tampered with. Intentional modification of the calibration can, for example, make large flows look small. However, a good material balance using a simulation software package may detect this type of tampering. One method of minimizing intentional tampering is to enclose the instrument and transmitter in a box which may be entered only by authorized personnel.

Other types of problems may involve transmission of the signal from the transmitter to the data collector. A break in the signal wire (intentional or accidental) can cause outage for a significant time period. Process-operating conditions during this time will be unknown and changes in production rates may go unnoticed.

Any hardware failure in the data collector, the communication equipment or the computer will result in lost data. Fortunately, this equipment is usually very reliable (greater than 99 per cent). However, the 'uptime' of the system is directly related to the ability of the maintenance personnel to quickly diagnose and repair the hardware. If the local-facility personnel are responsible for maintaining the monitoring systems, as well as the plant operation, their priorities will address their employer's obligations first. If the plant is not well staffed, this can result in significant downtime for the monitoring systems. The plant personnel know that the 'non-company' monitoring system is not needed to properly operate their plant.

Another problem is one of technical knowledge 'giveaway'. Many small companies and Third World countries do not have the technical expertise to properly instrument the chemical process. Use of sophisticated electronic and solid-state hardware is rare. Use of sophisticated software simulation programs is unknown. What are the implications of installing (giving) this type of expertise to companies which compete with large, modernly operated companies? Can they be protected so that the unsophisticated company does not use the 'gift' against its sophisticated competitors? In many cases, it is a small difference in expertise which gives one company the competitive edge over its competition--small differences which can 'make or break' a company's balance sheet.

An important aspect of remote process monitoring as described above is the need to standardize the type of equipment and software employed throughout the verification system. This will reduce the span of technical knowledge required to maintain the systems. The net result will be improved 'uptime' for the entire system.

An additional issue is cheating. Cheating can range from the ongoing production of large quantities of chemicals to a quick campaign to make a few tonnes. Someone who wants to cheat can try to hide the operation in a facility being monitored or use an unmonitored site. Speciality-chemicals facilities with corrosion-resistant equipment which can be readily adapted to make precursors of/or chemical weapons exist throughout the world. Additional similar facilities to produce the ever-increasing number of new speciality chemicals (polymer, agricultural, pharmaceutical) will be built in the future. Use of unmonitored equipment would be very possible and prevention of this type of cheating will be very difficult to control. If cheating were not a concern, less confidential information would be lost by discontinuing monitoring when making non-treaty-regulated products and by using plant personnel to service monitoring equipment The use of plant personnel to service monitoring equipment would greatly reduce the number of service personnel needed by the treaty-verification agency.

Conclusion

Remote process monitoring is a viable method of learning about the activities of a chemical plant. It can be very useful in assisting plant operators in running the plant efficiently and determining that it is being run correctly for chemical-weapon monitoring purposes. However, if the remote monitoring systems are not specified and installed correctly, or if they are not properly maintained, the information that they collect will be worthless. The work of dedicated people in specifying, installing and maintaining these systems is necessary to ensure a system which will carry out the extremely important function for which it is designed.

V. Summary

The chemical industry is supportive of exploring the use of instruments to monitor chemical-weapon systems and precursors as a means of replacing or supplementing use of personnel only. The instruments should be designed and employed in a manner which will minimize or eliminate intrusion into the normal technical and commercial practices of a facility and company.

Current monitoring practices for normal industrial use can serve as the foundation for instrumentation and monitoring technology which can be designed for chemical-weapon monitoring only. Finally, any monitoring system must also include means of safeguarding intellectual property by controlling the collection, storage, accessibility and dissemination of data collected by the monitors.

149

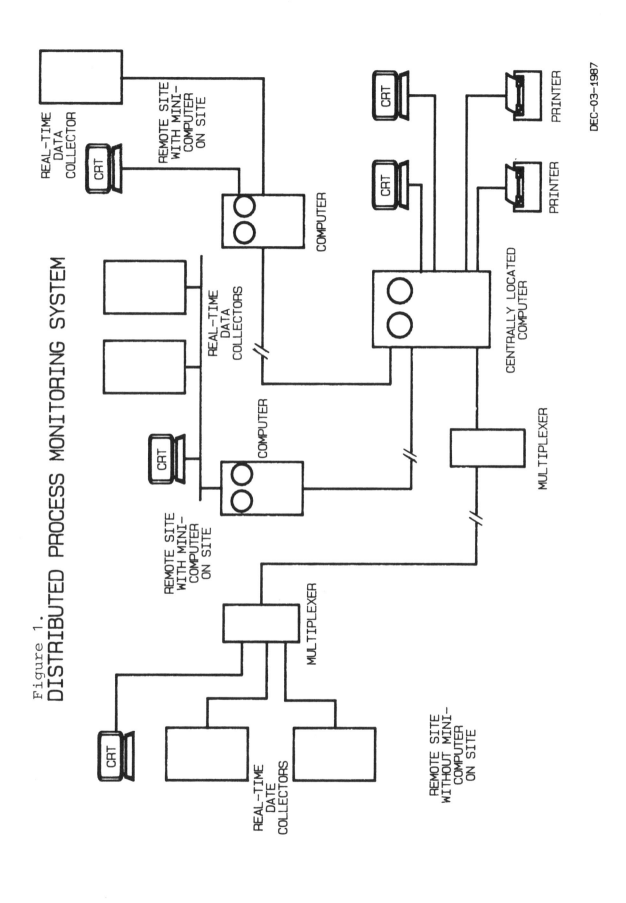

Figure 1.
DISTRIBUTED PROCESS MONITORING SYSTEM

DEC-03-1987

IV. COLLECTION AND USE OF PRODUCTION STATISTICS, HANDLING OF SENSITIVE INFORMATION

Considerations on the collection of production statistics and handling
of sensitive information under a Chemical Weapons Convention
K. NISHIKAWA, Japan

Remarks on data collection and handling of sensitive information
under a future Chemical Weapons Convention
O. V. PERRONI, Brazil

The data-reporting system in verification of non-production
SUN XIANGYIN, China

CONSIDERATIONS ON THE COLLECTION OF PRODUCTION STATISTICS AND HANDLING OF SENSITIVE INFORMATION UNDER A CHEMICAL WEAPONS CONVENTION

K. NISHIKAWA, Japan*

I. Introduction

The draft Convention on Chemical Weapons (CWC) being drawn up at the Conference on Disarmament (CD) currently in session in Geneva is intended to be applied to the precursors of super-toxic lethal chemicals (STLCs) and the chemicals which may be used as their basic raw materials, regardless of whether they are actually related to the production of chemical weapons or not, as a means to ensure the effectiveness of the Convention.

The chemical industry seems to be opposing the production, holding and use of chemical weapons from the viewpoint of world peace and humanitarianism and supporting the early signing of the Convention. When the Convention comes into force, the chemical industry will do its best to co-operate in its application. However, in the drafting of this Convention, care should be taken so that the Convention would not impose unduly strict restrictions on the activities of the chemical industry which have nothing to do with the production of chemical weapons so that the chemical industry could co-operate fully in its enforcement. In this respect, it will be necessary to have the opinions of the chemical industry, derived from its practical experiences, duly reflected in the process of negotiation of the Convention.

The author has been invited by SIPRI to write a paper representing his personal views on the provisions of Article VI of the Convention entitled 'Production Report'. Since the items which affect the chemical industry are the chemicals listed in Schedules 2 and 3, the discussion here will be in regard to the provisions on those chemicals.

II. Problems of restrictions imposed by the Convention in relation to the chemical industry

A fundamental perception

Among the chemicals included in the lists of Schedules 2 and 3 are those produced by the chemical industry which are used for applications unrelated to chemical weapons. The chemical industry understands that monitoring of the production of chemicals for peaceful purposes will also be necessary to increase the effectiveness of the CWC as relates to the non-production of chemical

---

*The views presented in this paper are those of the author. He is employed by the Japan Chemical Industry Association.

weapons, which is one of its primary objectives. However, it should be recognized that international monitoring of chemical production for peaceful purposes should never be the primary objective of the Convention but merely an auxiliary measure.

International monitoring of the chemical industry is claimed to be necessary for the verification of non-production of chemical weapons, but the STLCs used for chemical weapons are normally not produced by chemical companies. The effect of international monitoring of the raw materials used for a wide scope of applications, in the assurance of non-production of chemical weapons, is rather limited. The possible effect would be only the following:

1. The creation of a psychologically inhibiting effect on the unlawful production of chemical weapons in those countries which are signatories of the Convention and the detection of indications of such production.

2. The detection of indications of export of these chemicals as the raw material for production of chemical weapons in the non-signatory nations.

These effects are rather indirect as a means of ensuring the non-production of chemical weapons. It is therefore suggested that these provisions should not be the primary focus of the Convention but rather auxiliary to it. The main focus of the Convention should be related to the prohibition of production, stockpiling and the use of chemical weapons. This would be assured by verified disposal of existing chemical weapons and production facilities for them; and by verification of non-production of STLCs which might be converted into chemical weapons. In regard to these items, strict provisions should be incorporated into the Convention.

On the other hand, the provisions for the chemicals listed in Schedules 2 and 3 might be deliberated from a different angle. In speculating about the future application of the Convention, at such time as the aforementioned main part of the Convention has fulfilled its role to eliminate chemical weapons from the world, the international monitoring of the chemical industry which would have been an auxiliary part of the Convention might well become the primary focus of the Convention. If that were to be the case, it can be anticipated that each clause might start to lead an independent life from the Convention and be applied strictly and precisely. Despite the fact that the companies which are producing those chemicals listed in Schedules 2 and 3 have nothing to do with chemical weapons, they might be placed under permanent international monitoring under the Convention.

If the Convention is drafted based on the suspicion that the chemical industry could be an independent participant in the production of chemical weapons, the Convention might become an unbearably heavy burden for the chemical industry. In the drafting and application of the provisions related to the chemical industry, consideration should be given to minimizing its influence upon the peaceful chemical industry with sufficient recognition of the considerations discussed above.

Possible hampering of the chemical industry

The possible hampering of the peaceful activities of the chemical industry by the Convention might include those discussed below.

Confidentiality

It is important to guarantee that the various kinds of information related to corporate activities be kept confidential so that a fair competitive relationship in the world market can be maintained. The information related to production capacity, output, production planning, export quantities and customer information which is likely to be required in the Production Report envisaged under the Convention is important and confidential business information. If such information is presented to an international organization under the Convention, one can fear that it may be difficult to maintain its confidentiality.

Restrictions on the business activities of corporations

The business activities of the peaceful chemical industry should be fundamentally free. The international monitoring of the Convention may impose certain restrictions on the activities of the chemical industry particularly as regards production of chemicals listed in Schedule 2. Such restriction would be the inevitable result of the verification inspections, reporting of production planning and the like suggested for the Convention. It is also possible that monitoring under the CWC could injure the corporate image of chemical companies and lead to decisions to stop production of such chemicals to avoid damage to their corporate images. If so, this would constitute a most serious restriction on business activities.

Costs owing to observance of the regulations

A corporation may be required to bear the burden of the costs related to data reporting and accepted on-site inspection. Such costs might be small each time but could become burdensome if the regulatory process were continued for a long time. Items that must be considered in order to minimize such burdens are: (a) the protection of confidentiality, and (b) the reporting only of the necessary, minimal amount of data.

III. Production statistics in Japan

As a point of reference in the discussion of a useful design for the Production Report, a description of the current state of production statistics being collected in Japan is presented below.

The Japanese system of statistics

Designated statistics

The production statistics prepared by the Government are classified into three types called *designated statistics, approved statistics* and *administrative statistics*. The designated statistics are designated by the Director-General of the Management and Co-ordination Agency based on the Statistics Law.[1] The Statistics Law aims at securing truthful statistics, establishing the system for statistical investigation and improving and developing the statistical system. It prescribes the designation process and enforcement of the collection of designated statistics. The Law prescribes the system of statistical officers and statistical research staffs in charge of designated statistics in the central and local government. It also provides for the obligation for submission of designated statistics, on-site investigation, preservation of secrecy and publishing of the results. The provisions regarding preservation of secrecy are as follows:

1. The confidentiality of matters which belong to the business secrecy of a person, legal person or an organization and which have become known to the officers as the result of the designated statistics investigation must be protected.

2. No one is allowed to use the questionnaire sheet returned for the preparation of designated statistics for purposes other than those of the statistics.

3. The provisions of the foregoing clause do not apply to the use of the data which have been approved and made public by the Director-General of the Management and Co-ordination Agency. Production statistics which belong to such designated statistics are called the *dynamic production statistics* prepared by the Ministry of International Trade & Industry which is described below.

Approved statistics

Based on the Statistical Report Adjustment Law,[2] any statistical reporting which is requested by the administrative offices of the government must be approved beforehand by the Director-General of the Management and Co-ordination Agency. These statistics are called *approved statistics*. Designated statistics and the statistical report required by the law or government ordinances are excluded from this category.

This system aims to reduce the burden of the preparation of statistical reports and to increase the efficiency of administrative work through adjustment of the method of collection of statistical reports, the form of the reports and other matters related to their collection. The criteria used for approving applications for collecting statistics are that such collection is deemed reasonable and there is no duplication of existing statistics.

Reports required by the law

In regard to certain laws there are instances where the collection of statistical reports is required by law in order to perform administrative work provided for in the law. These statistics are called *administrative statistics*. Examples of these in production statistics are described below.

Chemical industry statistics in the dynamic production statistics

Dynamic production statistics are collected according to the Rule for Investigation of Dynamic Production Statistics of the Ministry of International Trade and Industry, which constitutes no. 11 of the designated statistics under the Statistics Law.[3] It reveals the dynamic state of mining and industrial production and aims at obtaining the basic data required for planning and implementing administrative measures for mining and industries.

The portion related to chemical industry in the dynamic production statistics is called the Chemical Industry Statistics[4] which will be discussed below.

The parties which are investigated by the Rule are all the workplaces which produce (including processing) the product items in the following ministerial ordinance list. The investigation is made by the use of reports covering each product sector. Items surveyed are: the amount of receipt, amount of production, amount of consumption, amount of shipment, value of shipment, inventory at the end of the month, amount of use of primary raw material, fuel and power, number of workers and production capacity for the month for each item of production.

The kinds of main reports and the number of product items are as follows:

1. Monthly report on ammonia and ammonia derivatives	9 items
2. Monthly report on calcium carbide and nitrous lime	2 items
3. Monthly report on phosphate fertilizers and compound fertilizers	8 items
4. Monthly report on sulfuric acid	1 item
5. Monthly report on soda industry chemicals	15 items
6. Monthly report on high pressure gases	11 items
7. Monthly report on inorganic chemicals, pigments and catalysts	83 items
8. Monthly report on explosives	11 items
9. Monthly report on coal-tar products	17 items
10. Monthly report on cyclic intermediates and synthetic dyes	27 items
11. Monthly report on organic chemicals	28 items
12. Monthly report on petrochemicals	65 items
13. Monthly report on plastics	47 items
14. Monthly report on oil and fat products and surface-active agents	38 items

15. Monthly report on photosensitizers .... 13 items
16. Monthly report on paints .... 26 items
17. Monthly report on printing inks .... 9 items

Chemicals listed in Schedules 2 and 3 are not found among these items because the product items are expressed in general names or product groups.

The contents of each report submitted by a company are kept strictly confidential but provision is made for publication of a summary of the results by the government office as soon as possible after the completion of the gathering and processing work. Chemical industry statistics are published according to the following schedules. A quick report of chemical industry statistics is made on the 23rd of the following month. A monthly report of chemical industry statistics is made 2 months later on the 15th. An annual report of chemical industry statistics is presented in June of the following year.

Investigation of the actual state of production, import of existing chemicals and the like

This investigation is an Approved Investigation (Approval no. 15640 of the Management and Co-ordination Agency). It is conducted by the Ministry of International Trade and Industry in order to ascertain the actual state of production, import and so on of what are known as the 'existing chemical substances' under the Law Concerning Examination and Regulation of Manufacture, etc. of Chemical Substances,[5] to thereby comply with the requirements of this Law.

This investigation requires that the workplaces where chemical substances are manufactured submit reports on the annual amounts of chemical substances manufactured and imported and amounts as classified by their use. Such an investigation is conducted once every three years. The Chemical Industry Statistics described above require the reporting of a number of items designated as 'production items' while this survey requests a report on each chemical substance which is indicated in the inventory of existing chemical substances under the Law Concerning Examination and Regulation of Manufacture, etc. of Chemical Substances. Since this investigation requests the reporting of sensitive information from chemical companies, which may belong to their business secrets, the results of the survey are kept strictly confidential and a summary of the results is not made public.

Notification of the amount of production and import based on the Law Concerning Examination and Regulation of Manufacture, etc. of Chemical Substances

An example of the reporting of production amounts as required by a law is the system of notification of the amount of production and import under the Law Concerning Examination and Regulation of Manufacture, etc. of Chemical Substances. This provision was first incorporated into a revision of this law in 1986.[6]

Designated chemical substance

The above-mentioned law designates the chemicals for which chronic toxicity is suspected based on the results of the minimum premarketing set of data (MPD) level tests as the 'designated chemical substance' and requires monitoring of the amount of production and import of such chemicals so that their residue in the environment does not build up to such a level as to influence human health. The parties which produce or import such designated chemical substances are obligated to report the annual amount of production and import of such chemicals to the Ministry of International Trade and Industry. The statistics of production and import of each designated chemical substance are published in the official gazette. At present 20 substances are listed as such designated chemical substances. A *partial* list of substances includes: trichloroethylene, tetrachloroethylene, chloroform, tetrachloromethane, 1,2-dichloroethane, 3,3-dichloro-4,4-diamino-diphenylmethane, 3,3-dichlorobenzidine, 1,4-dioxane, 2,4-dichloro-3-methylphenol and organic tin compounds (8 substances).

Class 2 specified chemical substances

Among the designated chemical substances, those which are deemed to cause remarkable environmental hazard and which may influence human health are subject to chronic toxicity tests. As a result, if their chronic toxicity is verified, they are designated as Class 2 specified chemical substances.

The Class 2 specified chemical substances are subject to such measures as improvement of the method of handling, restriction of their total production amount and so on in order to prevent environmental hazard. The enterprises must notify the amount of production or import (actual record) and the planned amount of production or import of such chemicals every year. When the production plan is changed, they must notify the authority beforehand. When they receive instructions regarding the change of production amount from the authority, they must follow such instructions.

IV. A suggestion for construction of the Production Report for the Convention on Chemical Weapons

The basic scheme of the report

According to the draft CWC, an authority of a State Party is obligated to monitor the chemical industry. In order to do so, it will be necessary for the State Party to incorporate provisions corresponding to Article VI of the Convention into its domestic law to provide for enforcement of the Convention.

Each State Party would be required to report to the international organization of the Convention concerning the chemicals listed in Schedules 2 and 3 and their production facilities in the form of both initial and annual declarations. Each State Party would be required not only to collect these data as required by domestic laws, but to abide by the Convention as well. In this case it would be appropriate to provide for submission of the necessary reports, but it would be excessive if the requirements would specify that the production in question be subject to approval or licence. These data belong to the category of confidential business information, and provisions for preservation of secrecy and prohibition of the use of confidential material for purposes other than monitoring under the CWC should be included in the domestic law.

The government would summarize and process the data submitted by each chemical company and then report to the international organization. A suggestion of how such a report to the international organization could be made is presented below.

Amount of production, import and export

In order to account for the amount of production in the preceding year, the total national production and the amount of production of each facility would be reported. The amount of production of each facility should be an approximate figure even for the chemicals listed in Schedule 2 so that confidential business information is protected. This should be sufficient for the purpose of 'International Monitoring' of the Convention.

The approximate amount might be expressed either by means of establishing a range of the amount or by means of round figures by setting significant figures. For example, in the case of range setting, a range of 10 tonnes would be available for an amount less than 100 tonnes, a range of 100 tonnes for 100 to 1000 tonnes and a range of 1000 tonnes for the tonnage over 1000 tonnes. Two significant figures might be sufficient.

When the chemicals in question are produced and consumed at the same site, it should be noted that the concept of annual production amount is not realistic. Therefore, it would be better to consider other methods, for example, in terms of tonnes/day. The amount of import and export should also be treated in the manner described above.

Application of chemicals

As for the chemicals listed in Schedule 2, the present rolling text of the CWC requests that the purpose of production of the chemical in question should be reported for each installation. As concerns use, however, the type of product for which the chemical is used may be reported but the exact chemical name of the product, the name of the consumer and the amount of the shipment could be excluded to preserve confidentiality. As concerns reporting of product type, the classification given in the Industrial Classification Table[7] used in each country might be suitable for use.

Planned production amount

In regard to the chemicals of Schedule 2, it has been discussed to ask for reporting of the planned production amount for the year following the year for which the annual declaration is made. This is probably because such a report is needed to prepare the on-site inspection plan for the year. If such is the case, it would be sufficient to report an approximate amount.

For chemical corporations, the plan for the following year represents only a tentative and approximate figure, and there is always the possibility that it will be revised owing to market changes or to changed circumstances for the customers of a company. When a company reports the planned amount of production, it would be required to report any modification of its reported production plan. Such frequent reporting would be cumbersome for the company. Even when the report of planned production is necessary, an approximate amount should be sufficient and correction of the report at a later time would not be appropriate. Another approach might be to report the planned amount by a range giving a maximum and a minimum amount; only when the actual production exceeded such a range would a correction report be presented.

Production capacity

There are various problems in regard to the reporting of production capacity. As the objective of the Convention is not the control of production capacity, it would be sufficient to report the approximate capacity.

In the calculation of production capacity, the performance of each item of equipment constituting the plant under normal operating conditions might be considered, but there are many assumptions in making such calculations. For example, production exceeding nominal capacity may well become possible as technology progresses even if no expansion of the plant is made. This means that the actual production capacity may change every year. Therefore it might be meaningless to report the production capacity as a precise figure. It would also not be necessary to verify the reported capacity. The reporting of production capacity should, therefore, be made by an approximate calculated capacity or by a range of maximum and minimum.

It may be difficult to express the capacity of a multi-purpose plant. Also in this case, it would be most practical to rely on the method of reporting in use at the chemical companies. When a plant manufactures several kinds of products, it is practical to calculate the annual-production capacity of each product on the basis of the number of days which the plant is occupied for production of that particular product.

V. Conclusion

The influence and burden of the proposed Chemical Weapons Convention on the peaceful chemical industry have been discussed above. As regards the so-called Production Report, the current state of Japanese chemical-industry statistics has been presented and the practical aspects of making such a report have been discussed.

Japanese production statistics are prepared very meticulously. It is because the applicable laws are properly implemented and the officials of the government strictly abide by the obligations for preservation of secrecy that they are trusted by the chemical industry. If the CWC becomes a part of Japanese domestic law, it may be supposed that the reporting of data from companies to the Japanese government can be properly made and the government would be able to sufficiently monitor non-production of chemical weapons in Japan. If the government of each country monitors its chemical industry so as to assure the non-production of chemical weapons, the reporting of data to the international organization and the international monitoring based on such data could be made fairly simple as far as the chemicals of Schedules 2 and 3 are concerned.

It is to be hoped that the persons engaged in the drafting of the Convention would pay sufficient attention to the possible damage and burden to the peaceful chemical industry which might be caused by the permanent application of this Convention.

References

[1] The Statistics Law, enacted 1947 (law no. 18) and revised 1968 (law no. 99).

[2] The Statistical Report Adjustment Law, enacted 1952 (law no. 148) and revised 1970 (law no. 111).

[3] The Rules for Investigation of Dynamic Production Statistics of the Ministry of International Trade and Industry, enacted 1953 (Ministerial Ordinance of the Ministry of International Trade and Industry no. 10) and revised 1976 (Ministerial Ordinance of the Ministry of International Trade and Industry no. 100).

[4] Research and Statistics Department, Minister's Secretariat, Ministry of International Trade and Industry, *Statistics on Japanese Industries 1988,* published by the International Trade and Industry Statistics Association [TSusan Tokei Kiyokai]; and *Kagakukogyo Kankei tokei chosa teiyo [The Manual for the Investigation of the Chemical Industry Statistics],* published March 1978 by the Chemical Industry Statistics and Research Office, Research and Statistics Department, Ministry of International Trade and Industry.

[5] Law Concerning Examination and Regulation of Manufacture, etc. of Chemical Substances, enacted 1973 (law no. 117) and revised 1986 (law no. 44). [A provisional English translation is published in *Kaisei Kashinho no zitumu* by Kagaku Kogyo Nippo, March 1987.]

[6] See note 5.

[7] Japan Standard Industrial Classification, revised 1984, published by Zenkoku Tokei Rengokai.

REMARKS ON DATA COLLECTION AND HANDLING OF SENSITIVE INFORMATION UNDER A FUTURE CHEMICAL WEAPONS CONVENTION

O. V. PERRONI, Brazil

I. Introduction

One of the purposes of the future Chemical Weapons Convention (CWC), presently under consideration, would be to regulate the manufacture of products which pose a risk to the Convention, but which may be produced for non-prohibited activities. Owing to this, the products would be listed in three (or four) Schedules each of which would correspond to a different regime of control and verification.

Schedule 1 would cover the super-toxic lethal chemicals (STLCs), the production of which would be restricted to a single small-scale facility per country, and limited to one tonne per year. The verification system would be permanent, that is, the facility would only be permitted to operate in the presence of international inspectors.

Schedule 2 would encompass the key precursors, the production of which, above a quantity yet to be defined (threshold), would be the object of periodic reporting in the form of data reports. Furthermore, the plants would remain subject to systematic on-site verification by international inspectors and monitoring by instruments.

Schedule 3 would contain products manufactured on a large scale, and which can be used as chemical weapons or their precursors. Production control of this category would be limited to periodic reporting via data reports.

Schedule 4 would likely include those STLCs not listed in Schedule 1. The list of products and the corresponding verification regime still remain to be determined.

In order to make control possible, the Parties would be obliged to provide sufficient data for the international authority of the CWC in order to keep track of production, sale, acquisition, use, transfer and storage of the listed substances.

Based on the understanding reached thus far, it can be taken as an accepted procedure that the necessary data would be collected by a national body which would process and transmit the information to the international authority. Among the data considered relevant would be included the plant capacity and the actual production. However, the concept of capacity and its meaning in relation to the actual production of the plant is a matter of debate. Moreover, it is questionable whether there is a need to indicate the capacity to the same degree as the actual production, or whether information on one of these areas would suffice. Also, it must be noted that the precision of the measuring methods and the degree of purity of the products have given rise to concern.

On the other hand, the collection of data, as well as the on-site inspections, would involve problems of the confidentiality of sensitive information. A satisfactory solution to this problem must be reached so that the Convention could function without conflicts or damage to the civil chemical industry. These points will be briefly discussed below.

II. The concept of capacity

The production capacity is the potential ability of a plant to manufacture a particular product. Thus, the capacity of the plant should be understood as the *maximum* output that is possible. As a general rule, two types of capacity can be defined: nominal capacity and actual capacity. The former is always theoretical and is a consequence of the calculation made by the designer of the equipment or the plant. It presupposes a particular definition of raw materials, of the efficiency of the chemical reactions involved, and of the so-called 'operational factor', that is, the number of working days in a calendar year.

In practice, however, owing to various factors, such as design margins, safety factors introduced into calculations and deviations in the behaviour of materials in relation to theoretical laws, the actual capacity of a plant is always different from its nominal capacity (generally greater). Therefore, it is not surprising when a certain plant produces 5, 10, 20 per cent, or more, above its nominal capacity.

Moreover, in complex plants the actual capacity is always limited by a particular section of the factory, or even a certain piece of equipment; this is known as a 'bottle-neck'. Once this bottle-neck has been eliminated, the actual capacity reaches a higher level, which is in turn, limited by a new bottle-neck. As a matter of fact, the actual capacity of a plant is not a constant value but one that varies over time as the bottle-necks of the plant are successively removed.

On the other hand, the definition of capacity can be made precise only when it refers to a plant that is dedicated to production of a single product (*single-purpose plant*).

However, when a plant is *multi-purpose* or *multi-component*, the concept needs to be qualified. A plant is multi-purpose when it is sometimes used to produce one product and at other times to produce others. In this case, for the objectives of the Convention, the capacity of a multi-purpose plant would be understood as if the plant were totally dedicated to the manufacture of the relevant product, that is, its maximum ability to make the product in question.

Multi-component plants would also require consideration. These are those plants in which, besides the main product, other by-products, isomers or other derivatives of the main product are simultaneously manufactured. Such is the case, for example, in the pyrolysis of liquid distillates of petroleum for the production of ethylene, with the simultaneous production of other olefins and of aromatic compounds. The same also occurs in the halogenation, nitration and acetylation of aromatic nuclei in which the product is always a mixture of isomers. Sometimes the problem becomes more complex because the proportions of these by-products vary according to the operational conditions or to the presence of specific catalysts. Also in these cases, for the purpose of the Convention, the capacity of the plant in relation to a certain product would be understood as the greatest production possible, achieved in the most favourable conditions for the manufacture of the product in question.

III. Actual production

As opposed to capacity--which defines the potential ability to produce--'actual production' is the quantity actually manufactured during a particular period.

In a material accountancy, the actual production should be equal to the sum of the amount used in the plant itself (captive use), plus the amount transferred (sold), plus the quantity stocked.

In continuous operation plants, when the product is a fluid, actual production is measured by a flow meter installed in the line that transports the final product. The most common flow meters, of the orifice-plate type, provide an accuracy of around 98 per cent. There are, however, turbine-type flow meters which provide even greater precision. More recently, micro-motion-meter flow meters, with no maintenance needs, have been developed which provide an accuracy of 99.6 per cent.

When the product is a solid, the instrument used to measure production is a balance, which is also of very high precision.

In batch operations, it is usual to measure production in the final-product storage tanks, where the measurement is carried out by level meters, the degree of precision of which (over 99 per cent) depends on the geometrical shape of the vessel. This would provide a quite acceptable range for the purposes of the Convention.

One has also to take into account the purity of the product so that the quantities produced are comparable, no matter what the sources of production may be. One way of making the data uniform is to express the result in terms of 100 per cent product purity.

The transmission of the data provided by each producer to the national control authority could, obviously, be accomplished by electronic means using terminals linked to a central computer, but the frequency and amount of information would not justify this procedure.

The central authority should, however, certainly store the information received in a data-processing machine so as to enable immediate reference to the data as necessary, and morever, to facilitate the aggregation or disaggregation of information sent to the international authority.

IV. Handling of confidential information

Plant owners normally have certain confidential information of a technical, economic or commercial nature the disclosure of which could place them at a disadvantage in relation to their competitors. Manufacturing secrets, production cost details or even a list of customers would be included here. Thus, on-site inspections and the data reporting will have to take into account the need to protect this confidential information.

The data collected by the inspectors would need to be treated in the strictest confidence, and *only* used for the purposes of the Convention. In other words, the inspectors should request only the data essential to carrying out the work they would be responsible for in accordance with the Convention. This would mean that the work of the inspectors should not go much beyond checking the instruments for measuring raw materials and products, checking the production records, and inspecting the storage tanks and warehouses for raw materials and finished products.

The greater the care taken in protecting confidential information, the greater will be the willingness of the industry to provide the data relevant to the purposes of the Convention. The Convention would take a large step in this direction if some working principles such as those indicated below were to be established:

1. Reporting should be restricted to that needed to meet the requirements of the Convention.

2. Monitoring by instruments should be maximized.

3. Sealed boxes should be installed in plants for use by the inspectors, so that the documents of restricted circulation could be handled without being taken outside the physical limits of the plant.

V. Summary and conclusions

The verification of the non-production of chemical weapons by the civil industry entails some difficulties concerning data collection and the protection of sensitive information. Nevertheless, these difficulties are not insurmountable and can be overcome provided that the necessary information is precisely defined and its handling is conducted with the proper care.

Capacity and production are distinct values, and both are necessary for the purpose of overall checking.

The declaration and verification of capacity should refer to actual capacity, expressed as the maximum production possible in the most favourable conditions for the product concerned (or the nominal capacity, when actual capacity is not available).

Actual production, measured by the usual methods (the precision of which is compatible with the purposes of the Convention) should be with reference to a 100 per cent pure product. Otherwise the degree of purity of the relevant product should be clearly indicated.

The confidentiality and protection of sensitive information are essential conditions for the smooth running of the Convention, and are not incompatible with a secure verification regime, provided that the appropriate measures are taken. These should include limiting the amount of reporting required, maximizing monitoring by instruments, and installing of sealed boxes inside plants to keep the circulation of documents restricted.

THE DATA-REPORTING SYSTEM IN VERIFICATION OF NON-PRODUCTION

SUN XIANGYIN, China*

I. Introduction

The destruction of existing chemical weapons and prevention of the emergence of new chemical weapons constitute the two main goals of the proposed Chemical Weapons Convention (CWC). The assurance of non-production of new chemical weapons, in particular, presents the more complex and arduous task. To accomplish this so as to make the Convention truly effective, it is essential to set up an effective verification regime designed to establish confidence among States Parties and to ensure complete compliance with and implementation of the Convention. The prevention of production of chemical weapons by the civilian chemical industries of the States Parties necessarily calls for supervision and control over all the key precursors and raw materials essential to the production of chemical weapons, so as to eliminate the possibility of production of chemical-warfare agents. The data-reporting system is a key component of such a verification regime.

II. Importance of the proposed data-reporting system

During the negotiations on the Convention, consideration has been given to the classification of chemical compounds into different categories according to factors such as the degrees of difficulty involved in turning them into chemical-warfare agents and the role each compound plays in the civilian chemical industry. Different supervision and verification regimes are being elaborated for each category of chemical compounds. At the present state of negotiation, initial agreement has been reached to classify chemical compounds according to the following three Schedules: 1. chemical compounds having the properties of chemical-warfare agents; 2. key precursors for the production of chemical-warfare agents, that is, chemicals which can be turned into chemical-warfare agents after one or two steps of reaction; and 3. chemical compounds which have extensive commercial applications and which can serve as raw materials for chemical-warfare agents. The risk to the Convention posed by these chemical compounds varies in degree. The higher the degree of risk, the stricter supervision over the compound and its verification measures must be. Following this principle, three types of verification measures have been worked out for the above three Schedules of compounds. In addition, discussions have occurred on the possible need to elaborate both a Schedule and verification measures for a fourth category--

---

* Sun Xiangyin is an expert in the Ministry of Chemical Industry of the People's Republic of China. The views expressed in this paper are personal.

toxic, lethal compounds that have commercial application. All these types of verification measures entail data reporting.

The data-reporting system will consist of routine collection of data on chemical compounds subject to supervision and control under the Convention, which must be reported regularly to the Convention-designated organ as proof that production and use of these compounds conform to Convention provisions. The data-reporting system will be the most widely used and most basic element in the verification regime.

Under the future CWC, many compounds will need to be monitored and controlled; the number will increase with the advancement of science and technology as will the number of facilities involved in the production, processing and consumption of these compounds. However, as human and material resources are limited, neither on-site inspection of these facilities nor cycles of routine inspections can be too frequent. Therefore, the data-reporting system will be the principal means of obtaining information on enterprises that produce, process and consume these compounds.

The data-reporting system will provide for analysis of use of the compounds reported. The data analysis, on the one hand, can serve to remove some doubts, thus contributing to mutual confidence; on the other hand, it can help to discover questions that need clarification and identify areas where routine on-site inspection will be needed. Therefore, the data-reporting system will be one of the corner-stones of the verification regime.

III. Some points for attention in the data-reporting system

The data-reporting system under consideration should centre on the objectives of the Convention, that is, to ensure that the key precursors and dual-purpose chemical compounds which have been produced are all used for purposes permitted under the Convention. The key aspect of the data-reporting system will be the information on quantities of production and consumption. However, in order to provide a precise indication of the quantities of production and consumption, additional data will be necessary. As the reporting expands its scope and content, it probably will involve more commercial and technological secrets and meet more difficulties in its application, hence, it will be difficult to be accepted by countries and enterprises. Therefore, the scope and content of data reporting should be determined by the degree of risk compounds pose to the objectives of the Convention. The greater the risk, the more information will be required so as to obtain a multi-aspect analysis for the most effective supervision over compounds listed in the Schedules. At the same time, caution will need to be taken so that excessive reporting demands may be avoided and so that commercial and technological secrets are not jeopardized, leading to economic losses for the enterprises.

The Schedule 2 compounds in the proposed Convention are the key precursors for the production of chemical-warfare agents. In general, these compounds are rarely used in civilian chemical industry and the enterprises involved are few. On the basis of these two considerations, it is both necessary and possible to apply a more stringent reporting system to this category of compounds.

The Schedule 3 compounds are those that have substantial commercial applications. They are produced and consumed in great quantities and many enterprises are involved. Thus, it would inevitably take substantial human and material resources to apply an overly stringent reporting system. The quantity and scope of these compounds would make it difficult to obtain any precise statistics. It is difficult to trace how these compounds are used, even if precise statistics have been obtained. Nevertheless, some of the compounds in this category serve as raw materials for the production of the compounds in Schedule 2. As a stringent reporting system is foreseen for Schedule 2 compounds, thereby effectively preventing civilian chemical industry from producing weapons, data reporting on Schedule 3 compounds could involve less information and be less precise.

In order to provide for cross-referencing of data and timely discovery of problems, it will be necessary to apply a 'dual reporting system'. The producer enterprises and the user enterprises will need to report simultaneously to confirm that monitored compounds that have been produced are all used for purposes permitted under the Convention.

Due to differences in raw material sources, in technological processes and levels of production technique as well as in product specification, the quantity of the product in both its actual and purified form could be provided in reporting so as to obtain more precise statistics on production and consumption quantities.

Differences in the final uses of the compounds monitored by the Convention may lead to great differences in reported production and consumption quantities, ranging from several dozens grams to several hundred thousand metric tonnes. This dictates a difference in the precision of the reporting as well. As previously stated, Schedule 2 compounds list the key precursors for the production of chemical-warfare agents. According to the text agreed upon initially, each State Party, for protective purposes, shall be allowed to produce and stockpile not more than one metric tonne of chemical-warfare agents in any calender year. Therefore, consumption of key precursors for production of these agents will not be too great. In order to ensure that these precursors are not used for the production of chemical-warfare agents, with the exception of a small quantity designated for 'protective purposes', it will be advisable to adopt *kilograms* as the reporting unit. Schedule 3 compounds have substantial commercial applications and are produced in great quantities; as they generally cannot be used directly for production of chemical-warfare agents, the adoption of metric tonnes as the reporting unit can be considered.

Some of the chemical compounds listed in the Convention Schedules are used for scientific research, others serve as industrial raw material; great disparity exists between them regarding amounts produced and consumed. It is neither possible nor necessary to cover all the producing and consuming facilities and their corresponding production and consumption quantities by the data reporting. Therefore, different thresholds may be determined for given chemical compounds in accordance with the difficulty with which the compound in question can be turned into chemical-warfare agents, the hazardousness of the agents thus produced, and the quantity of the compound needed for production of specified amounts of the chemical-warfare agents.

As the chemical compounds in Schedule 3 have wide commercial application, the amounts produced and consumed are enormous. These compounds can be turned into chemical-warfare agents only after many reaction steps, therefore, they may be allowed a higher threshold level, ranging from tens of tonnes to several hundred tonnes. Individual facilities with production below the threshold might be exempted from individual data reporting, but data reporting on the total number of such enterprises, their total production output and consumption quantity would be required so as to forestall the potential risk to the Convention which might be caused by an excessive number of below-the-threshold facilities producing and consuming excessive quantities of chemical compounds subject to supervision and control.

Chemical production is extremely complicated. In certain chemical-production processes, chemical compounds proceed to the next phase of reaction while simultaneously becoming compounds that would be subjected to supervision and control under the Convention. The intermediates thus produced are not separated, measured or counted. For instance, in the chemical-production process involving phosgene, the moment phosgene is produced, it proceeds to the next phase of reaction. In the production process of cyanuric chloride, the cyanogen chloride is absorbed by alkali immediately upon production in certain processes, thus turning into sodium cyanate. The quantity of these intermediates can only be worked out according to the output of end-products. Since the intermediates are neither separated nor sold as commodities, there is no question of using them for purposes prohibited by the Convention. Therefore, the facilities producing and using such chemical compounds would not need to be subject to data reporting.

IV. Content and format of data reporting

The future Convention may stipulate that data reporting include 'the aggregate volume of the production, consumption, import and export' of the chemical compounds listed in the supervision and control schedules of the Convention. In calculating total production and consumption, enterprises could themselves submit the required reports to ensure precision of the data, and separate statements of annual production and consumption of each facility could be made. The reporting could also include volume of commodities marketed, whether produced from raw materials prepared by the enterprise itself, or supplied from outside sources. Standard products resulting from pilot-plant production could be added to the output, provided they have been certified to meet quality specifications set by the enterprise and are in conformity with ordered technical specifications. Product output for the reporting period should equal the quantity of products that have been transferred into storage or for which paperwork for transfer into storage has been completed by the last day of the reporting period. Product-output figures thus would be obtained from calculations.

Product-output reports could include information on quantities of products in both purified form and as the actual product. The quantity of an actual product constitutes the basis for calculating the standard output. With regard to products that have different specifications and different levels of quality standard, outputs should be indicated for each level of the quality standard.

In data reporting on chemical compounds whose use and consumption are controlled by the Convention, major areas for accurate reporting may be as follows: quantity of use, including identification of the user; purpose (identifying the measurable products directly synthesized from the compounds controlled by the Convention); and gross quantity of compounds consumed. The list of these figures could include the total quantity consumed in the whole production process from material input to synthesis of the said products, irrespective of whether or not they meet the required quality standard; consumption of raw materials and semi-finished products in the course of storage and transportation; maintenance, commencement and termination of equipment operation; consumption caused by reprocessing or adapting shoddy products; and losses due to production accidents. Irregular consumption, which is not included in production consumption, could be reported separately.

Calculation of chemical compounds controlled by the Convention which are used repeatedly in a technological process should be based upon their first input quantity. Reused materials should not be re-counted if they are reused for the production of the same products in the same process. A separate report should, however, be made on the use of any significant quantity of recycled materials for purposes other than the production of the said products.

At every reporting phase in a continuous production process, there are materials left over from the previous phase and materials to be carried over to the next phase. They are calculated in the following manner: materials left over from the preceding phase + materials involved in the current phase - materials to be carried over to the next phase.

For the purpose of facilitating comparison between the various producer and consumer enterprises, production and consumption of chemical compounds controlled under the Convention must be calculated according to their purified equivalent. Two ways of conversion present themselves:

For dry base chemicals:

Quantity in purified form = actual material quantity (1 - water content percentage) x percentage purity of the dry base chemicals.

For wet base chemicals:

Quantity in purified form = actual material quantity x percentage purity of the wet base chemicals.

Total consumption should be defined as the sum of all batches of production or consumption as converted into purified form.

V. Compilation, processing and publication of data

As a large number of enterprises are involved in the data-reporting system, it may be necessary to set up channels for data reporting in order to ensure timely collection of relevant data. In this connection, the most effective and efficient channel might be for all enterprises, irrespective of their nature, affiliation and location to report to the designated authority of the respective State Party.[1] For its part, the designated authority will process and compile the data reported by enterprises before submitting them to the competent organ of the Convention; the latter, in turn, would process, compile and analyse data from States Parties and regularly inform them through their respective national authorities of the operation of the data-reporting system.

In order to reduce the possible leakage of information submitted by enterprises and prevent any subsequent losses to those enterprises, the competent organ of the Convention would not publicize the data it had processed and compiled. The information would only be made available to the institutions of States Parties responsible for data reporting, or to the authorities designated by them, for analysis by professional personnel so as to ensure effective compliance with the provisions of the Convention.

Note

[1]This paper does not deal with questions related to matters of 'jurisdiction and control'.

V. EXPERIENCES FROM IAEA

The Chemical Weapons Convention and some IAEA experiences
A. von BAECKMANN, IAEA

THE CHEMICAL WEAPONS CONVENTION AND SOME IAEA EXPERIENCES

A. von BAECKMANN, IAEA*

I. Introduction

Whereas the use of chemical weapons in the battlefield was possibly one of the most inhuman developments during World War I, the use of nuclear weapons against civilian targets was certainly the most terrifying event of World War II. In contrast to the development of chemical weapons, which was a side-product of a long-established and prosperous chemical industry, nuclear energy was introduced into our world as a means of threat and destruction.

It took more than 10 years until the constructive role nuclear energy can play in delivering reliable, low-cost electricity and in promoting science, medicine and technology was fully appreciated; and even now--43 years later-- nuclear energy is still stigmatized by the events of Hiroshima and Nagasaki.

It must, however, be realized that because of this dramatic first use of nuclear energy, its utilization for peaceful purposes was carefully controlled from its very beginning. The initial policy of complete denial of any transfer of nuclear technology was only later followed by the 'atoms for peace'- programme, accompanied by a widely accepted policy of striving for the non-proliferation of nuclear weapons.

The system of IAEA** safeguards to verify the peaceful utilization of nuclear energy is an important part of this international non-proliferation policy. Entrusted by its Statute, by the Treaty for the Prohibition of Nuclear Weapons in Latin America, by the Treaty on the Non-Proliferation of Nuclear Weapons (NPT) and most recently by the South Pacific Nuclear Free Zone Treaty, the IAEA has developed its safeguard system during the last 25 years into a powerful instrument aimed at verifying that states are complying with certain fundamental non-proliferation undertakings.

---

*This paper reflects the opinion of the author. It does not represent the official view of the IAEA nor of its Department of Safeguards.

**The International Atomic Energy Agency (IAEA) was founded in 1957 with the objective 'to seek to accelerate and enlarge the contribution of atomic energy to peace, health and prosperity throughout the world'.[1] The Agency is authorized to establish and administer safeguards to ensure that nuclear material, . . . is not used in such a way as to further any military purpose. Other major activities of the IAEA relate to the promotion of nuclear power and its fuel cycle; of nuclear applications in human health, industry and earth sciences, physical and chemical sciences, nuclear safety and radiation protection as well as technical assistance and co-operation.

The system embodies components of assurance as well as components of deterrence. It is designed to detect in a timely way any diversion of significant quantities of nuclear material from peaceful nuclear activities to the manufacture of nuclear weapons, or of other nuclear explosive devices (or for purposes unknown) that might occur, to deter a diversion by the risk of early detection, in case a diversion is contemplated; and to give assurance that the states are in compliance with their safeguard obligations. IAEA safeguards are absolutely unique. It is the first time in the history of humankind that 97 sovereign states, comprising a majority of those countries which use nuclear energy, have agreed to accept international control, on their territories by an international organization in an area of important industrial development, thereby voluntarily accepting some interference with their sovereignty. This is without any doubt a very significant contribution to nuclear arms limitation and thereby to world peace.

By the end of 1987, a total of 166 safeguards agreements were in force with 97 states including the four nuclear-weapon states: France, the UK, the USA and the Soviet Union. Through these agreements the following quantities of nuclear material were subject to IAEA safeguards: 9.4 tonnes of separated plutonium; 12.2 tonnes of high-enriched uranium ($\geq 20\%$ U-235); 224.2 tonnes of plutonium contained in irradiated fuel; 29 252 tonnes of low-enriched uranium; and 50 867 tonnes of source material (natural and depleted uranium and thorium).

In 1987 the Agency's Department of Safeguards spent about US $43.8 million and employed about 470 people (out of an IAEA budget of US $133 million and a total of about 1700 IAEA staff). More than 2100 inspections were carried out at about 600 facilities in 56 states by about 150 inspectors. More than 320 automatic-photo or television-surveillance systems operated in the field and more than 12 000 seals were applied. About 1300 samples from nuclear materials were analysed, and about 3600 analytical results were reported.

Although many, mostly minor, discrepancies and anomalies were found, all cases were satisfactorily solved. In 1987, as in previous years, no anomaly was detected which would indicate the diversion of a significant amount of safeguarded nuclear material. In essence, 95 per cent of all nuclear material in peaceful nuclear activities in the non-nuclear weapon states and some material in the civil fuel cycles in four nuclear-weapon states were subjected to IAEA safeguards which were applied successfully to it. Whereas between 1946 and 1968 the US policy of denial had not prevented the development of nuclear weapons in four additional states, only one additional country has exploded a nuclear explosive device since 1968 when the Non-Proliferation Treaty came into being.

II. Some experience with the safeguards system of the IAEA that might be pertinent to the verification of a Chemical Weapons Convention

Much experience has been gained and many lessons have been learned by establishing and operating the IAEA Inspectorate which might be of use in other arms control-verification organizations, in particular for the control related to a Chemical Weapons Convention (CWC). In this article only four related subjects are discussed: IAEA safeguards agreements and subsidiary arrangements, the inspector, the development and implementation of verification equipment and techniques, and the protection of sensitive information.

IAEA safeguards agreements and subsidiary arrangements

IAEA safeguards are implemented on the basis of safeguards agreements concluded between the IAEA and individual states or groups of states. Depending on the circumstances, these Agreements follow either the safeguards scheme described in INFCIRC/66[2] or the one described in INFCIRC/153.[3] The INFCIRC/66 scheme is used if the scope of IAEA is limited to such nuclear materials, other materials, equipment and facilities which are listed in a special inventory usually because they have been imported or their construction or use is related to imported relevant technological information. This scheme is characterized by the limited scope, according to the inventory described above, and the IAEA undertaking to apply its safeguards to all items on the inventory 'so as to ensure that no such item is used for the manufacture of any nuclear weapon or to further any other military purpose or for the manufacture of any other nuclear explosive device'. The INFCIRC/153 scheme is used in all non-nuclear weapon states party to the Treaty on the Non-Proliferation of Nuclear Weapons. It covers 'all source or special fissionable material in all peaceful nuclear activities', and IAEA safeguards under this scheme are applied 'for the exclusive purpose of verifying that such material is not diverted to nuclear weapons or other nuclear explosive devices'. This scheme is also used for the conclusion of safeguards agreements with states party to the Treaty for the Prohibition of Nuclear Weapons in Latin America and the South Pacific Nuclear Free Zone Treaty.

In these agreements the principles of safeguards to be applied are explained, the rights, privileges, immunities and obligation of the inspectors are described and guidance on the implementation of safeguards are provided. INFCIRC/66 is, in effect, a general description of the main components of the safeguards agreement. The individual agreements following this scheme may vary quite substantially reflecting the specific range of application, for example, on a specific facility delivered from another country. The texts of INFCIRC/66 agreements also vary because this scheme has significantly developed since it was first used in 1966. INFCIRC/153 is a model agreement, and its text is to a large extent identical with the text of the individual agreements. The agreements with Japan and with the non-nuclear weapons states of the European Community and EURATOM deviate from the standard text through the addition of a protocol recognizing the specific features of the Japanese safeguards system and of the EURATOM safeguards system. The safeguards agreements with nuclear-weapon states--which are usually called 'voluntary offer agreements'--follow mainly the INFCIRC/153 scheme with certain adaptations reflecting the use of nuclear energy in nuclear weapons in these states.

Safeguards agreements are usually complemented by subsidiary arrangements describing, in their general parts, those components of the safeguards system which are relevant for the entire state, for example channels and procedures for the flow of information, the national system of accounting for and control of nuclear material, co-ordination of inspection programmes and report forms and explanations of their use. The facility-specific safeguard measures are described in facility attachments which are individually negotiated and concluded for each facility. These facility attachments are prepared and negotiated on the basis of facility-specific design information provided by the state and a design-information verification visit by some inspectors. For many facility types, model-facility attachments have been developed with the assistance of international groups of experts and are being used within the IAEA.

The inspector

The inspector is the most important element in any scheme of verification through human observation. All assurances provided, all questions regarding results and all potential detection of deviations from international, binding undertakings devolve upon the inspector. His capabilities, reliability, integrity, and also his reputation and credibility are the ultimate pillars of the verification regime. This key role of the inspector must be kept in mind whenever international verification is being discussed.

IAEA inspectors are recruited from the widest possible geographical distribution; technical competence and experience in the nuclear field are essential criteria for recruitment.[4] During the first 3 months, new inspectors are trained in the basic aspects of safeguards, including Non-Destructive Assay (NDA) measurement technology, record auditing and the use of statistical-sampling plans. In the following 6 to 9 months inspectors receive in-field training under the supervision of experienced senior inspectors. Depending on their experience and training they may be employed on a P-2, P-3 or P-4 level.[5] P-5 level senior inspectors have usually long-term IAEA experience or special safeguards experience in a national or multi-national system for nuclear-material accountancy and control. If possible and if good performance permits it, the IAEA tries to secure the services of inspectors for an extended period of time. However, there are no permanent contracts available. After a first three-year and a subsequent two-year contract, 5 year extensions are usually possible.

The work of an inspector is not easy and puts a great strain on his health and his family relations. Heavy travel schedules and long absences from home characterize his work. The professional requirements are high: technical knowledge and competence, diplomatic skill, language capabilities, reliability, integrity, good health, flexibility and so on. The trend in the UN system for more economy, the decreasing quality of working conditions, the increasing uncertainty with respect to long-term employment and the limited prospects for career development hamper the recruitment of qualified staff and have led to some early resignations.

The standards for inspectors employed for the verification of compliance with a CWC may even be higher: more travelling to more remote places, direct handling of highly toxic substances, detailed technical knowledge of several completely different types of chemical compounds, and the related micro-analytical detection methods. Knowledge of chemical-weapon design and their employment may be additional important requirements.

Furthermore, it must be recognized that because of the present stagnation in the nuclear industry in developed countries enough qualified persons with nuclear experience can be found. The chemical industry, however, is in good health, and qualified persons will relatively easily find satisfactory or attractive positions in chemical enterprises. Specific training will be indispensable and good prospects for career development should be available. In addition, long-term (permanent) contracts might be required in order to ensure the necessary staff loyalty to the organization.

Development and implementation of verification equipment and methods

The verification of any advanced, highly sophisticated technology, such as the nuclear industry or chemical industry, requires well-developed and reliable instruments and methods.

In 1970, when the IAEA was entrusted, through the NPT, with the task of designing, implementing and successfully maintaining an extended international system for safeguarding nuclear materials in all peaceful applications, only very limited experience in nuclear-material safeguards was available. Furthermore, this experience was mainly based upon safeguards at nuclear-power reactors and research reactors. The main task for the following years was to develop procedures and techniques for applying safeguards throughout the nuclear fuel cycle including large bulk-handling facilities. Extensive research and development (R&D) activities were initiated covering, *inter alia*: (a) studies on safeguards concepts and approaches; (b) the development, testing, implementation and maintenance of safeguards instruments, methods and techniques; (c) the development of safeguards information and data-treatment capabilities; (d) the assessment and evaluation of safeguards results; (e) the training of safeguards inspectors; and (f) the performance of safeguards inspections.

In principle, there were two possible ways of tackling the first three tasks: 1. to provide the IAEA with the required (and very high) budgetary resources to build its own R&D facilities and to employ a large number of researchers; or 2. to conduct the necessary work in national R&D facilities in close co-operation with the IAEA and to provide the IAEA with the necessary limited resources and funds required for the co-ordination of the work and for the proper utilization of the results.

It is not surprising that, in a situation of financial shortage and a certain over-capacity in national nuclear R&D programmes and facilities, most Member States preferred to have the work done in their own facilities. Several formalized routes have been established and used for the co-ordination of the work and the transfer of results to the IAEA. These include: (a) conclusion of safeguards research agreements and contracts (inside or outside formalized co-ordinated research programmes); (b) participation in safeguards consultant or advisory-group meetings and working groups; (c) establishment of national programmes in support of IAEA safeguards; and (d) participation in multinational programmes aimed at the improvement of IAEA safeguards.

The last two routes turned out to be extremely useful and most of the R&D work related to IAEA safeguards has been carried out and continues to be performed under national or multinational programmes in support of IAEA safeguards.

Thus far 11 states (Australia, Belgium, Canada, France, the FRG, Italy, Japan, the UK, the USA, the USSR and Sweden) and EURATOM have entered into formalized safeguards support programmes with the IAEA and 4 major multinational programmes for promoting safeguards in specific situations (IWG-RPS,[6] TASTEX,[7] RECOVER,[8] HEXAPARTITE[9]) have been executed. Practically all instruments, methods and techniques which the IAEA employs in implementing its safeguards are a result of these programmes. In addition numerous cost-free experts and other expertise have been made available to the IAEA in the framework of these programmes. The co-ordination of these programmes with the requirements of the IAEA and the proper co-operation is a major task of the IAEA Division of Development and Technical Support, and represents about 7 full man-years of work per year.

Consultant and advisory-group meetings are important complementary means of obtaining expert advice and information. Once every four years, the IAEA organizes a major safeguards symposium which usually attracts some 300 experts, covering the development in all fields of safeguards R&D and implementation experience.

Safeguards research agreements and contracts played a major role in the early 1970s, before the support programmes were initiated. Now they are only used in rare cases where the required expertise or equipment cannot be obtained otherwise.

Safeguards instruments and the procedures for their use during inspection are not readily available and frequently require development[10] over several years in specialized research and development facilities. The steps leading to a fully suitable instrument include:

(a) definition of the purpose of the instrument and the conditions under which it shall be used;

(b) development of a laboratory device to demonstrate the feasibility of the technique under ideal laboratory conditions;

(c) production of a development prototype for evaluation, limited field testing, development of provisional procedures, manuals and safety analysis;

(d) production of field-evaluation units for testing the technique under routine field conditions, training of inspectors, determination of the range of applicability, for reliability and tamper-resistance analysis and for the development of specifications, production drawings, operation manuals, maintenance and preventive-maintenance procedures;

(e) production of commercial instruments for routine use; and

(f) equipment-performance monitoring for further improvement, continuous training of inspectors in the use of the equipment and, if possible, adaptation of the instrument and operating procedures to new situations and developments in the field.

Each of these steps may take many months to several years, depending on available resources, expertise and testing possibilities.

For the chemical analysis of samples taken from process lines in nuclear facilities, the IAEA operates its own Safeguards Analytical Laboratory (SAL) and co-operates with a network of safeguards analytical laboratories in 14 Member States.[11] The IAEA's Safeguards Analytical Laboratory is equipped with the necessary instruments to analyse about 1200 safeguards samples a year. Since the handling of plutonium and other radioactive materials requires careful protection of the operators and the environment, glove boxes, air-control systems with filters and shielding are installed. The measurement equipment is computerized to a large extent.

Although the analytical procedures used in SAL are the standard procedures used in nuclear industry, certain modifications and adaptations were required in order to take care of the relatively long transportation time for the samples, the different sample-preparation techniques used in different countries and the specific composition of the material from which the samples are taken. Sample transportation frequently requires particular attention since the rules and regulations for the safe transport of plutonium and other radioactive materials are very stringent and sometimes differ in different countries.

R&D for verification techniques related to a CWC will be very essential. Again a decision will be necessary about whether the organization should have its own major R&D facilities or whether it should rely mainly on the R&D work done in the Member States. Some countries (for example, Finland, The Netherlands and Norway) have already done some research for CWC purposes, and it will be essential that the available results are properly transferred into practical application by the inspectorate. But much more work needs to be done. At this time about US $15 million are being spent annually in the R&D activities covered by national programmes in support of IAEA safeguards, a continuing activity that started in 1976. Related activities in Member States may easily exceed this annual spending.

A comprehensive system of instruments, methods and techniques for the purpose of the CWC will certainly require the same effort--if not more. In addition, analytical laboratories capable of handling and analysing the samples collected by the inspectors need to be available to the organization. Even if most R&D work and analytical services are done in Member States, a sufficiently large group of staff is required within the organization in order to co-ordinate the work, to evaluate the results obtained and to perform routine services.

The implementation of verification equipment and methods is not always easy. Equipment must comply with national regulations and must work reliably under field conditions. Neither is trivial and specific adaptation may be required. For example, the colour-coding of cables connected to the main electricity supply is different in different countries. National regulations require the use of correct colours and that means that a specific instrument which is cabled in accordance with the rules of a particular country may not be used in other countries. Frequency and voltage of electricity is different in different areas of the world, but also the ranges of the frequency and voltage actually available may vary considerably. Power shortages may lead to 20 per cent below normal voltage and reduced frequency and in some countries to power cuts for several hours every day. In addition, electrical noise is quite significant in certain facilities. Robust, preferably battery-operated, instrumentation might be the only solution to this kind of problem. On the other side, the inspection activities must not interfere with safety, security or economic requirements of the inspected facility. The question of liability may come up if inspection activities require unusual handling or operation. Sampling of material may cause leakages or contamination. Items may be damaged during measurement or movement to or from measurement. In principle, any kind of verification is intrusive and may interfere with normal operation. Through careful planning and preparation the potential damage can, however, be minimized or at least reduced to an acceptable level. The IAEA has occasionally reported on the difficulties it experienced when a new verification instrument or technique was implemented. Not all instruments and methods can be used equally everywhere--indeed differences in national regulations or licensing conditions provide for more flexibility in some countries than in others. It has, however, usually been possible to avoid this kind of difficulty by using alternative safeguards instruments and procedures.

Protection of sensitive information

During the discussion of verification measures for a CWC, concern has been expressed that commercially sensitive information and/or industrial secrets may become known to the inspectors and/or the organization and could be misused for illegitimate purposes. Similar concern has been expressed repeatedly with respect to the implementation of IAEA safeguards since the nuclear industry is considered a technologically sensitive area. Thus the question of protection of information and the measures taken by the IAEA may be taken as a model for a CWC. Measures taken by the IAEA include:

Statutory and contractual obligations

The Statute of the IAEA requires that only persons of the 'highest standards of efficiency, technical competence and integrity' (Article 7 D) be recruited and employed and that 'In performance of their duties . . . the staff shall not seek or receive instructions from any source external to the Agency . . . they shall not disclose any industrial secrets or other confidential information coming to their knowledge by reason of their official duties for the Agency . . . (Article 7 F). In addition, all safeguards agreements include provisions obligating the Agency to keep confidential information secret. Relevant requirements are contained in Articles 5 and 9. of the safeguards model agreement for non-nuclear weapon States Parties to the NPT, reproduced in document INFCIRC/153.

Article 5 requires, *inter alia*, that 'the Agency shall take every precaution to protect commercial and industrial secrets and other confidential information coming to its knowledge in the implementation of the Agreement. The Agency shall not publish or communicate to any State, organization or person any information obtained by it in connection with the implementation of the Agreement, except that specific information . . . may be given to such Agency staff members as require such knowledge by reason of their official duties . . . but only to the extent necessary . . .' Article 9 contains the requirement that 'the visits and activities of Agency inspectors shall be arranged as to . . . ensure protection of industrial secrets as any other confidential information coming to the inspectors' knowledge'.

In addition, other procedures and measures are foreseen in the model. For example it is stated in Article 8 that 'the Agency shall require only the minimum amount of information and data consistent with carrying out its responsibilities under the Agreement. Information pertaining to facilities shall be the minimum necessary for safeguarding nuclear material subject to safeguards under the Agreement. In examining design information the Agency shall . . . be prepared to examine on premises of the State design information which the State regards as being of particular sensitivity' and so on. Two measures to protect information or secrets are explicitly mentioned here: minimizing the (sensitive) information available to the Agency and examining of information on the premises of the state--thereby minimizing the distribution by the state and controlling access of Agency staff to such information.

Furthermore, the state has to give its consent to the designation of inspectors that may perform inspections on its territory (Article 9). Process steps involving commercially sensitive information may be protected by establishing a special material-balance area around them (Article 46b IV). Access of inspectors is limited to 'locations where nuclear material is present' (Article 76a) or 'only to strategic points specified in a subsidiary arrangement' (Article 76c). If unusual circumstances require extended limitations on access by the Agency, arrangements have to be made--and reported to the Board-- which enable the Agency to discharge its safeguards responsibilities in the light of these limitations (Article 76d). The state has the right to have inspectors accompanied during their inspection by representatives of the state (Article 87) and the number, intensity, duration and timing of routine inspections is to be kept to the minimum consistent with the effective implementation of the safeguards procedures (Article 78). With respect to a non-proscribed military use of material to which safeguards are not being applied while the material is used in such an activity, it is explicitly stated that: 'The Agency's Agreement . . . shall not involve any . . . classified knowledge of the military activity' [in which the material is being used] (Article 14C).

Related administrative procedures

Related administrative procedures are contained in the Provisional Staff Regulations and Staff Rules, the other chapters of the Administrative Manual, the Safeguards Manual and specific instructions issued by the Head of the Department of Safeguards, Directors or other supervisors.

Staff Regulation 1.01 states: 'Members of the Secretariat are international civil servants. . . . By accepting the appointment they pledge themselves to perform their duties . . . with the interest of the IAEA only in view'. Regulation 1.06 requires that 'Members of the Secretariat shall exercise the utmost discretion in regard to all matters of official business. They shall not communicate to any person or Government any information known to them by reason of their official position which has not been made public, except in the course of the performance of their duties or by authorization of the Director General. They shall not at any time use such information to private advantage . . . These obligations shall not cease upon separation from the Secretariat'.

The oath or declaration to which members of the Secretariat shall subscribe states, *inter alia*, 'I solemnly swear . . . to exercise in all loyalty, discretion and conscience the functions entrusted to me as an international civil servant . . .' (Regulation 1.11) and Regulation 11.01 states that 'The Director General may impose such disciplinary measures as are in his opinion appropriate on staff members whose conduct is unsatisfactory. He may summarily dismiss a staff member for serious misconduct'.

Rule 1.06.1 on classified information reads as follows:

A. The Director General may from time to time establish
a. classes of information to be subjected to safekeeping, and
b. procedures to be followed by staff members for the safekeeping, handling and release of information so classified
B. Non-compliance with procedures established under para A. above shall constitute a conduct calling for appropriate action under Provisional Staff Regulation 11.01.

The classes and procedures mentioned in Rule 1.06.1 have been established by the Director General (SEC/NOT/956) and a *Manual of Standards for the Classification, Routing and Safekeeping of Safeguards Information* has been issued by the Head of the Department of Safeguards. These two documents contain instructions on classification, protection procedures, destruction, declassification, security officers, file stations for confidential information, safes, electric locks and so on. Thus far their implementation, although sometimes inconvenient, has not led to major problems. It should be noted that similar procedures apply to the protection of confidential information on magnetic tapes, disks or stored in computers.

Experience with the protection of sensitive information

In general it can be stated that the relevant obligations and administrative procedures are considered sufficient. It must moreover be realized that the best rules and procedures cannot absolutely exclude the possibility of illegal access to confidential information through robbery, accidents or misconduct of individual staff members, but those events are rare and have not thus far led to major controversies. Although it might be difficult for an international organization to prosecute staff guilty of misconduct and to hold someone accountable in the case of defection, it can be expected that the involved Member States would take the appropriate actions to protect the interests of the organization.

In some cases, Member States have requested unnecessarily stringent protection measures: for example, the Agency was requested to keep information confidential which was publicly available in brochures or scientific publications. In very few cases the standard rules were considered insufficient and additional security procedures have been agreed upon. These special procedures included, *inter alia*: (a) the development and review of surveillance films in the facility or in the state, without physical transfer of the films to IAEA offices; and (b) special-access procedures to areas containing commercially sensitive information, such as procedures for announcement of inspections, limited frequency of access, limitations on the number of inspectors, reduced duration of access, predetermined routes for inspectors, recording by an accompanying representative of the state only and the like.

In general, one can observe that the concern that the IAEA may not properly treat confidential information is declining. There is also a visible trend to ask the Agency to give more and more detailed information on safeguards implementation to its Board of Governors and through its Annual Report to the public. It is widely accepted that the advantages of providing confidence for the IAEA safeguards system through a higher degree of transparency may outweigh the disadvantages of releasing some less sensitive summary information. From this trend one can only hope that the sometimes over-emphasized concerns with respect to the treatment of sensitive information by the CWC control organization will disappear once the system has been established and brought into operation.

III. Outlook

The inspectorate envisaged for the verification of compliance with the basic undertakings related to a CWC will have an important and challenging task. In some respects, this task will have certain similarities with the IAEA system for safeguarding nuclear material; in other respects, the task will be new and unprecedented. Application of IAEA safeguards is strictly limited to the peaceful utilization of nuclear energy. None of these activities are related to nuclear arms or other uses of nuclear energy in military applications. The chemical-weapon verification inspectorate will have to deal not only with the verification of non-production of certain substances but also directly with the control of storage and destruction of chemical weapons and the termination of their production in chemical-weapon factories. In addition, nuclear-material safeguards are based on material accountancy related to three chemical elements: thorium, uranium and plutonium, with thorium having little importance. All three elements are radioactive and can therefore be detected and measured by non-destructive assay techniques. Uranium and plutonium are used practically exclusively in nuclear activities and therefore--except for material in military application--in most non-nuclear weapon states are fully under IAEA safeguards. In contrast, the verification of non-production of chemical weapons is based on the agreement that certain compounds are not being produced, or only being produced in small quantities for non-proscribed purposes. The elements from which these compounds are synthesized are easily available everywhere and uncontrollable, and compounds similar to those used in chemical weapons are widely used in the pharmaceutical industry, the chemical industry and in agriculture. Facilities and equipment used for the production of weapon-usable chemicals are identical to those used for the production of insecticides, herbicides and other chemical products.

And finally, the primary purpose of the IAEA safeguards system is to build up confidence that the non-nuclear weapon states accepting full-scope safeguards are not diverting nuclear material and technology for the production of nuclear weapons or other nuclear explosive devices, thereby providing a basis for international co-operation and technology transfer and eliminating the need for other (neighbouring) countries to enter into a nuclear-arms competition. This is significantly different from the main purpose of a CWC which is to reduce and eventually eliminate existing stockpiles of chemical weapons. A very high degree of confidence and assurance will be required to convince the states armed with chemical weapons that the dismantling of their chemical arsenals is in the best interest of everybody and not placing their legitimate national interests in jeopardy. It is obvious that one cannot simply copy the IAEA safeguards system in the CWC inspectorate; the environment of the system, the determining parameters external to it and the assurance to be provided through it are substantially different. However, IAEA experience in international co-operation in setting up an international-verification inspectorate, its structure, staff rules, working procedures, evaluation criteria and so on may serve as a model for the organization of the CWC. Other models less close to the IAEA safeguards system could be developed, for example those emphasizing bilateral-verification arrangements with little international verification. In this article the attempt has been made to describe, in four specific areas, how the functioning and organization of the IAEA might be of use in developing structures and concepts for the verification organization required in the context of the Chemical Weapons Convention.

References

[1] *Statute* of the International Atomic Energy Agency.

[2] *The Agency's Safeguards System*, INFCIRC/66/rev.2 (IAEA: Vienna, 1968).

[3] *The Structure and Content of Agreements between the Agency and States Required in Connection with the Treaty on the Non-Proliferation of Nuclear Weapons*, INFCIRC/153 (corrected) (IAEA: Vienna, 1972).

[4] Buechler, C. and Lichliter, W., *Career Prospects in the IAEA Safeguards Inspectorate*, IAEA SM 293/114 (IAEA: Vienna, 1987).

[5] *Report of the International Civil Service Commission for the Year 1987*, UN Official Records Supplement, no. 30(A/42/30), New York, 1987, p. 107.

[6] *International Working Group on Reprocessing Plant Safeguards, Overview Report to the Director General* (IAEA: Vienna, 1987).

[7] *Tokai Advanced Safeguards Technology Exercise*, Technical Report Series, no. 213 (IAEA: Vienna, 1982).

[8] Sanatani, S. and Neilsen, C. J., *A Remote Verification System for International Safeguards: Status of the RECOVER Programme in the IAEA*, IAEA SM 260/110 (IAEA: Vienna, 1983).

[9] Brown, F., *The Hexapartite Safeguards Project: A Review by the Chairman*, IAEA SM 260/57 (IAEA: Vienna, 1983).

[10] Rundquist, D., 'Improving technical support to IAEA safeguards', *IAEA Bulletin* (Vienna), vol. 28, no. 4 (1986), p. 29.

[11] Deron, S. and Wenzel, U., 'Safeguards analytical services: their role in verification', *IAEA Bulletin* (Vienna), vol. 28, no. 4 (1986), p. 24.

VI. CONCLUSION

Concluding remarks
S. J. LUNDIN, SIPRI

CONCLUDING REMARKS

S. J. LUNDIN, SIPRI

Article VI of the Chemical Weapons Convention (CWC) and its appendices will be the basis for the verification measures to be taken with regard to the chemical industry once the CWC enters into force. The present study addresses a number of important aspects for these verification measures concerning concrete problems which will have to be solved in connection with the ongoing negotiation process.

The problem areas covered in this study fall under the following headings: (a) organizational aspects; (b) verification concepts; (c) verification experiments; (d) technical verification methods and their applicability; and (e) the handling of technical and commercial secrets. The different contributions to this study each treat one or more of these aspects. Rather than attempting to edit the contributions so as to avoid repetition, it has been considered useful to retain the variety of points of view in order to provide as full as possible treatment of the modern concepts of verification of compliance with a CWC as regards the chemical industry. No attempt to sum up the various papers will be made in these concluding remarks. The reader is, instead, recommended to consult the conclusions in the individual contributions. These concluding remarks will only attempt to present an impression of the general trends in the contributions as perceived by the Editor.

A prominent aspect of the contributions from the representatives of the chemical industry is the constructive approach and willingness of the chemical industry to address problems which even, at the best, will create still new burdens of compliance with national and international verification regulations. This readiness is presumably also based on the fact that the chemical industry will ultimately benefit from the CWC regulations. The most important advantage may be the reinforcement of the perception that the chemical industry does not, in fact, desire to produce chemical weapons on its own initiative. The representatives of the chemical industry would also obtain an instrument which would allow them to decline production orders of chemicals the misuse of which could be suspected.

In this context, it should be emphasized that the increase in security provided by the regulation of the chemical industry under a future CWC represents for many countries only a minor part of the overall assurances required to be given and maintained under the CWC. The destruction of chemical weapons and of existing chemical-weapon stockpiles is of more immediate interest to the parties to a Chemical Weapons Convention. As pointed out in the introduction, it must be recognized that the production of chemical-warfare agents is not the only or most important limiting factor if a country wishes to acquire a militarily significant chemical-warfare capability.

Some of the contributors to this study express the opinion that only relatively small portions of the chemical industry may be affected by the inspection measures under the future CWC. Even so, it is of utmost importance that the routines and methods for meeting the verification objectives be worked out in such a fashion that they furnish as clear and unambiguous answers as possible on those occasions where and when they are applied. It is, for example, demonstrated in this study that, under certain production conditions, neither on-site inspection nor monitoring by instruments may provide sufficiently reliable data unless additional measures are taken. Under other circumstances, on-site inspection and monitoring by instruments would be adequate.

The various 'inspection experiments' which have been performed in some countries' chemical plants in the past, of which several are presented in this study, provide examples of the types of problems which may be met in the actual performance of routine or challenge inspections at production facilities. These endeavours have also underlined the need for a continued theoretical approach with respect to such concepts as the aims of the verification as well as the technical methods to be used. In this context, experiences from the IAEA, presented in Dr von Baeckmann's contribution, are useful, even if only partly applicable.

Concrete work on the evaluation of, and decision on, the actual verification methods to be applied would need to be begun as soon as possible, and be performed in direct connection with the ongoing negotiations. Several practical suggestions concerning this matter were suggested in the introduction to this study. A number of informal national and international groups have addressed these problems over a period of many years, but co-ordination of these efforts has been lacking. Information about this work and future work needs to be spread to both governments and the chemical industry. The future work will need to attend to two main areas: which technical methods are available and applicable today; and which methods will be needed and require further development.

Many technical methods exist today which can be applied to verification tasks. Their applicability is, however, dependent on factors which, to some extent, will have to be evaluated and decided upon in the technical-political iterative process called for above, and the following questions will need to be answered.

Should verification concern the presence or absence of individual, listed chemicals, or of classes of chemicals?

What emphasis should be given to the presence of inspectors on-site and to automatic-registration methods, respectively?

Need suggested 'spot-check' verification imply interruption of production processes?

To what extent does the need for maintenance of the verification equipment influence the reliability of the verification activities?

What efforts should be placed on standardizing the methods and instruments to conform to a common standard?

Will chemical analysis of products preferably be done on-site or, after sampling, at a central laboratory of the international authority?

What manpower resources and equipment will be needed and available?

What technical expertise will be required to perform the inspections and technical work at a central facility?

How will the technical personnel be trained and educated?

An in-depth evaluation has yet to be made which estimates and categorizes the various kinds and number of facilities which will be affected by the different verification methods. Such evaluation presupposes that the threshold amounts of the chemicals to be subject to the regime have previously been subjected to analysis and tentative agreement. In this context multi-purpose plants, as well as multi-purpose pilot plants and development laboratories, constitute important problems which need to be discussed further, as is made quite clear in the contribution by Dr Schröder and Professor Dr Hoffmann. Another important activity will be the working out of the model agreements and the ensuing facility agreements which will constitute the basis for the implementation of the verification measures on each particular site to be subject to on-site inspections or continuous monitoring, by instruments, of production activities.

With respect to the gathering of production data and its submission to national and international authorities, much emphasis has been given in this study to the need for data confidentiality to the extent necessary and to the possible methods for ensuring this. The national authority, or authorities, which will presumably be instituted or appointed as the national counterpart(s) to the international organization of the Convention will be indispensable in this respect.

Many of the contributors to this study have suggested that the role of the national authority should be to gather, organize and transmit the necessary data to the international authority in order that the latter not be overburdened by irrelevant data. Some consider this procedure to constitute an important means of preserving the confidentiality of the technical and commercial secrets of the national chemical industries. Whether such a system gives sufficient assurance of compliance remains to be evaluated. It might be of interest to have a more thorough discussion of the manner in which such a national body (bodies) might operate and how it would proceed in its transmission of relevant information.

The precision of the obtainable data which would serve as the basis for the reporting of production does not seem to be a technical problem. Sufficiently reliable registering instruments exist. However, other production factors may complicate the picture. For example, is production by batch or continuous; is it for immediate, internal consumption or for storing and selling? Which are the statistical errors; are the ranges given by statistical errors acceptable in relation to the risk to the Convention of possibly missing amounts of the given chemical? What are the possibilities of obtaining independent data which can reinforce each other, and so on?

A particular problem, touched upon by several of the contributors to this study, is the need to evaluate the possibility of using material accountancy balances. Although this approach is theoretically feasible, and has been applied under the IAEA Safeguards, the variations in production methods in the chemical industry and the very wide ranges of production volumes may limit its applicability under the CWC.

The influence of trading with chemicals on the international market with respect to the reliability of production statistics will probably have to be studied further, and the role of the national authorities in this context will have to be given increased attention.

Although the present study does not argue for any specific solutions, it presents a broad overview of the problems to be addressed, and--it is particularly important to note--provides detailed reasoning which explains the suggestions made. It is hoped that this study will thus constitute a valuable inventory of problems and suggestions for solutions that can benefit the remaining work on the Chemical Weapons Convention, not only in the context of the ongoing negotiations but also when the Preparatory Commission starts its work, and when implementation and future adjustments or revisions are undertaken under the final Chemical Weapons Convention.

VII. ANNEXES

Annex I: The table of contents and Article VIII from CD/831

Annex II: Article VI and its Annexes 0 to 4 from CD/831

Annex III: Bibliography of publications of relevance to this study

Annex IV: Excerpts from *OECD Environment Monographs*, no. 4

Annex V: Tables 1 to 6, presenting the relation between verification aims, methods, requirements and resources

Preliminary structure of a Convention on chemical weapons

Preamble

I.   General provisions on scope

II.   Definitions and Criteria

III.   Declarations

IV.   Chemical weapons

V.   Chemical weapons production facilities

VI.   Activities not prohibited by the Convention

VII.   National implementation measures

VIII.   The Organization

IX.   Consultations, co-operation and fact finding

X.   Assistance

XI.   Economic and technological development

XII.   Relation to other international agreements

XIII.   Amendments

XIV.   Duration, withdrawal

XV.   Signature, ratification, entry into force

XVI.   Languages

Annexes and other documents

CD/831
page 26
Appendix I

VIII.   THE ORGANIZATION 1/

A.   General Provisions

1.   The States Parties to the Convention hereby establish the Organization for the Prohibition of Chemical Weapons, to achieve the objectives of the Convention, to ensure the implementation of its provisions, including those for international verification of compliance with it, and to provide a forum for consultation and co-operation among States Parties. 2/

2.   All States Parties to the Convention shall be members of the Organization.

3.   The seat of the headquarters of the Orgnaization shall be ...

4.   There are hereby established as the organs of the Organization the [Consultative Committee] [General Conference], the Executive Council and the Technical Secretariat.

B.   [The Consultative Committee] [The General Conference]

(a)   Composition, procedure and decision-making

1.   The [Consultative Committee] [General Conference] shall be composed of all the States Parties to this Convention. Each State Party to the Convention shall have one representative in the [Consultative Committee] [General Conference], who may be accompanied by alternates and advisers.

2.   The first session of the [Consultative Committee] [General Conference] shall be convened by the Depository at (venue) not later than 30 days after the entry into force of the Convention.

3.   The [Consultative Committee] [General Conference] shall meet in regular sessions which should be held annually unless it decides otherwise. It shall meet in special sessions, as the [Consultative Committee] [General Conference] may decide, at the request of the Executive Council or at the request of any State Party supported by [8-10] 3/ [one third of] the States Parties. When necessary a special session shall be convened at short notice.

1/   One delegation has expressed reservations with regard to the approach being given to the concept of an Organization for the Prohibition of Chemical Weapons, or any other similar solution for this purpose, and has expressed the view that before proceeding further in the examination of this question, there is a need to define the principles that will govern the financing of such an Organization.

2/   A view was expressed that the achievement of these objectives should be sought in close co-operation with the United Nations.

3/   A view was expressed that a smaller number of States Parties supporting such a request could also be sufficient.

4.   Sessions shall take place at the headquarters of the Organization unless the [Consultative Committee] [General Conference] decides otherwise.

5.   The [Consultative Committee] [General Conference] shall adopt its rules of procedure. At the beginning of each regular session, it shall elect its Chairman and such other officers as may be required. They shall hold office until a new Chairman and other officers are elected at the next regular session.

6.   A majority of the members of the [Consultative Committee] [General Conference] shall constitute a quorum.

7.   Each member of the [Consultative Committee] [General Conference] shall have one vote.

8.   Decisions on questions of procedure, including decisions to convene special sessions of the [Consultative Committee] [General Conference], shall be taken by a simple majority of the members present and voting. Decisions on questions of substance shall be taken by a two-thirds majority of the members present and voting unless otherwise specifically provided for in the Convention. When the issue arises as to whether a question is one of substance or not, that question shall be treated as one of substance unless otherwise decided by the [Consultative Committee] [General Conference] by the majority required for decisions on questions of substance. 1/ 2/

(b) Powers and functions

1.   The [Consultative Committee] [General Conference] shall be the [principal] [supreme] organ of the Organization. It shall consider any questions, matters or issues within the scope of the Convention, including those relating to the powers and functions of the Executive Council and Technical Secretariat. It may make recommendations and take decisions 2/ on any questions, matters or issues related to the Convention raised by a State Party or brought to its attention by the Executive Council.

2.   The [Consultative Committee] [General Conference] shall oversee the implementation of the Convention, and promote and [assess] review compliance with it. It shall also oversee the activities of the Executive Council and the Technical Secretariat and may issue guidelines in accordance with the Convention to either of them in the exercise of their functions.

     1/   It has also been proposed that decisions should be taken by consensus, except as specified elsewhere and, if a consensus were not possible within 24 hours, by a simple majority of the members present and voting. It has also been pointed out that there should be no differentiation between decisions on questions of procedure and those of substance.

     2/   A view was expressed that the report of a fact-finding inquiry should not be put to a vote, nor should any decision be taken as to whether a Party is complying with the provisions of the Convention.

CD/831
page 28
Appendix I

3.   In addition, the powers and functions of the [Consultative Committee]
[General Conference] shall be:

   (i)   To consider and adopt at its regular sessions the report of the
          Organization, consider other reports 1/ and consider and adopt the
          programme and budget of the Organization, submitted by the Executive
          Council;

   (ii)   to [encourage] [promote] international co-operation for peaceful
          purposes in the chemical field;

   (iii) to review scientific and technological developments which could
          affect the operation of the Convention;

   (iv)   to decide on the scale of financial contributions to be paid by
          States Parties; 2/

   (v)   to elect the members of the Executive Council;

   (vi)   to appoint the Director of the Technical Secretariat; 3/

   (vii) to approve the rules of procedure of the Executive Council submitted
          by the latter;

   (viii) to establish such subsidiary organs as it finds necessary for the
          exercise of its functions in accordance with this Convention. 4/ 5/

   (ix)   ... 6/

   1/   It has been proposed that reports should be sent to the
United Nations.

   2/   The entire problem of the costs of the Organization needs to be
considered.

   3/   The option of candidates being proposed by the Executive Council and
by States Parties for appointment should be discussed.

   4/   It has been proposed that a Scientific Advisory Council be
established as a subsidiary body.

   5/   It has been proposed that a Fact-finding Panel be established as a
subsidiary body.

   6/   The question of functions relating to the implementation of
Articles X and XI will be considered at a later stage. Other functions,
e.g. the action to be taken in the event of non-compliance by a State Party,
could be included as well.

4.   The [Consultative Committee] [General Conference] shall, after the expiry of 5 and 10 years from the date of entry into force of this Convention and at such other times within that time period as may be agreed on, meet in special sessions to undertake reviews of the operation of this Convention. Such reviews shall take into account any relevant scientific and technological developments.   At intervals of five years thereafter, unless otherwise agreed upon by a majority of the States Parties, further sessions of the [Consultative Committee] [General Conference] shall be convened with the same objective. 1/

[5.   The Chairman of the [Consultative Committee] [General Conference] shall serve as non-voting Chairman of the Executive Council.]

C.   The Executive Council

(a)   Composition, procedure and decision-making

(To be elaborated)

(b)   Powers and functions

1.   The Executive Council shall be the executive organ of the [Consultative Committee] [General Conference], to which it shall be responsible.   It shall carry out the powers and functions entrusted to it under the Convention and its Annexes, as well as such functions delegated to it by the [Consultative Committee] [General Conference].   In so doing, it shall act in conformity with the recommendations, decisions and guidelines of the [Consultative Committee] [General Conference] and assure their continuous and proper implementation.

2.   In particular, the Executive Council shall:

(a)   promote the effective implementation of, and compliance with, the Convention;

(b)   supervise the activities of the Technical Secretariat;

(c)   co-operate with the appropriate national authorities of States Parties and facilitate consultations and co-operation among States Parties at their request;

1/   The placement and wording of this provision as well as the possible need for separate review conferences require further consideration.

(d)   consider any issue or matter within its competence, affecting the Convention and its implementation, including concerns regarding compliance,and cases of non-compliance, 1/ and, as appropriate, inform States Parties and bring the issue or matter to the attention of the [Consultative Committee] [General Conference];

(e)   consider and submit to the [Consultative Committee] [General Conference] the draft programme and budget of the Organization;

(f)   consider and submit to the [Consultative Committee] [General Conference] the draft report of the Organization on the implementation of the Convention, the report on the performance of its own activities and such special reports as it deems necessary or which the [Consultative Committee] [General Conference] may request;

(g)   conclude agreements with States and international organizations on behalf of the Organization, subject to approval by the [Consultative Committee] [General Conference], and approve agreements relating to the implementation of verification activities, concluded by the Director-General of the Technical Secretariat with States Parties;

(h)   (i)   meet for regular sessions. Between regular sessions, it shall meet as often as may be required for the fulfilment of its functions;

[(ii)   elect its Chairman;]

(iii)   elaborate and submit its rules of procedure to the [Consultative Committee] [General Conference] for approval;

(iv)   make arrangements for the sessions of the [Consultative Committee] [General Conference] including the preparation of a draft agenda.

3.   The Executive Council may request the convening of a special session of the [Consultative Committee] [General Conference]. 2/

1/   A view was expressed that the report of a fact-finding inquiry should not be put to a vote, nor should any decision be taken as to whether a Party is complying with the provisions of the Convention.

2/   It has been proposed that the Executive Council should request the convening of a special session of the [Consultative Committee] [General Conference] whenever obligations set forth in Article I of the Convention are violated.

D. Technical Secretariat

1.   A Technical Secretariat shall be established to assist the [Consultative Committee] [General Conference] and the Executive Council in the performance of their functions. The Technical Secretariat shall carry out the functions entrusted to it under the Convention and its Annexes, as well as such functions assigned to it by the [Consultative Committee] [General Conference] and the Executive Council.

2.   In particular, the Technical Secretariat shall:

(a) address and receive communications on behalf of the Organization to and from States Parties on matters pertaining to the implementation of the Convention;

(b) negotiate the subsidiary agreements with States Parties relating to systematic international on-site verification for approval by the Executive Council;

(c) execute international verification measure provided for in the Convention; 1/

(d) inform the Executive Council of any problems which have arisen with regard to the execution of its functions, and of [doubts, ambiguities or uncertainties about compliance with the Convention] which have come to its notice in the performance of its verification activities and/or which it has been unable to resolve or clarify through its consultations with the State Party concerned;

(e) provide technical assistance and technical evaluation to States Parties [in accordance with] [in the implementation of the provisions of] the Convention; 2/

(f) prepare and submit to the Executive Council the draft programme and budget of the Organization;

(g) prepare and submit to the Executive Council the draft report of the Organization on the implementation of the Convention and such other reports as the Executive Council and/or the [Consultative Committee] [General Conference] may request;

(h) provide administrative and technical support 2/ to the [Consultative Committee] [General Conference], the Executive Council and other subsidiary bodies.

_____

1/ It has been suggested that the International Inspectorate may request inspections for some insufficiently clear situations in the context of their systematic verification activities.

2/ The phrasing of this paragraph needs to be considered further in the light of the elaboration of the relevant provision of the Convention. It has been suggested that the technical assistance or evaluation may relate, inter alia, to developing technical procedures, improving the effectiveness of verification methods, and revising lists of chemicals.

202

3.   The International Inspectorate shall be a unit of the Technical Secretariat and shall act under the supervision of the Director-General of the Technical Secretariat.   Guidelines on the International Inspectorate are specified in ... 1/

4.   The Technical Secretariat shall comprise a Director-General, who shall be its head and chief administrative officer, and inspectors and such scientific, technical and other personnel as may be required.

5.   The Director-General of the Technical Secretariat shall be appointed by the [Consultative Committee] [General Conference] [upon the recommendation of the Executive Council] 2/ for [4] [5] years [renewable for one further term, but not thereafter].   The Director-General shall be responsible to the [Consultative Committee] [General Conference] and the Executive Council for the appointment of the staff and the organization and functioning of the Technical Secretariat.   The paramount consideration in the employment of the staff and in the determination of the conditions of services shall be the necessity of securing the highest standards of efficiency, competence and integrity.   Only citizens of States Parties shall serve as international inspectors or as other members of the professional and clerical staff.   Due regard shall be paid to the importance of recruiting the staff on as wide a geographical basis as possible.   Recruitment shall be guided by the principle that the staff shall be kept to a minimum necessary for the proper execution of its responsibilities.

6.   In the performance of their duties, the Director-General of the Technical Secretariat, the inspectors and other members of the staff shall not seek or receive instructions from any Government or from any other source external to the Organization.   They shall refrain from any action which might reflect on their positions as international officers responsible only to the [Consultative Committee] [General Conference] and the Executive Council.   In particular, subject to such responsibilities, they shall not disclose to any unauthorized persons any confidential information coming to their knowledge in the performance of their official duties.   The Director-General shall establish a régime governing the handling and protection of confidential data by the Technical Secretariat.

7.   Each State Party shall undertake to respect the exclusively international character of the responsibilities of the Director-General of the Technical Secretariat, the inspectors and the other members of the staff and not seek to influence them in the discharge of their responsibilities.

1/   Because of considerations under way in some capitals, the question of how to approach these guidelines will be decided later.   For the convenience of delegations Attachment (A) of the Report of the Co-ordinator for Cluster IV (CD/CW/WP.175) is included as Addendum I to this Appendix.

2/   It has been proposed that the Director-General of the Technical Secretariat be appointed by the [Consultative Committee] [General Conference] upon the recommendation of the Secretary-General of the United Nations.

VI. ACTIVITIES NOT PROHIBITED BY THE CONVENTION 1/ 2/

1.   Each State Party:

(a) has the right, subject to the provisions of this Convention, to develop, produce, otherwise acquire, retain, transfer and use toxic chemicals and their precursors for purposes not prohibited by the Convention.

(b) shall ensure that toxic chemicals and their precursors are not developed, produced, otherwise acquired, retained, transferred, or used within its territory or anywhere under its jurisdiction or control for purposes prohibited by the Convention.

2.   Toxic Chemicals and their Precursors:

(a) Toxic chemicals and their precursors considered in the Annexes to Article VI [1], [2], [3] and [...], 3/ which could be used for purposes prohibited by the Convention, as well as facilities which produce, process or consume these toxic chemicals or precursors, shall be subject to international monitoring as provided in those annexes:

Annex to Article VI [1] Schedule [1]:   Super-Toxic Lethal Chemicals and [especially dangerous key precursors] [key components of chemicals weapons systems].

Annex to Article VI [2] Schedule [2]:   Key Precursors.

Annex to Article VI [3] Schedule [3]:   Chemicals produced in large commercial quantities and which could be used for chemical weapons purposes.

Annex to Article VI [...]:   Production of super-toxic lethal chemicals not listed in Schedules [1].

1/   One delegation considers that the terminology used in this article and its annexes should be consistent with the final definition of chemical weapons to be agreed upon.

2/   One delegation expressed the view that the question of collection and forwarding of data and other information to verify non-production requires further consideration. This delegation made reference to the Working Paper CD/CW/WP.159 of 19 March 1987, which includes draft elements for inclusion in the rolling text.

3/   Some delegations consider that these chemicals should be dealt with in the Annex to Article VI [2] Schedule [2]. Other delegations consider that a separate Annex [4] is required. Until this issue is resolved, the designation Annex to Article VI [...] is used.

(b) The schedules of chemicals contained in the annexes may be revised. Modalities for revision are contained in the Annex to Article [VI] [O.]. 1/

3. Within 30 days of the entry into force of it, each State Party shall declare data on relevant chemicals and the facilities which produce them, in accordance with the Annex to Article VI [1], [2], [3] and [...].

4. Each State Party shall make an annual declaration regarding the relevant chemicals in accordance with the Annex to Article VI [1], [2], [3] and [...].

5. Each State Party undertakes to subject the chemicals and [facility] [facilities] under the Annex to Article VI [1] to the measures contained in that Annex.

6. Each State Party undertakes to subject the chemicals and facilities under the Annex to Article VI [2] and [...] to monitoring by data reporting and routine systematic international on-site verification, through on-site inspection and use of on-site instruments as long as production and processing are not impaired.

7. Each State Party undertakes to subject the chemicals and facilities under the Annex to Article VI [3] to monitoring by data reporting.

8. The provisions of this article shall be implemented in a manner designed in so far as possible to avoid hampering the economic or technological development of parties to the Convention and international co-operation in the field of peaceful chemical activities including the international exchange of scientific and technical information and chemicals and equipment for the production, processing or use of chemicals for peaceful purposes in accordance with the provisions of the Convention. 2/ 3/

9. In conducting verification activities, the (Consultative Committee) shall:

(a) avoid undue interference in the State Party's peaceful chemical activities;

(b) take every precaution to protect confidential information coming to its knowledge in the implementation of the Convention; 2/ and

(c) require only the minimum amount of information and data necessary for the carrying out of its responsibilities under the Convention.

10. For the purpose of on-site verification, each State Party shall grant to the (Consultative Committee) access to facilities as required in the Annex to Article VI [1], [2], [3] and [...].

1/ Furthermore, work was carried out on guidelines for considering inclusion of chemicals in Schedule [1]. The result of this work is enclosed in Appendix II to serve as a basis for future work.

2/ It was agreed that provisions to ensure the confidentiality of the information provided should be elaborated.

3/ The inclusion of this paragraph in this Article is to be considered further.

ANNEX TO ARTICLE VI [O.]

MODALITIES FOR REVISION OF LISTS

1. The revisions envisaged would consist of additions to, deletions, from, or shifts between the lists.

2. A revision could be proposed by a State Party. [If the Technical Secretariat has information which in its opinion may require a revision of the lists of chemicals, it should provide that information to the [Executive Council] which should communicate it to all States Parties.] A State Party may request the assistance of the Technical Secretariat in the substantiation of its proposal.

3. A proposal for revision should be submitted to [the International Authority] [the Executive Council] [the Depositary of the Convention].

4. [The International Authority] [The Executive Council] [The Depositary of the Convention], upon receipt of a proposal for revision, will be responsible for informing States Parties about it.

5. The proponent should substantiate its proposal with the necessary information. Any State Party and, as requested, the Technical Secretariat, could also provide relevant information for the evaluation of the proposal.

6. Technical evaluations of a proposal may be made by the International Authority, [the Executive Council], any State Party [and the Technical Secretariat].

7. The decision on a proposal should be taken by the International Authority [the Consultative Committee] by [a majority vote] [consensus] [tacit approval of all States Parties 60 days after they have been informed of the proposal by the International Authority. If there is no tacit approval, the matter should be reviewed by the [Consultative Committee] at its next meeting.] [If urgent consideration is requested by five or more Parties, a special meeting of the Consultative Committee should be promptly convened.]

8. The revision procedure should be concluded within [60 days] after the receipt of the proposal. Once a decision is taken, it should enter into force after a period of [30 days].

9. The Technical Secretariat should provide assistance to any State Party, when requested, in evaluating an unlisted chemical. This assistance should be confidential [unless it is established in the evaluation that the chemical has chemical weapon properties].

ANNEX TO ARTICLE VI [1]

GENERAL PROVISIONS

1.   A State Party shall not produce, acquire, retain, transfer or use chemicals in Schedule [1] unless:

(i)   the chemicals are applied to research, medical or protective purposes, 1/ and

(ii)   the types and quantities of chemicals are strictly limited to those which can be justified for research, medical or protective purpose, and

(iii)   the aggregate amount of such chemicals at any given time for [permitted] [protective] purposes is equal to or less than one metric tonne, and

(iv)   the aggregate amount for [permitted] [protective] purposes acquired by a State Party in any calendar year through production, withdrawal from chemical weapons stocks and transfer is equal to or less than one metric tonne.

TRANSFERS

2.   A State Party may transfer chemicals in Schedule [1] outside its territory only to another State Party and only for research, medical or protective purposes in accordance with paragraph 1.

3.   Chemicals transferred shall not be retransferred to a third State.

4.   Thirty days prior to any transfer to another State Party both States Parties shall notify the Consultative Committee.

5.   Each State Party shall make a detailed annual declaration regarding transfers during the previous calendar year. The declaration shall be submitted within ... months after the end of that year and shall for each chemical in Schedule [1] include the following information:

(i)   the chemical name, structural formula and Chemical Abstracts Service Registry Number (if assigned);

(ii)   the quantity acquired from other States or transferred to other States Parties. For each transfer the quantity, recipient and purpose should be included.

1/   A view was expressed that for consistency in this Annex, "permitted purposes" should be used instead of "research, medical or protective purposes". The view was also expressed that use of the term "permitted" would broaden considerably the sphere of use of super-toxic lethal chemicals which could be used as chemical weapons and that this was very undesirable.

SINGLE SMALL-SCALE PRODUCTION FACILITY

Each State Party which produces chemicals in Schedule [1] for [permitted] [protective] purposes shall carry out the production at a single small-scale facility, the capacity of which shall not exceed [one] metric tonne per'year, as measured by the method established in [   ]. 1/

I.   Declarations

A.   Initial declarations

Each State Party which plans to operate such a facility shall provide the Consultative Committee with the location and a detailed technical description of the facility, including an inventory of equipment and detailed diagrams. For existing facilities, this information shall be provided not later than 30 days after the Convention enters into force for the State Party. Information on new facilities shall be provided six months before operations are to begin.

B.   Advance notifications

Each State Party shall give advance notification to the [international authority] of planned changes related to the initial declaration. The notification shall be submitted not later than ... months before the changes are to take place.

C.   Annual declarations

(a) Each State Party possessing a facility shall make a detailed annual declaration regarding the activities of the facility for the previous calendar year. The declaration shall be submitted within ... months after the end of that year and shall include:

1.   Identification of the facility

2.   For each chemical in Schedule [1] produced, acquired, consumed or stored at the facility, the following information:

   (i)   the chemical name, structural formula and Chemical Abstracts Service Registry Number (if assigned);

   (ii) the methods employed and quantity produced;

   (iii) the name and quantity of precursor chemicals listed in Schedules [1], [2] or [3] used for production of chemicals in Schedule [1];

   (iv) the quantity consumed at the facility and the purpose(s) of the consumption;

1/   The view was expressed that the single small-scale production facility should be State-owned.

(v)   the quantity received from or shipped to other facilities
within the State Party. For each shipment the quantity,
recipient and purpose should be included;

(vi)   the maximum quantity stored at any time during the year;

(vii)   the quantity stored at the end of the year.

3.   Information on any changes at the facility during the year compared
to previously submitted detailed technical descriptions of the
facility including inventories of equipment and detailed diagrams.

(b)   Each State Party possessing a facility shall make a detailed annual
declaration regarding the projected activities and the anticipated production
at the facility for the coming calendar year. The declaration shall be
submitted not later than ... months before the beginning of that year and
shall include:

1.   Identification of the facility

2.   For each chemical in Schedule [1] produced, consumed or stored at
the facility, the following information:

(i)   the chemical name, structural formula and Chemical Abstracts
Service Registry Number (if assigned);

(ii)   the quantity anticipated to be produced and the purpose of the
production.

3.   Information on any anticipated changes at the facility during the
year compared to previously submitted detailed technical
descriptions of the facility including inventories of equipment and
detailed diagrams.

II.   Verification

1.   The aim of verification activities at the facility shall be to verify
that the quantities of Schedule [1] chemicals produced are correctly declared
and, in particular, that their aggregate amount does not exceed one metric
tonne.

2.   The single small-scale production facility shall be subject to systematic
international on-site verification, through on-site inspection and monitoring
with on-site instruments.

3.   The number, intensity, duration, timing and mode of inspections for a
particular facility shall be based on the risk to the objectives of the
Convention posed by the relevant chemicals, the characteristics of the
facility and the nature of the activities carried out there. The guidelines
to be used shall include: (to be developed)

4.   Each facility shall receive an initial visit from international
inspectors promptly after the facility is declared. The purpose of the
initial visit shall be to verify information provided concerning the facility,

including verification that the capacity will not permit the production, on an annual basis, of quantities [significantly] above one metric tonne, and to obtain any additional information needed for planning future verification activities at the facility, including inspection visits and use of on-site instruments.

5.   Each State Party possessing or planning to possess a facility shall execute an agreement, based on a model agreement, with the [international authority] before the facility begins operation or is used, covering detailed inspection procedures for the facility. Each agreement shall include: (to be developed) 1/

OTHER FACILITIES

[Facilities which synthesize, acquire or use chemicals in Schedule [1] for research or medical purposes shall be approved by the State Party. Synthesis at each such facility for research and medical purposes shall be limited per annum to a total maximum of [..]g and to [..]g of any one chemical on the Schedule.]

[Facilities which acquire or use chemicals in Schedule [1] for permitted purposes shall be approved by the State Party. Each transfer from the single small-scale production facility to such facilities shall be notified to the Consultative Committee by inclusion in the annual data reporting, with an indication of the chemical or chemicals involved, the amount transferred and the purpose of the transfer.]

I.   Declarations

A.   Initial declarations

The location of the facilities approved by the State Party shall be provided to the Consultative Committee.

B.   Advance notifications

C.   Annual declarations

II. Verification

Facilities shall be monitored through annual data reporting to the Consultative Committee. The following information shall be included: (to be developed)

_____

1/   The view was expressed that pending conclusion of the agreement between a State Party and the [International Authority] there would be a need for provisional inspection procedures to be formulated.

ANNEX TO ARTICLE VI [1]
SCHEDULE [1]

PROVISIONAL LIST 1/

1.   O-Alkyl alkylphosphonofluoridates

     e.g.   Sarin: O-isopropyl methylphosphonofluoridate   (107-44-8)
            Soman: O-pinacolyl methylphosphonofluoridate   (96-64-0)

2.   O-Alkyl N,N-dialkylphosphoramidocyanidates

     e.g.   Tabun: O-ethyl N,N-dimethylphosphoramidocyanidate   (77-81-6)

3.   O-Alkyl S-2-dialkylaminoethylalkylphosphonothiolates

     e.g.   VX: O-ethyl S-2-diisopropylaminoethylmethyl-
                  phosphonothiolate   (50782-69-9)

4.   Sulphur mustards:

     e.g.   Mustard gas (H):   bis(2-chloroethyl)sulphide   (505-60-2)
            Sesquimustard (Q):   1,2-bis(2-chloroethylthio)ethane   (3563-36-8)
            O-Mustard (T):   bis(2-chloroethylthioethyl)ether   (63918-89-8)

5.   Lewisites

     Lewisite 1:   2-chlorovinyldichloroarsine   (541-25-3)
     Lewisite 2:   bis(2-chlorovinyl)chloroarsine   (40334-69-8)
     Lewisite 3:   tris(2-chlorovinyl)arsine   (40334-70-1)

6.   Nitrogen mustards

     HN1:   bis(2-chloroethyl)ethylamine   (538-07-8)
     HN2:   bis(2-chloroethyl)methylamine   (51-75-2)
     HN3:   tris(2-chloroethyl)amine   (555-77-1)

7.   3-Quinuclidinyl benzilate (BZ)   (6581-06-2)

8.   Alkylphosphonyldifluorides

     e.g.   DF   (676-99-3)

9.   Ethyl O-2-diisopropylaminoethyl alkylphosphonites

     e.g.   QL   (57856-11-8)

1/   Some of the chemicals on the Schedules exist in more than one
stereoisomeric form. It is proposed that, where assigned, the Chemical
Abstracts Service Registry Numbers be stated for each of them.

To be discussed further

1. Saxitoxin

2. 3,3-Dimethylbutan-2-ol (pinacolyl alcohol)

3. CS

4. CR

5. Chloro Soman and Chloro Sarin

6. Sulphur Mustards: to include compounds listed below.

   2-chloroethylchloromethylsulphide

   bis(2-chloroethyl)sulphone

   bis(2-chloroethylthio)methane

   1,3-bis(2-chloroethylthio)-n-propane

   1,4-bis(2-chloroethylthio)-n-butane

ANNEX TO ARTICLE VI [2]

KEY PRECURSOR CHEMICALS

DECLARATIONS

The Initial and Annual Declarations to be provided by a State Party under paragraphs [3] and [4] of Article VI shall include:

1.   Aggregate national data on the production, processing and consumption of each chemical listed in Schedule [2], and on the export and import of the chemicals in the previous calendar year with an indication of the countries involved.

2.   The following information for each facility which, during the previous calendar year, produced, processed or consumed more than [ ] tonnes per annum of the chemicals listed in Schedule [2]:

Key Precursor Chemical(s)

   (i)   The chemical name, common or trade name used by the facility, structural formula, and Chemical Abstracts Service Registry Number (if assigned).

  (ii)   The total amount produced, consumed, imported and exported in the previous calendar year. 1/

 (iii)   The purpose(s) for which the key precursor chemical(s) are produced, consumed or processed:

      (a)   conversion on-site (specify product type)

      (b)   sale or transfer to other domestic industry (specify final product type)

      (c)   export of a key precursor (specify which country)

      (d)   other.

   1/   Whether the total amount is to be expressed as an exact figure or within a range is to be discussed.

Facility 1/ 2/

(i) The name of the facility and of the owner, company, or enterprise operating the facility.

(ii) The exact location of the facility (including the address, location of the complex, location of the facility within the complex including the specific building and structure number, if any).

(iii) Whether the facility is dedicated to producing or processing the listed key precursor or is multi-purpose.

(iv) The main orientation (purpose) of the facility.

(v) Whether the facility can readily be used to produce a Schedule [1] chemical or another Schedule [2] chemical. Relevant information should be provided, when applicable.

(vi) The production capacity 3/ for the declared Schedule [2] chemical(s).

(vii) Which of the following activities are performed with regard to the key precursor chemicals:

(a) production

(b) processing with conversion into another chemical

(c) processing without chemical conversion

(d) other - specify.

(viii) Whether at any time during the previous calendar year declared key precursors were stored on-site in quantities greater than [   ] [tonnes].

_____

1/ One delegation suggested that, in the case of a multi-purpose facility currently producing key precursor chemicals, the following should be specified:

- general description of the products;
- detailed technological plan of the facility;
- list of special equipment included in the technological plan;
- type of waste treatment equipment;
- description of each final product (chemical name, chemical structure and register number);
- unit capacity for each product;
- use of each product.

2/ The view was expressed that a definition of a chemical production facility was needed and thus should be elaborated.

3/ How to define production capacity remains to be agreed upon. Some consultations with technical experts have taken place on this issue. A report on these consultations is enclosed in Appendix II to facilitate further work by delegations.

Advance notifications

3.   (a) Each State Party shall annually notify the (international authority) of facilities which intend, during the coming calendar year, to produce, process or consume more than ... of any chemical listed in Schedule [2]. The notification shall be submitted not later than ... months before the beginning of that year and shall for each facility include the following information:

(i)   The information specified under paragraph 2 above, except for quantitative information relating to the previous calendar year;

(ii)   For each chemical listed in Schedule [2] intended to be produced or processed, the total quantity intended to be produced or processed during the coming calendar year and the time period(s) when the production or processing is anticipated to take place.

(b) Each State Party shall notify the (international authority) of any production, processing or consumption planned after the submission of the annual notification under paragraph 3 (a), not later than one month before the production or processing is anticipated to begin. The notification shall for each facility include the information specified under paragraph 3 (a).

Verification 1/

Aim

4.   The aim of the measures stipulated in Article VI, paragraph 6 shall be to verify that:

(i)   Facilities declared under this Annex are not used to produce any chemical listed in Schedule [1]. 2/

(ii)   The quantities of chemicals listed in Schedule [2] produced, processed or consumed are consistent with needs for purposes not prohibited by the Chemical Weapons Convention. 3/

(iii) The chemicals listed in Schedule [2] are not diverted or used for purposes prohibited by .the Chemical Weapons Convention.

1/   Some of the provisions contained in this section have general application throughout the Convention. It is understood that the retention of these will be reviewed at a later stage in the negotiations.

2/   It was suggested that "or for any other purposes prohibited by the Convention" should be added.

3/   Opinions were expressed on the need to consider the question of the existence in a facility of excessive capacity for the production of chemicals in Schedule [2].

Obligation and Frequency

5.   (i)   Each facility notified to the [international authority] under this
          Annex shall be subject to systematic international on-site
          verification on a routine basis.

     (ii) The number, intensity, duration, timing and mode of inspections and
          monitoring with on-site instruments for a particular facility shall
          be based on the risk to the objectives of the Convention posed by
          the relevant chemical, the characteristics of the facility and the
          nature of the activities carried out there. 1/ 2/ The guidelines to
          be used shall include: (to be developed). 3/

Selection

6.   The particular facility to be inspected shall be chosen by the
[international authority] in such a way to preclude the prediction of
precisely when the facility is to be inspected.

Notification

7.   A State Party shall be notified by the [international authority] of the
decision to inspect a facility referred to in paragraphs 2 and 3 .... hours
prior to the arrival of the inspection team.

Host State Party

8.   The host State Party shall have the right to designate personnel to
accompany an international inspection team. The exercise of this right shall
not affect the right of inspectors to obtain access to the facility, as
provided by the Convention, nor shall it delay or otherwise impede the
carrying out of the inspection.

1/   One delegation suggested that the number of such inspections could
be from 1 to 5 per year.

2/   A number of possible factors that could influence the number,
intensity, duration, timing and mode of inspections have been identified and
discussed. The result of this work is enclosed in Appendix II to serve as a
basis for future work.

3/   It was noted that a "weighted approach" might be taken in
determining the inspection régime for specific chemicals. The importance of
establishing a threshold(s) in this context was also noted. It was mentioned
that a threshold(s) should relate to "military significant quantities" of the
relevant chemical(s).

Initial Visit

9.   Each facility notified to the [international authority] under this Annex shall be liable to receive an initial visit from international inspectors, promptly after the State becomes a Party to the Convention.

10.   The purpose of the initial visit shall be to verify information provided concerning the facility to be inspected and to obtain any additional information needed for planning future verification activities at the facility, including inspection visits and use of on-site instruments.

Agreement on Inspection Procedures

11.   Each State Party shall execute an agreement, based on a model agreement, with the [international authority], within [6] months after the Convention enters into force for the State, governing the conduct of the inspections of the facilities declared by the State Party. The agreement shall provide for the detailed subsidiary arrangements which shall govern inspections at each facility. 1/

12.   Such agreements shall be based on a Model Agreement and shall specify for each facility the number, intensity, duration of inspections, detailed inspection procedures and the installation, operation and maintenance of on-site instruments by the International Authority. The Model Agreement shall include provisions to take into account future technological developments.

    States Parties shall ensure that the systematic international on-site verification can be accomplished by the International Authority at all facilities within the agreed time frames after the convention enters into force. 2/

Verification Inspections

13.   The areas of a facility to be inspected under subsidiary arrangements may, inter alia, include: 3/

    1/   Several delegations considered that the model agreement should be elaborated as part of the negotiations on the Convention. A draft for such a model agreement is contained in Appendix II.

    2/   Procedures to ensure the implementation of the verification scheme within designated time frames are to be developed.

    3/   Opinions were expressed on the need to consider the question of the existence in a facility of excessive capacity for the production of chemicals on Schedule [2].

217

(i) areas where feed chemicals (reactants) are delivered and/or stored;

(ii) areas where manipulative processes are performed upon the reactants prior to addition to the reaction vessel;

(iii) feed lines as appropriate from subparagraph (i) and/or subparagraph (ii) to the reaction vessel, together with any associated valves, flow meters, etc.;

(iv) the external aspect of the reaction vessel and its ancillary equipment;

(v) lines from the reaction vessel leading to long- or short-term storage or for further processing of the designated chemical;

(vi) control equipment associated with any of the items under subparagraphs (i) to (v);

(vii) equipment and areas for waste and effluent handling;

(viii) equipment and areas for disposition of off-specification chemicals.

14. (a) The International Authority shall notify the State Party of its decision to inspect or visit the facility [48] [12] hours prior to the planned arrival of the inspection team at the facility for systematic inspections or visits. In the event of inspections or visits to resolve urgent problems, this period may be shortened. The International Authority shall specify the purpose(s) of the inspection or visit.

(b) A State Party shall make any necessary preparations for the arrival of the Inspectors and shall ensure their expeditious transportation from their point of entry on the territory of the State Party to the facility. The agreement on subsidiary arrangements will specify administrative arrangements for Inspectors.

(c) International Inspectors shall, in accordance with agreements on subsidiary arrangements:

- have unimpeded access to all areas that have been agreed for inspection. While conducting their activity, Inspectors shall comply with the safety regulations at the facility. The items to be inspected will be chosen by the Inspectors;

- bring with them and use such agreed instruments as may be necessary for the completion of their tasks;

- receive samples taken at their request at the facility. Such samples will be taken by representatives of the State Party in the presence of the Inspectors;

- perform on-site analysis of samples;

- transfer, if necessary, samples for analysis off-site at a laboratory designated by the International Authority, in accordance with agreed procedures; 1/

- afford the opportunity to the Host State Party to be present when samples are analysed; 1/

- ensure, in accordance with procedures (to be developed), that samples transported, stored and processed are not tampered with; 1/

- communicate freely with the International Authority.

(d) The State Party receiving the inspection shall, in accordance with agreed procedures:

- have the right to accompany the International Inspectors at all times during the inspection and observe all their verification activities at the facility;

- have the right to retain duplicates of all samples taken and be present when samples are analysed;

- have the right to inspect any instrument used or installed by the International Inspectors and to have it tested in the presence of its personnel;

- provide assistance to the International Inspectors, upon their request, for the installation of the monitoring system and the analysis of samples on-site;

- receive copies of the reports on inspections of its facility(ies);

- receive copies, at its request, of the information and data gathered about its facility(ies) by the International Authority.

15. The Technical Secretariat may retain at each site a sealed container for photographs, plans and other information that it may wish to refer to in the course of subsequent inspection.

Submission of Inspectors' Report

16. After each inspection or visit to the facility, International Inspectors shall submit a report with their findings to the International Authority which will transmit a copy of this report to the State Party having received the inspection or visit. Information received during the inspection shall be treated as confidential (procedures to be developed).

17. The International Inspectors may request clarification of any ambiguities arising from the inspection. In the event that any ambiguities arise which cannot be resolved in the course of the inspection, the Inspectors shall inform the International Authority immediately.

1/   The view was expressed that all questions related to analysis off-site required further discussion.

ANNEX TO ARTICLE VI [2]
SCHEDULE [2]

PROVISIONAL LIST

1. Chemicals containing one P-methyl, P-ethyl, or P-propyl (normal or iso) bond.

2. N,N-Dialkylphosphoramidic dihalides.

3. Dialkyl N,N-dialkylphosphoramidates.

4. Arsenic trichloride.   (7784-34-1)

5. 2,2-Diphenyl-2-hydroxyacetic acid.   (76-93-7)

6. Quinuclidin-3-ol   (1619-34-7)

7. N,N-Diisopropylaminoethyl-2-chloride.   (96-79-7)

8. N,N-Diisopropylaminoethan-2-ol.   (96-80-0)

9. N,N-Diisopropylaminoethane-2-thiol.   (5842-07-9)

TO BE DISCUSSED FURTHER

(1) The following compounds:

Bis(2-hydroxyethyl)sulphide   (thiodiglycol)

3,3-Dimethylbutan-2-ol   (pinacolyl alcohol)

(2) Expanded groups for compounds 5, 6, 7, 8 and 9, as follows:

(No. 5):   2-phenyl-2-(phenyl, cyclohexyl, cyclopentyl or cyclobutyl)-2-hydroxyacetic acids and their methyl, ethyl, n-propyl and iso-propyl esters.

(No. 6):   3- or 4-hydroxypiperidine and their [derivatives] and [analogs].

(Nos. 7,8,9): N,N-Disubstituted aminoethyl-2-halides
               N,N-Disubstituted aminoethan-2-ols
               N,N-Disubstituted aminoethane-2-thiols

220

ANNEX TO ARTICLE VI [3]

Chemicals which are produced in large commercial quantities and which could be used for chemical weapons purposes

DECLARATIONS

1.   The Initial and Annual Declarations to be provided by a State Party under paragraph [4] of Article VI shall include the following information for each of the chemicals listed in Schedule [3]:

   (i)   The chemicals name, common or trade name used by the facility, structural formula and Chemical Abstracts Service Registry Number.

  (ii)   The total amount produced, consumed, imported and exported in the previous calendar year.

 (iii)   The final product or end use of the chemical in accordance with the following categories (to be developed),

  (iv)   for each facility which during the previous calendar year produced, processed, consumed or transferred more than [30] tonnes of a chemical listed in Schedule [3]. 1/

      (a)   The name of the facility and of the owner, company, or enterprise operating the facility.

      (b)   The location of the facility.

      (c)   The capacity (to be defined) 2/ of the facility.

      (d)   The approximate amount of production and consumption of the chemical in the previous year (ranges to be specified).

1/   It was proposed that a threshold for the dual purpose agents (Phosgene, Cyanogen chloride, Hydrogen cyanide, Chloropicrin) could be established at [50 tonnes/year] [500 tonnes/year] and for precursors at [5 tonnes/year] [50 tonnes/year]. The proposal was presented in an informal discussion paper dated 30 March 1987, prepared on the request of the Chairman of the Committee, by Dr. Peroni (Brazil), Lt. Col. Bretfeld (German Democratic Republic) and Dr. Ooms (Netherlands).

2/   Some consultations with technical experts have taken place on this issue. A report on these consultations is enclosed in Appendix II to facilitate further work by delegations.

2.   A State Party shall notify the (International Authority) of the name and location of any facility which intends, in the year following submission of the Annual Declaration, to produce, process or consume any of the chemicals listed in Schedule [3] (on an industrial scale - to be defined).

VERIFICATION

The verification régime for chemicals listed in Schedule [3] will comprise both the provision of data by a State Party to the [International Authority] and the monitoring of that data by the [International Authority]. 1/

1/   Some delegations consider that provision should be made for resort to an on-site "spot-check" inspection, if required, to verify information supplied by a State Party. Other delegations believe that the provisions of Articles VII, VIII and IX of the Convention are sufficient in this respect.

ANNEX TO ARTICLE VI [3]
SCHEDULE [3]

Phosgene   (75-44-5)

Cyanogen chloride   (506-77-4)

Hydrogen cyanide   (74-90-8)

Trichloronitromethane (chloropicrin)   (76-06-2)

Phosphorus oxychloride   (10025-87-3)

Phosphorus trichloride   (7719-12-2)

Di- and Trimethyl/Ethyl Esters of
  Phosphorus [P III] Acid:

        Trimethyl phosphite   (121-45-9)

        Triethyl phosphite   (122-52-1)

        Dimethyl phosphite   (868-85-9)

        Diethyl phosphite   (762-04-9)

Sulphur monochloride   (19925-67-9)

Sulphur dichloride   (19545-99-0)

ANNEX TO ARTICLE VI [...] 1/

Production of super-toxic lethal chemicals not listed in Schedule [1]

The provisions of this Annex cover:

- chemicals with an LD_{50} equal to or less than 0.5 mg per kg bodyweight 2/ or an LCt_{50} equal to or less than 2,000 mg-min/m^3;

- facilities which

(a) produce or process more than [10] [100] [1 000] kg 3/ per annum 4/ of any such chemical; 5/

[(b) have a production capacity 6/ for any such chemical exceeding 1 000 kg 7/ per annum. 8/]

1/ Some delegations consider that the chemicals in this Annex should be dealt with in the Annex to Article VI [2] Schedule [2]. Other delegations consider that a separate Annex [4] is required.

2/ It is understood that further discussion is needed with regard to chemicals with a somewhat lower toxicity. In this context various ideas were put forward, i.a.:

- that chemicals falling within a deviation-range of 10-20 per cent could be considered;

- that chemicals with an LD_{50} close to 0.5 mg/kg bodyweight could be included as exceptions;

- that the modalities for revisions of lists could be made use of to take care of possible concerns in this regard.

3/ Some delegations felt that the thresholds for production and production capacity should correspond to militarily significant quantities.

4/ The question of production or processing not occurring annually requires further discussion.

5/ Some delegations expressed the view that additional criteria of suitability for chemical weapons purposes should be added.

6/ How to define production capacity remains to be agreed upon. In this context reference was made to the proposal contained in CD/CW/WP.171, as well as the report contained in Appendix II to this document.

7/ It is understood that the quantitative value of the threshold for production capacity remains to be discussed.

8/ One delegation expressed the view that the question of production capacities should be considered in accordance with the relevant provisions in the Annex to Article VI, Schedules [2] and [3] (cf. CD/CW/WP.167 pp. 62, 68).

DECLARATIONS 1/

The Initial and Annual Declarations to be provided by a State Party under Article VI shall include:

1.   Aggregate national data on the production or processing of each chemical [listed in] [covered by] this Annex, 2/ and on the export and import of the chemicals in the previous calendar year with an indication of the countries involved.

2.   The following information for each facility which, during the previous calendar year, produced or processed more than [10] [100] [1 000] kg 3/ of any chemical [listed in] [covered by] this Annex.

Chemical(s)

(i)   The chemical name, common or trade name used by the facility, structural formula, and Chemical Abstracts Service Registry Number (if assigned).

(ii)   The total amount produced, processed, imported and exported in the previous calendar year. 4/ 5/

(iii)   The purpose(s) for which the chemical(s) are produced or processed:

(a)   conversion on-site (specify product type)

(b)   sale or transfer to other domestic industry (specify final product type)

(c)   export of a chemical (specify which country)

Facility

(i)   The name of the facility and of the owner, company, or enterprise operating the facility.

1/   The information to be reported on chemicals will depend largely on what aims are eventually agreed for verification under paragraph 4 of this Annex.

2/   A proposal for a list of chemicals, to be included in the Convention under this category, is contained in CD/792.

3/   Some delegations felt that the thresholds for production and production capacity should correspond to militarily significant quantities.

4/   Whether the total amount is to be expressed as an exact figure or within a range is to be discussed.

5/   One delegation expressed the view that aggregate national data on the production of any such chemical should also be provided.

> (ii) The exact location of the facility (including the address, location of the complex, location of the facility within the complex including the specific building and structure number, if any).
>
> (iii) Whether the facility is dedicated to producing or processing the declared chemical or is multi-purpose.
>
> (iv) The main orientation (purpose) of the facility.
>
> [(v) Whether the facility can readily be used to produce a Schedule [1] chemical.' Relevant information should be provided, when applicable.]
>
> (vi) The production capacity for the declared chemical(s) 1/
>
> (vii) Which of the following activities are performed with regard to chemicals
>
>> (a) production
>>
>> (b) processing with conversion into another chemical
>>
>> (c) processing without chemical conversion
>>
>> (d) other - specify.
>
> (viii) Whether at any time during the previous calendar year declared chemicals were stored on-site in quantities greater than [ ] [tonnes].

Advance notifications

3. (a) Each State Party shall annually notify the [International Authority] of facilities which anticipate, during the coming calendar year, to produce or process more than .... of any chemical [listed in] [covered by] this Annex. The notification shall be submitted not later than ... months before the beginning of that year and shall for each facility include the following information:

> (i) The information specified under paragraph 2 above, except for quantitative information relating to the previous calendar year;
>
> (ii) For each chemical, the total quantity anticipated to be produced or processed during the coming calendar year and the time period(s) when the production or processing is anticipated to take place.

(b) Each State Party shall notify the [International Authority] of any production, processing planned after the submission of the annual notification under paragraph 3 (a), not later than one month before the production or processing is anticipated to begin. The notification shall for each facility include the information specified under paragraph 3 (a).

_____

1/ How to define production capacity remains to be agreed upon.

226

VERIFICATION 1/

Aim 2/

4.   The aim of the measures stipulated in Article VI, paragraph 6 shall be to verify that:

(i)   facilities declared under this Annex are not used to produce any chemical listed in Schedule [1];

(ii)   the quantities of declared chemicals produced or processed are consistent with needs for purposes not prohibited by the Chemical Weapons Convention;

(iii)   the declared chemicals are not diverted or used for purposes prohibited by the Chemical Weapons Convention.

Obligation and frequency

5.   (i)   Each facility notified to the [International Authority] shall be liable to receive an initial visit from international inspectors, promptly after the State becomes a Party to the Convention.

(ii)   The purpose of the initial visit shall be to verify information provided concerning the facility to be inspected and to obtain any additional information, [including on the capacity of the facility, needed for planning] [to determine whether systematic on-site verification on a routine basis is necessary, and, if so, to plan] future verification activities at the facility, including inspection visits and use of on-site instruments.

(iii)   Each facility notified to the [International Authority] under this Annex shall be subject to systematic international on-site verification on a routine basis.

(iv)   The number, intensity, duration, timing and mode of inspections and monitoring with on-site instruments for a particular facility shall be based on the risk to the objectives of the Convention posed by the relevant chemical, the characteristics of the facility including its capacity and the nature of the activities carried out there. 3/ The guidelines to be used shall include: (to be developed).

1/   Some of the provisions contained in this section have general application throughout the Convention. It is understood that the retention of these will be reviewed at a later stage in the negotiations.

2/   This aim requires further consideration. Some delegations have raised in this context the issue of suitability for chemical weapons purposes.

3/   One delegation suggested that the number of such inspections might be one to three per year.

Selection

6.   The particular facility to be inspected shall be chosen by the [International Authority] in such a way to preclude the prediction of precisely when the facility is to be inspected.

Host State Party

7.   The Host State Party shall have the right to designate personnel to accompany an international inspection team. The exercise of this right shall not affect the right of inspectors to obtain access to the facility, as provided by the Convention, nor shall it delay or otherwise impede the carrying out of the inspection.

Agreement on Inspection Procedures

8.   Each State Party shall execute an agreement, based on a model agreement, with the [International Authority] within [6] months after the Convention enters into force for the State, governing the conduct of the inspections of [the facilities declared by the State Party] [those facilities which are determined by the Technical Secretariat on the basis of the initial visit of international inspectors to warrant systematic international on-site verification on a routine basis]. The agreement shall provide for the detailed subsidiary arrangements which shall govern inspections at each facility.

9.   Such agreements shall be based on a Model Agreement and shall specify for each facility the number, intensity, duration of inspections, detailed inspection procedures and the installation, operation and maintenance of on-site instruments by the [International Authority]. The Model Agreement shall include provisions to take into account future technological developments.

States Parties shall ensure that the systematic international on-site verification can be accomplished by the [International Authority] at all facilities within the agreeed time frames after the Convention enters into force.

Verification Inspections

10.   The areas of a facility to be inspected under subsidiary arrangements, may, inter alia, include:

(i)   areas where feed chemicals (reactants) are delivered and/or stored;

(ii)   areas where manipulative processes are performed upon the reactants prior to addition to the reaction vessel;

(iii)   feed lines as appropriate from subparagraph (i) and/or subparagraph (ii) to the reaction vessel, together with any associated valves, flow meters;

(iv)   the external aspect of the reaction vessel and its ancillary equipment;

(v)   lines from the reaction vessel leading to long- or short-term
       storage or for further processing of the designated chemical;

(vi)   control equipment associated with any of the items under
       subparagraphs (i) to (v);

(vii) equipment and areas for waste and effluent handling;

(viii) equipment and areas for disposition of off-specification chemicals.

11.   (a)   The [International Authority] shall notify the State Party of its
decision to inspect or visit the facility [48] [12] hours prior to the planned
arrival of the inspection team at the facility for systematic inspections or
visits.

       (b)   A State Party shall make any necessary preparations for the arrival
of the Inspectors and shall ensure their expeditious transportation from their
point of entry on the territory of the State Party to the facility.   The
agreement on subsidiary arrangements will specify administrative arrangements
for Inspectors.

       (c)   International Inspectors shall, in accordance with agreements on
subsidiary arrangement:

   -   have unimpeded access to all areas that have been agreed for inspection.
       While conducting their activity, Inspectors shall comply with the safety
       regulations at the facility.   The items to be inspected will be chosen by
       the Inspectors;

   -   bring with them and use such agreed instruments as may be necessary for
       the completion of their tasks;

   -   receive samples taken at their request at the facility.   Such samples
       will be taken by representatives of the State Party in the presence of
       the Inspectors;

   -   perform on-site analysis of samples;

   -   transfer, if necessary, samples for analysis off-site at a laboratory
       designated by the [International Authority], in accordance with agreed
       procedures;

   -   afford the opportunity to the Host State Party to be present when samples
       are analysed;

   -   ensure, in accordance with procedures (to be developed), that samples
       transported, stored and processed are not tampered with;

   -   communicate freely with the [International Authority].

       (d)   The State Party receiving the inspection shall, in accordance with
agreed procedures:

- have the right to accompany the International Inspectors at all times during the inspection and observe all their verification activities at facility;

- have the right to retain duplicates of all samples taken and be present when samples are analysed;

- have the right to inspect any instrument used or installed by the International Inspectors and to have it tested in the presence of its personnel;

- provide assistance to the International Inspectors, upon their request, for the installation of the monitoring system and the analysis of samples on-site;

- receive copies of the reports on inspections of its facility(ies);

- receive copies, at its request, of the information and data gathered about its facility(ies) by the [International Authority].

12.   The Technical Secretariat may retain at each site a sealed container for photographs, plans and other information that it may wish to refer to in the course of subsequent inspection.

Submission of Inspectors' Report

13.   After each inspection or visit to the facility, International Inspectors shall submit a report with their findings to the [International Authority] which will transmit a copy of this report to the State Party having received the inspection or visit. Information received during the inspection shall be treated as confidential (procedures to be developed).

14.   The International Inspectors may request clarification of any ambiguities arising from the inspection. In the event that any ambiguities arise which cannot be resolved in the course of the inspection, the Inspectors shall inform the [International Authority] immediately.

Annex 3

BIBLIOGRAPHY OF PUBLICATIONS OF RELEVANCE TO THIS STUDY

I. Intergovernmental and governmental sources

Australia, 'Regimes to ensure non-diversion of super-toxic lethal chemicals: possible approaches', Conference on Disarmament document CD/CW/WP.131, 24 Mar. 1986.

--, 'Verification of non-production of chemical weapons and their precursors by the civilian chemical industry: trial inspection of an Australian chemical facility', Conference on Disarmament document CD/698, 4 June 1986.

Belgium, 'Order of elimination of chemical weapons stocks and method for comparing these stocks: elements of a possible solution', Conference on Disarmament document CD/697, 20 May 1986.

Canada, 'Identification of chemical substances', Conference on Disarmament document CD/679, 13 Mar. 1986.

Committee on Disarmament, 'Compilation of material on chemical warfare from the Conference of the Committee on Disarmament and the Committee on Disarmament working papers and statements, 1972-1979' (prepared by the Secretariat at the request of the Committee on Disarmament), Conference on Disarmament document CD/26, 1 July 1979.

--, 'Report of the Ad Hoc Committee on Chemical Weapons to the Conference on Disarmament', Conference on Disarmament document CD/727, 21 Aug. 1986.

--, 'Report of the Ad Hoc Committee on Chemical Weapons on its work during the period 13-31 January 1986', Conference on Disarmament document CD/651, 31 Jan. 1986.

Finland, *Identification of Degradation Products of Potential Organophosphorus Warfare Agents* (Ministry for Foreign Affairs: Helsinki, 1980).

--, *Trace Analysis of Chemical Warfare Agents* (Ministry for Foreign Affairs: Helsinki, 1981).

--, *Systematic Identification of Chemical Warfare Agents* (Ministry for Foreign Affairs: Helsinki, 1982).

--, *Systematic Identification of Chemical Warfare Agents* (Ministry for Foreign Affairs: Helsinki, 1983).

--, *Technical Evaluation of Selected Scientific Methods for the Verification of Chemical Disarmament* (Ministry for Foreign Affairs: Helsinki, 1984).

--, *Air Monitoring as a Means for Verification of Chemical Disarmament* (Ministry for Foreign Affairs: Helsinki, 1985).

--, *Systematic Identification of Mycotoxins* (Ministry for Foreign Affairs: Helsinki, 1986).

--, *Report of the Workshop on Automatization of Verification Analysis*, Helsinki, 13-14 Feb. 1987 (later published as Conference on Disarmament document CD/765, 29 June 1987).

--, 'Summary of the discussions in Working Group 1: role and architecture of a global system of automated monitors', *Report of the Workshop on Automatization of Verification Analysis,* Helsinki, 13-14 Feb. 1987.

--, 'Summary of the discussions in Working Group 3: automatic monitoring of non-production', *Report of the Workshop on Automatization of Verification Analysis,* Helsinki, 13-14 Feb. 1987.

France, 'Chemical weapons: elimination of stocks of chemical weapons, irreversible neutralization of means of production', Conference on Disarmament document CD/630, 5 Aug. 1986.

German Democratic Republic, 'National verification measures to implement the Convention on the Prohibition of Chemical Weapons', Conference on Disarmament document CD/620, 23 July 1985.

Germany, Federal Republic of, 'Some aspects of international verification of non-production of chemical weapons: experience gained in the Federal Republic of Germany', Conference on Disarmament document CD/37, 12 July 1979.

--, 'The impact of on-site Inspections of current civilian production on the chemical industry', Conference on Disarmament document CD/CW/WP.5, 11 July 1980.

--, 'Principles and rules for verifying compliance with a Chemical Weapons Convention', Conference on Disarmament document CD/265, 24 Mar. 1982.

--, 'Proposals on "prohibition of transfer" and "permitted transfers" in a future CW Agreement', Conference on Disarmament document CD/439, 24 Feb. 1984.

--, 'Verification of the destruction of chemical weapons', Conference on Disarmament document CD/518, 17 July 1984.

--, 'Verification of the non-production of chemical warfare agents by means of inspections in the civilian chemical industry', Conference on Disarmament document CD/627, 1 Aug. 1985.

Japan, 'Some quantitive aspects of a Chemical Weapons Convention', Conference on Disarmament document CD/713, 14 July 1986.

The Netherlands, 'Verification of non-production of chemical weapons: scenario for an experimental inspection', Conference on Disarmament document CD/CW/WP.141, 10 June 1986.

--, 'Verification of non-production of chemical weapons: observations on the scenario for an experimental inspection as laid down in CD/CW/WP.141', Conference on Disarmament document CD/CW/WP.142, 13 June 1986.

--, 'Size and structure of a chemical disarmament Inspectorate', Conference on Disarmament document CD/445, 7 Mar. 1984.

--, 'Verification of non-production of chemical weapons', Conference on Disarmament document CD/706, 20 June 1986.

Norway, 'Verification of a Chemical Weapons Convention: procedures for verification of alleged use of chemical weapons', Conference on Disarmament document CD/703, 16 June 1986.

--, 'Verification of a Chemical Weapons Convention: evaluation of methods for identification of arsenic containing chemical warfare agents', Conference on Disarmament document CD/704, 16 June 1986.

Pakistan, 'Fact-finding under the future Chemical Weapons Convention', Conference on Disarmament document CD/664, 13 Feb. 1986.

Sweden, 'A comprehensive approach for elaborating regimes for chemicals in a future Chemical Weapons Convention', Conference on Disarmament document CD/632, 20 Aug. 1985.

United Kingdom of Great Britain and Northern Ireland, 'Verification of non-production of chemical weapons', Conference on Disarmament document CD/353, 8 Mar. 1983.

--, 'Verification of non-production of chemical weapons', Conference on Disarmament document CD/514, 10 July 1984.

--, 'Verification of non-production of chemical weapons: proposals for inspection procedures and data exchange', Conference on Disarmament document CD/575, 6 Mar. 1985.

United States of America, 'Draft Convention on the Prohibition of Chemical Weapons', Committee on Disarmament document CD/500, 18 Apr. 1984.

--, 'Amendment to CD/500, Draft Convention on the Prohibition of Chemical Weapons', Conference on Disarmament document CD/685, 3 Apr. 1986.

--, 'Movement of chemical weapons stocks', Conference on Disarmament document CD/CW/WP.147, 25 July 1986.

USSR/USA, 'Joint USSR-United States report on progress in the bilateral negotiations on the prohibition of chemical weapons', Conference on Disarmament document CD/48, 7 Aug. 1979.

II. Non-governmental sources: Reports of Pugwash CW Workshops

Report of the 3rd Pugwash CW Workshop, London, 12-14 Apr. 1976, *Pugwash Newsletter*, vol. 13, no. 4 (Apr. 1976), pp. 188-95.

Report of the 4th Pugwash CW Workshop, Muehlhausen, 22-23 Aug. 1976, *Pugwash Newsletter*, vol. 14, nos 1 & 2 (July & Oct. 1976), pp. 62-66.

Report of the 5th Pugwash CW Workshop, Cologne/Leverkusen, 17-19 Aug. 1977, *Pugwash Newsletter*, vol. 15, no. 3 (Jan. 1978), pp. 84-90.

Report of the 6th Pugwash CW Workshop, Salt Lake City/Tooele, Utah and Kansas City, Missouri, 8-12 May 1978, *Pugwash Newsletter*, vol. 16, no. 1 (July 1978), pp. 4-12.

Report of the 8th Pugwash CW Workshop, Geneva, 2-4 Apr. 1981, *Pugwash Newsletter*, vol. 18, no.4 (Apr. 1981), pp. 106-109.

Robinson, J. P. and Lohs, Kh., 'Impressions on the eighth Workshop on Chemical Warfare', *Pugwash Newsletter*, vol. 19, no. 1 (July 1981), pp. 3-5.

Lohs, Kh. and Robinson, J. P., 'Impressions on the ninth Workshop on Chemical Warfare (CW)' [Geneva 12-14 Mar. 1982] *Pugwash Newsletter*, vol. 19, no. 4 (Apr. 1982), pp. 152-57.
--, 'Report on the tenth Workshop on Chemical Warfare' [Geneva 19-20 Feb. 1983], *Pugwash Newsletter*, vol. 20, no. 4 (Apr. 1983), pp. 133-36.

III. Non-governmental sources: individuals and institutions

Akiyama, I., 'Regulatory procedures on chemicals in the Japanese chemical industry', *The Chemical Industry and the Projected Chemical Weapons Convention*, SIPRI Chemical & Biological Warfare Studies no. 5 (Oxford University Press: Oxford), pp. 1-9.

Binenfeld, Z., 'Some thoughts on the problem of national and international control regarding organophosphorus compounds', SIPRI, *The Problem of Chemical and Biological Warfare: Vol. 6, Technical Aspects of Early Warning and Verification* (Almqvist & Wiksell: Stockholm, 1975), pp. 165-71.

Borrmann, D., 'Can chemical weapons be produced in plants designed for the production of normal insecticides?', *Pugwash Newsletter*, vol. 15, no. 3 (Jan. 1978), p. 91.

Burstall, M. L., 'The industrial context of chemical warfare', *The Chemical Industry and the Projected Chemical Weapons Convention*, SIPRI Chemical & Biological Warfare Studies no. 4 (Oxford University Press: Oxford, 1986), pp. 35-54.

Carpenter, W. D., 'Government regulation of chemical manufacturing in the USA as a basis for surveillance of compliance with the projected Chemical Weapons Convention', *The Chemical Industry and the Projected Chemical Weapons Convention*, SIPRI Chemical & Biological Warfare Studies no. 5 (Oxford University Press: Oxford, 1986), pp. 11-32.

234

Cooper, G. H., 'Verification of the non-production of chemical weapons: The United Kingdom approach', *The Chemical Industry and the Projected Chemical Weapons Convention*, SIPRI Chemical & Biological Warfare Studies no. 5 (Oxford University Press: Oxford, 1986), pp. 33-82.

Coppock, R., *Regulation of Chemical Hazards in Japan, West Germany, France, The United Kingdom, and The European Community: A Comparative Examination*, Board on Environmental Studies and Toxicology Commission on Life Sciences National Research Council (National Academy Press: Washington, D C, 1986).

Elstner, P., Lohs, Kh. and Stephan, U., *Umgang mit gefaehrlichen Stoffen: Rechtsvorschriften* (Verlag Tribune: Berlin (GDR), 1982).

Ezz, E., 'The chemical industry in the developing countries and the projected Chemical Weapons Convention', *The Chemical Industry and the Projected Chemical Weapons Convention*, SIPRI Chemical & Biological Warfare Studies no. 5 (Oxford University Press: Oxford, 1986), pp. 83-70.

Herbig, Statement at the 12th Pugwash CW Workshop, Berlin, 5-8 Mar. 1987.

Hoffmann, H., 'Some aspects of verification from the viewpoint of the chemical industry of the Federal Republic of Germany', *The Chemical Industry and the Projected Chemical Weapons Convention*, SIPRI Chemical & Biological Warfare Studies no. 5 (Oxford University Press: Oxford, 1986), pp. 97-104.

Jacchia, E., 'Twenty years experience in multinational verification: the system of nuclear safeguards of the European Community', *The Chemical Industry and the Projected Chemical Weapons Convention*, SIPRI Chemical & Biological Warfare Studies no. 5 (Oxford University Press: Oxford, 1986), pp. 105-11.

Jeschke, H.-J., Statement at the 12th Pugwash CW Workshop, Berlin, 5-8 Mar. 1987.

Kammueller, J. G., 'Safety aspects in the production and formulation of pesticides of high mammalian toxicity', SIPRI, *The Problem of Chemical and Biological Warfare: Vol. 6, Technical Aspects of Early Warning and Verification* (Almqvist & Wiksell: Stockholm, 1975), pp. 171-77.

Koehler, H., Statement at the 12th Pugwash CW Workshop, Berlin, 5-8 Mar. 1987.

Kurata, H., 'Lessons learned from the destruction of the chemical weapons of the Japanese Imperial Forces', SIPRI, *Chemical Weapons: Destruction and Conversion* (Taylor and Francis: London, 1980), pp. 77-93.

Lau, A., 'A comprehensive approach for elaborating regimes for chemicals in a future Chemical Weapons Convention', *The Chemical Industry and the Projected Chemical Weapons Convention*, SIPRI Chemical & Biological Warfare Studies no. 5 (Oxford University Press: Oxford, 1986), pp. 113-20.

Lohs, Kh., 'Destruction or conversion of chemical warfare agents: possibilities and alternatives', SIPRI, *Chemical Weapons: Destruction and Conversion* (Taylor and Francis: London, 1980), pp. 67-75.
--, 'Verification of the non-production of chemical weapons: a view from the GDR', *The Chemical Industry and the Projected Chemical Weapons Convention*, SIPRI Chemical & Biological Warfare Studies no. 5 (Oxford University Press: Oxford, 1986), pp. 121-28.

Lohs, Kh., Stock, T. and Kläss, V., 'Internationale und nationale Methoden der Verifikation regionaler und globaler Vereinbarungen zum Verbot chemischer Waffen', *Zeitschrift für Chemie*, vol. 27 (Oct. 1987).

Lundin, S. J., 'The inhibition of cholinesterase activity by organophosphorus compounds as a means in an inspection procedure', SIPRI, *The Problem of Chemical and Biological Warfare: Vol. 6, Technical Aspects of Early Warning and Verification* (Almqvist & Wiksell: Stockholm, 1975), pp. 177-83.
--, 'Confidence-building measures and a chemical weapons convention', SIPRI, *Chemical Weapons: Destruction and Conversion* (Taylor and Francis: London, 1980), pp. 139-51.

Mate, L., 'The verification of non-production: questions and doubts', *The Chemical Industry and the Projected Chemical Weapons Convention*, SIPRI Chemical & Biological Warfare Studies no. 5 (Oxford University Press: Oxford, 1986), pp. 129-34.

Matousek, J., 'Verification of the non-production of chemical weapons by the civilian chemical industry in the projected Chemical Weapons Convention', Working Paper, 12th Pugwash CW Workshop, Berlin, 5-8 Mar. 1987.

Melnikov, N. N., 'Future consumption patterns of elemental phosphorus in the USSR', SIPRI, *The Problem of Chemical and Biological Warfare: Vol. 6, Technical Aspects of Early Warning and Verification* (Almqvist & Wiksell: Stockholm, 1975), pp. 183-87.

Miettinen, J. K., 'A mobile laboratory for verification of alleged manufacture of chemical warfare agents', SIPRI, *The Problem of Chemical and Biological Warfare: Vol. 6, Technical Aspects of Early Warning and Verification* (Almqvist & Wiksell: Stockholm, 1975), pp. 187-90.

Mikulak, R., 'Destruction of US chemical weapons production and filling facilities', SIPRI, *Chemical Weapons: Destruction and Conversion* (Taylor and Francis: London, 1980), pp. 57-66.

Moravec, J., 'Some aspects of the problem of possible convertibility of organophosphorus plants', SIPRI, *The Problem of Chemical and Biological Warfare: Vol. 6, Technical Aspects of Early Warning and Verification* (Almqvist & Wiksell: Stockholm, 1975), pp. 190-200.

Ooms, A. J. J., 'On the possibility to delimitate nerve gases within the field of organophosphorus compounds', SIPRI, *The Problem of Chemical and Biological Warfare: Vol. 6, Technical Aspects of Early Warning and Verification* (Almqvist & Wiksell: Stockholm, 1975), pp. 200-208.
--, 'Verification of the destruction of stockpiles of chemical weapons', SIPRI, *Chemical Weapons: Destruction and Conversion* (Taylor and Francis: London, 1980), pp. 123-28.
--, 'The CW Convention and the chemical industry', *The Chemical Industry and the Projected Chemical Weapons Convention*, SIPRI Chemical & Biological Warfare Studies no. 5 (Oxford University Press: Oxford, 1986), pp. 135-85.

Osa, T. and Fukushima, Y., 'Some aspects of the organophosphorus industry in Japan', SIPRI, *The Problem of Chemical and Biological Warfare: Vol. 6, Technical Aspects of Early Warning and Verification* (Almqvist & Wiksell: Stockholm, 1975), pp. 208-17.

Pittaway, A. R., Roberts, R. E. and Epp, D., 'Volume I of Paper prepared for discussion of the working group meeting on 16-18 December 1972', SIPRI, *Chemical Disarmament: Some Problems of Verification* (Almqvist & Wiksell: Stockholm, 1973), pp. 51-130.
--, 'Volume II (statistical annexes)', SIPRI, *Chemical Disarmament: Some Problems of Verification* (Almqvist & Wiksell: Stockholm, 1973), pp. 131-72.
--, 'Production of organophosphorus chemical warfare agents', SIPRI, *The Problem of Chemical and Biological Warfare: Vol. 6, Technical Aspects of Early Warning and Verification* (Almqvist & Wiksell: Stockholm, 1975), pp. 217-26.

Ramachandran, P. K., 'Regulatory practices in the Indian chemical industry', *The Chemical Industry and the Projected Chemical Weapons Convention*, SIPRI Chemical & Biological Warfare Studies no. 5 (Oxford University Press: Oxford, 1986), p. 187.

Rautio, M. and Miettinen, J. K., 'Measures to establish the non-production of chemical-warfare agents and related banned compounds by the civilian chemical industry', *The Chemical Industry and the Projected Chemical Weapons Convention*, SIPRI Chemical & Biological Warfare Studies no. 5 (Oxford University Press: Oxford, 1986), pp. 189-95.

Rehak, W. W., 'Theses on the verification of the non-production of chemical weapons from the viewpoint of nuclear material safeguards', 12th Pugwash CW Workshop, Berlin, 5-8 Mar. 1987.

Reutov, O. A. and Babievsky, K. K., 'Some aspects of the problem of the destruction of chemical warfare agents', SIPRI, *Chemical Weapons: Destruction and Conversion* (Taylor and Francis: London, 1980), pp. 117-21.

Reutov, O. A. and Melnikov, N., 'On the problem of verification of the production of chemical weapons', SIPRI, *The Problem of Chemical and Biological Warfare: Vol. 6, Technical Aspects of Early Warning and Verification* (Almqvist & Wiksell: Stockholm, 1975), pp. 226-31.

Reutov, O. A., Melnikov, N. N. and Moravec, J., 'Paper prepared for discussion at the working group meeting on 16-18 December 1972', *Chemical Disarmament: Some Problems of Verification* (Almqvist & Wiksell: Stockholm, 1973), pp. 36-50.

Riess, J. G., 'Some aspects of phosphorus chemistry related to the preparation and transformation of toxic esters', SIPRI, *The Problem of Chemical and Biological Warfare: Vol. 6, Technical Aspects of Early Warning and Verification* (Almqvist & Wiksell: Stockholm, 1975), pp. 232-39.

Roberts, E. R., 'Verification problems--monitoring of conversion and destruction of chemical-warfare agent plant', *SIPRI, Chemical Weapons: Destruction and Conversion* (Taylor and Francis: London, 1960), pp. 129-36.

Roberts, R., 'Economic data monitoring for production of organophosphorus compounds', SIPRI, *The Problem of Chemical and Biological Warfare: Vol. 6, Technical Aspects of Early Warning and Verification* (Almqvist and Wiksell: Stockholm, 1975), pp. 240-53.

Robinson, J. P. P., 'Near-site verification technique: its place in a confidence-building strategy of verification', *Pugwash Newsletter*, vol.15, no. 3 (Jan. 1978), p. 94.
--, *Chemical Warfare Arms Control: A framework for considering policy alternatives*, SIPRI Chemical & Biological Warfare Studies no. 2 (Taylor and Francis: London, 1985).
--, 'The chemical industry and chemical-warfare disarmament: categorizing chemicals for the purpose of the projected Chemical Weapons Convention', *The Chemical Industry and the Projected Chemical Weapons Convention*, SIPRI Chemical & Biological Warfare Studies no. 4 (Oxford University Press: Oxford, 1986), pp. 55-104.

Robinson, J. P. P. and Trapp, R. with Mårtensson, K., 'Summary report of the proceedings', *The Chemical Industry and the Projected Chemical*

Weapons Convention, SIPRI Chemical & Biological Warfare Studies no. 4 (Oxford University Press: Oxford, 1986), pp. 1-34.

Rosival, L., 'Biomedical aspects of the destruction and conversion of chemical warfare agents', SIPRI, *Chemical Weapons: Destruction and Conversion* (Taylor and Francis: London, 1980), pp. 107-111.

Rylov, V., 'Comparative analysis of verification methods of non-production of chemical weapons at commercial enterprises', *Automatic Monitoring in Verification of Chemical Disarmament,* Proceedings of a Workshop, Helsinki, Finland, 12-14 Feb. 1987, pp. 37-43.

Scoville, H., Jr, 'The objectives of inspection in a limitation on the production of CW agents', SIPRI, *The Problem of Chemical and Biological Warfare: Vol. 6, Technical Aspects of Early Warning and Verification* (Almqvist & Wiksell: Stockholm, 1975), pp. 254-59.

SIPRI, *Chemical Disarmament: Some Problems of Verification* (Almqvist & Wiksell: Stockholm, 1973).
--, *The Problem of Chemical and Biological Warfare: Vol. 6, Technical Aspects of Early Warning and Verification* (Almqvist & Wiksell: Stockholm, 1975).
--, *Chemical Weapons: Destruction and Conversion* (Taylor and Francis: London, 1980).
--, *The Chemical Industry and the Projected Chemical Weapons Convention: Proceedings of a SIPRI/Pugwash Conference,* SIPRI Chemical & Biological Warfare Studies no. 4 (Oxford University Press: Oxford, 1986).
--, *The Chemical Industry and the Projected Chemical Weapons Convention: Proceedings of a SIPRI/Pugwash Conference,* SIPRI Chemical & Biological Warfare Studies no. 5 (Oxford University Press: Oxford, 1986).

Spigarelli, J., 'A discussion of the near-site verification technique', *Pugwash Newsletter,* vol. 15, no. 3 (Jan. 1978), pp. 94-95.

Stock, T., 'Some aspects of verification of the non-production of chemical weapons', Working Paper, 12th Pugwash CW Workshop, Berlin, 5-8 Mar. 1987.

Trapp, R., 'The Geneva talks on chemical weapons and attitudes displayed there towards the chemical industry', *The Chemical Industry and the Projected Chemical Weapons Convention,* SIPRI Chemical & Biological Warfare Studies no. 4 (Oxford University Press: Oxford, 1986), pp. 105-39.

Urbanski, T., 'Phosphorus pesticides--suggested principles for the control of their production', SIPRI, *The Problem of Chemical and Biological Warfare: Vol. 6, Technical Aspects of Early Warning and Verification* (Almqvist & Wiksell: Stockholm, 1975), pp. 260-63.

Verweij, A., Degenhardt, C. E. A. M. and Boter, H. L., 'Determination of PCH3-containing compounds in a Rhine water sample and in a waste water sample', *Pugwash Newsletter,* vol. 15, no. 3 (Jan. 1978), p. 95.

Vilceanu, R., 'New developments in the chemistry of organophosphorus pesticides', SIPRI, *The Problem of Chemical and Biological Warfare: Vol. 6, Technical Aspects of Early Warning and Verification* (Almqvist & Wiksell: Stockholm, 1975), pp. 264-71.

Vincken, J., 'Review of current regulatory obligations and practices as experienced by a speciality chemicals producer in the Netherlands', *The Chemical Industry and the Projected Chemical Weapons Convention,* SIPRI Chemical & Biological Warfare Studies no. 5 (Oxford University Press: Oxford, 1986), pp. 197-202.

Voepel, K. H., 'The production of organophosphorus insecticides in the Federal Republic of Germany and their control by government authorities and the Western European Union', SIPRI, *The Problem of Chemical and Biological Warfare: Vol. 6, Technical Aspects of Early Warning and Verification* (Almqvist & Wiksell: Stockholm, 1975), pp. 271-89.

Vojvodic, V. and Minic, D., 'Civil Industry and permitted activities in production of lethal and other harmful chemicals', *The Chemical Industry and the Projected Chemical Weapons Convention,* SIPRI Chemical & Biological Warfare Studies no. 5 (Oxford University Press: Oxford, 1986), pp. 203-29.

Voprsal, J., 'Technology and possible control', SIPRI, *The Problem of Chemical and Biological Warfare: Vol. 6, Technical Aspects of Early Warning and Verification* (Almqvist & Wiksell: Stockholm, 1975), pp. 269-94.

Wiezorek, W.D., 'National experience in controlling chemical substances', Working Paper, 12th Pugwash CW Workshop, Berlin, 5-8 Mar. 1987.

Åberg, B., 'Implications for the projected Chemical Weapons Convention of new industries such as those using gene technology', *The Chemical Industry and the Projected Chemical Weapons Convention,* SIPRI Chemical & Biological Warfare Studies no. 5 (Oxford University Press: Oxford, 1986), pp. 231-33.

Excerpts from

OECD

ENVIRONMENT
MONOGRAPHS

No 14

FINAL REPORT OF THE EXPERT GROUP ON

MODEL FORMS OF AGREEMENT FOR THE EXCHANGE OF

CONFIDENTIAL DATA ON CHEMICALS

MARCH 1988

ENVIRONMENT MONOGRAPHS

This series is designed to make available to a
wide readership selected technical reports
prepared by the OECD Environment Committee and
Directorate. Following a recommendation by the
Environment Committee, this report has been
derestricted by the Secretary-General on his own
responsibility. Additional copies of Monographs
on a limited basis can be forwarded on request.

This Monograph is also available in French.

ORGANISATION FOR ECONOMIC CO-OPERATION AND DEVELOPMENT

242

TABLE OF CONTENTS

IV. CHECKLIST OF ISSUES TO CONSIDER WHEN NEGOTIATING AN AGREEMENT TO EXCHANGE CONFIDENTIAL INFORMATION ON CHEMICALS

Scope of Agreement

To establish the scope of the agreement the following items should be considered:

-- purpose of information/data exchange;

-- types of chemicals covered (e.g.: industrial chemicals; pesticides; food additives; drugs; transformation products; byproducts; preparations; consumer products);

-- types of information/data to be exchanged (e.g.: toxicological data; human and environmental data; production and trade figures relevant to assessment of exposure; use patterns; composition of a preparation or a product; production methods; exposure data; epidemiological information).

Legal Support and Background Regulations

Negotiating countries should discuss the particulars of their national practice as well as problems concerning management and exchange of confidential data. In this respect they should exchange information on:

-- existing legislation, regulations or administrative practices regarding information/data gathering, public disclosure and confidentiality in their respective countries;

-- what information/data is required to be held confidential; criteria for defining confidential information;

-- in what circumstances information/data required to be held confidential may be disclosed;

-- what procedures and restrictions are applicable to disclosure of information/data including actions that might be taken and sanctions that may be applied;

-- liability issues.

Form of the Agreement

The following should be discussed to determine what form the agreement will take:

-- would there be a need for new legislation or altering of existing national legislation to allow exchange of confidential information;

12

-- what other existing international obligations also have to be taken into account;

-- what type of instrument is appropriate (e.g. convention, treaty, agreement, memorandum of understanding, arrangement between governmental departments).

Procedures

Having considered the scope of the agreement, and the legal support and background regulations within which each country operates, the procedures of practical implementation of the exchange under the agreement should be discussed. In this context the following should be considered:

General procedures

-- which authority or authorities (focal points), in each country, will have the responsibility for conducting the exchange of information/data;

-- what will be the procedure for requesting information/data;

-- how will the request for the information/data be substantiated;

-- what will be the procedure for the transmission of information/data to the requesting country (ensuring confidentiality);

Procedures within the requesting country

-- what procedures, including security measures, will be used to ensure at least the same degree of confidentiality as is practised in the transmitting country;

-- under what procedures may the requesting country make information/data available to national, regional or local authorities;

-- what procedures are necessary to ensure that the information/data received is used solely for the purpose of the assessment of hazards with a view to the protection of man and the environment;

-- what procedures, including consultation with the transmitting country, are to be followed in the event of the requesting country needing to disclose confidential information/data in unanticipated circumstances (e.g. emergency situations).

Procedures within the solicited country

-- how the solicited country consults the submitter of the information/data concerning transmission of the requested information/data;

-- what should be done if the information/data given no longer is treated as confidential by the solicited country (e.g. information ceasing to be confidential after a period of time, or confidentiality claim being withdrawn by the submitter of the information).

Other Considerations

Other practical aspects may warrant discussion during the negotiations. These concern, but are not limited to the following:

-- relationship to other agreements;

-- keeping of records of the information/data transmitted;

-- dates and modality of entry into force;

-- duration;

-- revision period;

-- termination, including effects on information/data already transmitted;

-- settlement of disputes.

V. MODEL AGREEMENT FOR THE EXCHANGE OF CONFIDENTIAL INFORMATION ON CHEMICALS

AGREEMENT
BETWEEN THE GOVERNMENT OF [COUNTRY A] AND THE GOVERNMENT
OF [COUNTRY B]
CONCERNING
THE EXCHANGE OF CONFIDENTIAL INFORMATION ON CHEMICALS

PREAMBLE

The Government of [Country A] and the Government of [Country B],

Having regard to the Recommendation of the OECD Council dated 26 July 1983 concerning the Exchange of Confidential Data on Chemicals [C(83)97(Final)],

Considering...

Considering it important for a country requesting information on chemicals to demonstrate fully and clearly to the solicited state its need for that information, the use to which it will be put and its capacity effectively to ensure respect for the confidential status of the information,

Considering...

Have agreed as follows:

ARTICLE 1

Object of the Agreement

The Parties agree to exchange confidential information on chemicals for the sole purpose of facilitating assessment of the hazards they present to man and the environment. Such exchanges of information shall take place in accordance with the procedures and conditions provided for in this Agreement.

ARTICLE 2

Scope of the Agreement

1. This Agreement applies to the exchange of confidential information on the following chemicals or categories of chemicals or products:

    (a) industrial chemicals;

    (b) agricultural chemicals;

  (c) consumer products;

  (d) food additives;

  (e) ....

2. The information exchanged may include:

  (a) toxicological data;

  (b) production and trade figures relevant to the assessment of exposure;

  (c) use patterns;

  (d) composition of preparations or products;

  (e) exposure data;

  (f) epidemiological information;

  (g) environmental data;

  (f) ....

ARTICLE 3

Definitions

In this Agreement:

  (a) "confidential" means protected under the laws and regulations of the solicited Party concerning trade, business, industrial or commercial secrecy;

  (b) "requesting Party" means the Party requesting the transfer of confidential information;

  (c) "solicited Party" means the Party to which a request for transfer of confidential information is made;

  (d) ....

ARTICLE 4

Focal point

1. Each Party shall nominate a national authority as the focal point through whom all communications under this Agreement shall be channelled.

2. The focal point for the requesting Party shall be responsible for, in particular:

    (a) transmitting requests for confidential information to the solicited Party; and

    (b) receiving confidential information from the solicited Party and disseminating it in accordance with any conditions specified.

3. The focal point for the solicited Party shall be responsible for, in particular:

    (a) receiving, and coordinating the response to, requests for confidential information from the requesting Party; and

    (b) transmitting such information to the requesting Party.

4. The focal points shall settle between them the details of their working arrangements, including procedures for reviewing and reporting on the activities carried out under this Agreement.

ARTICLE 5

Substantiation of requests for information

Requests for confidential information under this Agreement shall be made in writing and shall indicate:

(3B)   (a) the reasons, in accordance with Article 1 above, for which the requesting Party needs the information;

(3A)   (b) whether the chemicals to which the requests relate are already present in the territory of the requesting Party or are shortly to be marketed there;

(5)   (c) the laws and regulations under which the public authorities of the requesting Party are empowered to collect and use equivalent information within their own territory; and

(4B)   (d) the laws and regulations under which the confidentiality of the information, if provided, will be protected by the requesting Party.

ARTICLE 6

Provision of information by solicited Party

1. Within [six weeks] of the date of receiving a request for confidential information made in accordance with Article 5, above, the solicited Party shall either:

(a) provide the information sought, or so much of it as it considers appropriate to provide, subject to such conditions regarding its dissemination by the requesting party as it deems necessary; or

(b) send in writing a refusal to provide the information, stating the reasons for the refusal.

2. Before providing information under paragraph 1(a), above, the solicited Party shall:

(6)

(a) consult, as necessary, the submitter of the information and other persons entitled to have the confidential status of the information maintained; and

(b) satisfy itself that the information sought:

(i) is necessary to enable, and has been requested solely to facilitate, assessment by the requesting Party of the hazards the chemical in question presents to man and the environment; and

(ii) relates to a chemical which is already present or is shortly to be marketed in the territory of the requesting Party.

3. In the case of a request for information made as a result of a public health or environmental emergency in the territory of the requesting Party, or the threat of such an emergency, the period of [six weeks] specified in paragraph 1, above, shall be reduced to as short a time as possible [and in any event to no longer than one week].

ARTICLE 7

Use of information transmitted

A requesting Party that receives confidential information under Article 6, above, shall:

(a) treat and protect the information provided with at least the same degree of confidentiality as that accorded to it in the territory of the solicited Party and ensure that any authority or other body to whom the information is transmitted treats it in the same way;

(4B)(4A)

(2) (b) use the information only for the reasons it indicated in making its request for the information;

(4C) (c) make the information available to its national, regional and local authorities, and to its courts and tribunals, only if, and to the extent that, it is satisfied that it is necessary to do so for purposes of the assessment of hazards to man and the environment; and

(4D) (d) not pass the information on to any third state.

ARTICLE 8

Settlement of disputes

The Parties agree that, if a dispute arises between them as to the interpretation or application of this Agreement, they will seek a solution by negotiation or by some other mutually acceptable method of dispute settlement.

ARTICLE 9

Relationship to other agreements

Nothing in this Agreement shall be interpreted as to diminish obligations arising under other agreements concluded between the Parties or between one of the Parties and a third state.

ARTICLE 10

Entry into force, duration and termination

1. This Agreement shall enter into force [on .....] [upon ....]. It shall continue in force [until] [unless] ....

2. It may be terminated by ....

3. Termination of this Agreement shall forthwith end the entitlement of the Parties to disseminate or otherwise use any confidential information provided to them in accordance with Article 6, above.

Terminal clause

In witness whereof the Undersigned, being duly authorised by their respective Governments, have signed this Agreement.

Done at .... this.......... day of .... [, in the .... and .... languages, both texts being equally authoritative.]

ANNEX 1

SUGGESTED PRINCIPLES TO GOVERN THE EXCHANGE OF CONFIDENTIAL ˙
DATA AND INFORMATION BETWEEN MEMBER COUNTRIES
[Appendix to C(83)97(Final)]

Preamble

1.   The Chemicals Group at its High Level Meeting in May 1980 stated that the exchange of health, safety and environmental data between Member countries was necessary for the purpose of assessing chemicals with the object of protecting man and the environment. It instructed the Group of Experts on the Confidentiality of Data to work out the principles applicable to the exchange of confidential data.

2.   The Group of Experts, in its discussions, defined the scope of such exchange; it was agreed that the exchange of information between the authorities in Member countries responsible for the control of chemicals should complement the company submissions to these authorities and secondly should allow for exchange on request when companies are not involved. Given the worldwide scarcity of material and intellectual resources for conducting tests, exchange, avoiding duplication of tests so far as possible, should enable better use to be made of existing data. Exchangeable data should be both for new chemicals and for existing chemicals.

3.   Member countries differ very widely in their assessment of the confidentiality of data submitted in response to regulations or administrative practice for chemicals control. While it is generally recognised that the notifier is entitled to claim confidentiality for some of the data he makes available to a competent authority, the final decision lies with the authority. As a result certain data, which cannot be disclosed in some countries, may be disclosable in others. The extent to which confidential data are circulated within government departments may also vary from one country to another. The exchange of data between countries therefore raises a problem of widening the access to confidential data.

   Confidentiality of data is certainly the factor most often limiting exchange of information on chemicals between countries. The Group therefore considered it opportune to recommend that certain types of data should not be designated as confidential and that their exchange should not be limited by principles.

4.   It would seem to be premature, at the present stage, to try to solve these problems by proposals aiming at international harmonization of the relevant laws. Even if greater harmonization of chemicals control regulations can be achieved, the purpose underlying the work of the OECD chemicals programme, the fact remains that concepts of administrative secrecy, and of industrial and commercial secrecy, in different countries derive from fundamental principles associated with national law, which must act as a curb on harmonization. The Group has pointed out that the OECD work towards harmonization should, in particular, encourage those Member countries which have not yet adopted legislation on chemicals control to do so in the years ahead.

5.   The exchange of confidential data between countries should be governed by principles taking account of the differences between legislation and administrative practice in different countries, and enable countries to participate in such exchange without infringing in the law or practice prevailing in their own territories.   Clearly, a list of principles extensively respecting the traditions of countries strictly applying the rule of administrative secrecy to any information imparted to the government imposes restrictions on the possibilities for exchange.   A competent authority will only transmit confidential information if it can be certain that the requesting authority will treat it at least with the same degree of confidentiality as is practised in the transmitting country.   Countries whose laws or administrative practices favour disclosure could agree to follow less restrictive principles in transmitting data which originated in these countries.

6.   The principles were defined by the Group on the following basis:

-   the exchange system must respect the sovereignty of the country transmitting information in its decision on the confidential nature of the information;

-   a competent authority must make every reasonable effort to obtain the information available in its country before requesting confidential information from the competent authority in another country;

-   exchanges of confidential data between competent authorities in different countries should not distort competition and in particular, should not have the effect:

     of subjecting nationals in the solicited country to a more severe testing or reporting requirement than would apply to a national of the soliciting country in the same situation;

     or exempting nationals of the soliciting country from conforming to the notification procedures prevailing in their country;

-   all data made available to a competent authority must remain the property of the submitter, even after exchange with competent authorities elsewhere, to the extent recognised in the original country.

The text of the principles drawn up by the Group is presented below, accompanied by explanatory comments reflecting the various opinions expressed during the work of the Group.

Principle No. 1

     The exchange of confidential information on chemicals between the competent authorities of countries is intended solely to facilitate the hazard assessment of chemicals and the protection of man and the environment.

Comments

7.   The Group distinguished three categories of confidential information that might be available to a competent authority and might be exchangeable between Member countries: data reported under chemical control legislation or regulation, or in the normal course of chemical control administration, data supplied by companies voluntarily or upon request, and data produced under the sponsorship of government departments and other public services. The Group was mainly interested in the exchange of data in the first category, pointing out that such exchange should not be an alternative to ordinary submissions by companies to competent authorities.

8.   It seemed difficult if not impossible to establish principles which could govern the exchange in the two other categories. The discretionary power exercised by the competent authority in deciding or declining to transmit its own data, or data provided voluntarily by companies, lends itself to no general rule and will be different from case to case. However, there should be nothing to prevent such data from being exchanged when appropriate.

9.   From the standpoint of protecting man and the environment, the Group considered that it should not define the term "chemicals". The Group also made no distinction between existing chemicals and new chemicals. This distinction becomes very difficult in an instance where data are exchanged between countries whose systems of notification of new chemicals are different in scope. For similar reasons, it did not appear desirable to distinguish chemicals in terms of the particular use made of them, and to exclude some categories from eligibility for exchange.

10.   Exchange is intended to transmit data already available to the competent authority, and not to have the transmitting authority gather and develop new data for this purpose.

Principle No. 2

A country naving received information in response to a request must in no circumstances use such information for any purpose other tnan the assessment of hazards of chemicals and the protection of man and the environment

Comments

11.   This limitation of tne uses that can be made of information transmitted accurately reflects the need recognised by the Chemicals Group at its May 1980 High Level Meeting. Any extension of the use of information received would prejudice the smooth running of the exchange and the maintenance of the commitment entered into by the countries participating in it.

Principle No. 3

A country, whenever requesting information about a chemical, must substantiate the need for the information, on the grounds that:

A) The chemicals is present or is shortly to be marketed in its territory; and

B) The information is necessary for the assessment of its hazards and the protection of man and the environment

Comments

12.   Automatic exchange of the available data among all Member countries would be an administrative burden and is not considered worthwhile. Such an exchange would also increase the risk of disclosure of confidential data. Therefore, data would be exchanged only in response to a substantiated request.

13.   Linking the acceptability of a request to the information needs as defined in the principle helps to avoid excessively frequent requests, making exchange impractical, and to avoid undue latitude in the reasons a country can give for declining it.

14.   The expression "present... in its territory" has been chosen to include not only the presence of a chemical on a country's market but also its presence in the country's territory due to transfrontier pollution. The expression "shortly to be marketed" was chosen to include chemicals for which the marketing process has been launched even though the chemical is not yet physically present in the territory.

15.   Several experts considered that the principle above would be too restrictive and reduce the value of the exchange of information in respect to hazard assessment. They suggested supplementing the principle by:

"or demonstrate the usefulness of the information because of a similarity in structure to a chemical present or shortly to be marketed in its territory"

However, other experts were of the opinion that the present state of scientific knowledge does not allow the establishment of a direct relationship between chemical structure and effect upon man and the environment which can be generally applied. Those experts also thought that the concept could harm the proprietary rights of a manufacturer of a chemical showing "similarity in structure" without its chemical being directly concerned or relevant to the case under consideration.

The Group agreed that Member countries could include a provision on structural similarity in bilateral exchange agreements.

Principle No. 4

A country requesting information

A) must abide by the decision made by the transmitting country in respect to the confidential nature of the information;

B) must treat the transmitted information with at least the same degree of confidentiality as is practised in the country from which the information has been requested;

C) may make the information available to national, regional or local authorities only when necessary for purposes of hazard assessment of chemicals or protection of man and the environment and only when such authorities are able to guarantee the same level of confidential treatment;

D) shall not transmit the information received to any other country

Comments

16. The national authority having recognised the confidentiality of information submitted to it has the first responsibility for ensuring that it is effectively safeguarded. The authority can only transmit such information if it is certain that the requesting country will respect the confidentiality of such information.

17. "Treat the transmitted information with at least the same degree of confidentiality as is practised in the country from which the information has been requested" means that the requesting country must treat the information in a manner that is the practical equivalent of the treatment of that information in the originating country. The Group understands that receiving countries will not have legisltion identical to that in originating countries.

18. The Group recognised that different authorities within a country's government may need access to information, and that to make it accessible only to one competent authority would remove much of the value of an exchange of confidential information.

19. Each country should designate an authority to be responsible for transmitting confidential data to another country. The receiving country shall not transmit them elsewhere.

Principle No. 5

The requesting country shall not ask for the transmission of confidential information which it does not have the authority to collect and use under its legislation or in the normal course of its administration

Comment

20. Exchangeable information would essentially be limited to data submitted under laws, regulations and practice of control of chemicals. It is therefore necessary to avoid a situation in which countries with stricter notification requirements than others find themselves constantly being asked to provide data.

21. OECD work under the chemicals programme, and especially work on exchanging confidential data, should be part of a broader effort to harmonize chemicals control procedures, and not be allowed to act as a substitute for harmonization. In particular, it should encourage Member countries which have not yet adopted legislation on the matter to do so over the coming years.

Principle No. 6

The solicited country should consult with the person who submitted the requested confidential data before transmitting them

Comments

22.   Since any exchange involves a further risk of disclosure, whose consequences cannot always be fully assessed by the government, it would seem normal to consult the submitter.

23.   However, it should be clearly understood that this is a consultation and that the final decision must be taken by the government, and that consultation is without prejudice to specific agreements already in force between some Member countries and in accordance with national or international provisions.

Annex 5

Table 1. Verification of declared stockpiles

Object or event	Aim	Requirement (information)	Method	Equipment, manpower
Stockpile site	Confirm location of site	Co-ordinates, address, etc., of site as declared	On-site inspection, check geographical location	Satellite surveillance, inspectors
Closure (for other than destruction transports)	Assurance that no unauthorized transports to and from the site take place	Access to site for inspectors and equipment	Perimeter surveillance, locks at storage units, checkpoints establishments, on-site inspection	Patrolmen, instruments for perimeter surveillance, optic locks with coding equipment, equipment for transmission of data
	Confirm accuracy of declaration of chemical weapons	Statistical significance of declaration	On-site inspection, statistical selection of samples for analyses	Detailed maps of area, sites of storage units, etc.
Weapons (devices, equipment)	Type	Distinguish all types	Description	Inspectors
	Number	Every item	Counting	Inspectors
	Quantity (kilo, liter)	Within X tonnes, cubic meter, of every type, or per cent	Measuring volumes, weighing empty and full containers and shells	Volume measuring equipment, balances, inspectors

Object or event	Aim	Requirement (information)	Method	Equipment, manpower
	Identify type of agent	Alternatively (a) Only type of agent	Chemical analysis	Military detection kit (declared new chemical-warfare agents may require new methods)
		(b) Percentage of active agent	Chemical or spectro-photometric analysis	Relatively simple spectrophotometric analysis
		(c) Binary components	Chemical or spectro-photometric analysis	Relatively simple spectrophotometric analysis
		(d) Other components (declared)	Chemical or spectro-photometric analysis	(Samples may be sent to central laboratory)
	Check transport to destruction site	1. Identify the contents of the transport	According to declaration, checked statistically	Detailed map of site, checklist according to statistical survey
		2. Identify its origin with the stockpile	Supervise loading, seal transport	Inspectors, lockable cargo containers (or continuous presence of inspectors during transport), possibility to communicate locking key to destruction site

Table 2. Verification of destruction facilities (familiarization)

Object or event	Aim	Requirement (information)	Method	Equipment, manpower
Declaration of facility	Confirm location of site	Co-ordinates, address of site, etc., as declared	Check position, on-site inspection	Satellite surveillance, inspectors
Declaration of destruction process	Confirm accuracy of construction: no false outlets, etc.	Building and operation plans	On-site inspection before start, check process flow by in-put/out-put measurements (materials balance accountancy)	Inspection, X-ray equipment, radioactive isotopes, radiation measuring equipment
	Confirm authenticity of measuring equipment (process-control equipment)	Processing manuals, etc.	Testing actual methods and equipment	Inspectors
			Installation of verification equipment	Flow meters, emission measuring instruments, etc.
	Confirm function of recording and reporting systems (automatic or manual)	Reports, manuals	Testing equipment	Recording equipment (black boxes?), communication links, inspectors

Table 3. Verification of destruction of declared stockpiles of chemical weapons[a]

Object or event	Aim	Requirement (information)	Method	Equipment, manpower
Arrival of chemical weapons to the destruction site	Check identity of transport of chemical weapons	According to coding, inspector reports	Check code, accept record	Decoding equipment, inspector (automatic recording ?)
Following the lot of chemical weapons until loaded into destruction facility	Check identity of transport of chemical weapons	According to coding, inspector reports	Check code	Decoding equipment (automatic recording?)
Planned destruction	Check destruction	According to agreed process	Materials accounting, reporting of processing times	Depends on process, automatic registering and reporting of in-put and out-put products
				Storing of records

[a] The question of 'destruction' of the stockpile *site* is not discussed here.

Table 4. Verification of chemical-weapon production facilities (familiarization)

Object or event	Aim	Requirement (information)	Method	Equipment, manpower
Declaration of production facility	Confirm location of site	Co-ordinates, address, etc., of site as declared	Check position, on-site inspection	Satellite surveillance, inspectors
Cessation of production	Certify cessation	That the production process has stopped (That the facility is not operating)	On-site inspection	Inspectors
Closure of production facility	Certify closure	That the production facility cannot operate	Sealing the processing equipment, etc., on-site inspection	Seals, alarm systems, reporting devices, inspectors

Table 5. Verification of destruction (conversion) of chemical-weapon facilities

Object or event	Aim	Requirement (information)	Method	Equipment, manpower
Destruction of production facility	That chemical weapons cannot be produced at the site	Removal of plant	On-site inspection	Satellites, inspectors
		Removal of critical parts enabling production of chemical weapons	On-site inspection	Inspectors
Conversion	That chemical weapons cannot be produced at the site	Only non-prohibited production is undertaken	On-site inspection	

Table 6. Verification (monitoring) of non-production of chemical weapons (toxic chemicals and their precursors, etc.)

Object or event	Aim	Requirements (information)	Methods	Equipment, manpower
Schedule 1 chemicals: super-toxic lethal chemicals, dangerous key precursors/components of chemical-weapon systems				
Declaration of single small-scale production facility (capacity, production plans)	Confirm site, capacity	Co-ordinates, addresses, etc. as declared	Check position, on-site inspection	Satellite surveillance, inspectors
Production of Schedule 1 chemicals at a single small-scale production facility as contained in declaration	That aggregate production is not more than one tonne per year	Assurance can be obtained that the margin of error in verification does not allow excess production by more than X per cent	On-site inspection, (systematic, permanent), check of production journals, equipment, control stockpiles, analyses of produced chemicals Regular reporting to central laboratory Continuous monitoring on-site	Inspectors Production journals, system for transmitting data Analytical chemical equipment, alternatively test samples to test the analytical equipment of the facility

Object or event	Aim	Requirement (information)	Methods	Equipment, manpower
Schedule 2 chemicals: key precursors				
Production of chemicals listed in Schedule 2	That declared facilities do not produce Schedule 1 chemicals	That it is possible to detect and reliably identify probably very few of the undertakings within large, normally on-going activities at a number of plants	Systematic on-site inspection according to weighted guide-lines	Qualified observations of relevant plant constructions, calculations of production capacity and capability Permanent on-site instrumentation (e. g., for remote monitoring) Chemical analysis of samples Qualified inspectors (chemical process engineers) Sampling equipment Systems for transmission of data Sealed containers for reference material for further inspection, production journals
Relevant production facilities as declared, annual data on produced amount and consumption of the chemicals, and on import and export of them	That their production of Schedule 2 chemicals is consistent with non-prohibited needs		Different production thresholds	
	That such chemicals are not diverted or used for prohibited purposes		Check declarations on production by evaluation of production, import/export statistics, etc. Continuous monitoring with on-site measurements	
Schedule 3 chemicals: produced in large quantities and usable for chemical-weapon purposes				
Annual declarations of facilities including capacity, amounts of chemicals produced, end use - - 'on an industrial scale'	See Schedule 2	That monitoring of declared data, etc. allows reliable detection of violations	Monitoring and analyses of statistical information, on-site inspection by challenge	Facilities for statistical analyses (computer), relevant equipment for chemical analyses Qualified inspectors

Schedule 4 chemicals: toxic chemicals not listed in Schedules 1 - 3, listed or other relevant toxic chemicals produced in quantities larger than 10 (?) kilograms per year

Object or event	Aim	Requirement (information)	Methods	Equipment, manpower
Amounts produced, exported				
Production facilities for Schedule 4 chemicals, locations	Facilities do not produce Schedule 1 chemicals	That such chemicals are not detected by agreed methods	Systematic on-site inspection	Inspectors, chemical analytical equipment
Single or multi-purpose facilities	Quantities produced consistent with non-prohibited needs	Materials accounting can be shown to be correct	Based on the risk for the Convention of a chemical on the basis of a 'weighting' system	
Capability[a] and capacity[a] of such facilities	No diversion to prohibited uses of produced chemicals		On-site instruments; Chemical analyses of samples	

[a] The terms 'capability' and 'capacity' need further clarification.